CHILDREN OF SIBERIA

MEMOIRS OF LITHUANIAN EXILES

Supplemented translation of the Lithuanian edition

Kaunas, 2013

UDK 821.172-94
Ch325

This book was compiled by
Irena Kurtinaitytė Aras and Vidmantas Zavadskis,
former child exiles in Siberia

Translated by Živilė Gimbutas
Illustrated by Marius Zavadskis

Cover photo: thirteen-year-old Aušra Juškaitė (above) and
fourteen-year-old Laimutė Juškaitė in the Raseiniai prison, 1949.

ISBN 978-9955-03-770-5

CONTENTS

TRANSLATOR'S NOTE

This translation of selected reminiscences of exile in Siberia is literal, except for changes necessitated by differences between Lithuanian and English syntax and grammar. Moreover, we have retained the feminine endings in surnames and the diminutive forms of names. We have kept the Lithuanian letters *č*, *š*, and *ž*, which would transliterate as *ch*, *sh*, and *zh* respectively, as well as *ė*, often the last letter in feminine names and surnames, producing a shortened *eh*.

Boys' surnames are the same as their fathers' whereas girls' surnames, or maiden names, vary according to the masculine endings, for instance, Vilkaitė for Vilkas, Kairytė for Kairys, Starkutė for Starkus. The suffix *-ienė* signifies a married woman, or "Mrs.," as in Juška and Juškienė, Zubinas and Zubinienė. Feminine forms (*-ienė, -aitė, -ytė, -utė, -iūtė*) predominate in the reminiscences because fathers were usually separated from their families in the event of deportation.

The diminutive forms of names are typically used for children, but they are also terms of endearment for adults. We have Aušrelė for Aušra, Onutė for Ona, Dainutė for Dainora, Elenytė for Elena, and Teresiukė, Teresytė, or Teresėlė for Teresė. Examples of diminutives for boys are Antanukas and Antanėlis for Antanas, Stasiukas for Stasys, and Levukas for Leonas. In Dainora T. Urbonienė's chapter, we find Arutis and Vygandėlis without mention of Aras and Vygandas, so habitual is the use of their diminutive forms. In Ona B. Švilpienė's chapter, Rev. Bučys is referred to as Bučelis, suggesting affection for the person. *Mama*, "mother," is often voiced in the endearing form *Mamytė*, one of many variants that might be translated as "Mummy."

The attainment of a fluent, precise translation was aided by Danutė Januta, who assisted by reading and correcting the translated text. Danutė frequently improved diction as well as sentence structure. For instance, she rendered *purée* as *glop*, *cheesecloth* as *gauze*, and *ointment* (for the hands) as *grease* (for machinery), with attentiveness to context. She researched geographical and other terminology on the internet. I am very thankful for her excellent, generous assistance throughout the translation process.

Ž.G.

FOREWORD

During the twentieth century, an unimaginably cruel wave of terror swept across the world. *The Black Book of Communism* by Stéphane Courtois, Nicolas Werth, Jean-Louis Panné, Andrzej Paczkowski, Karel Bartosek, and Jean-Louis Margolin (translated from the original French and published in Lithuania, as *Juodoji komunizmo knyga*, in 2000) summarizes the crimes of world-wide communism as follows: "20 million victims in the USSR, 65 million in China, 1 million in Vietnam, 2 million in North Korea, 2 million in Cambodia, 1 million in Eastern Europe, 150,000 in Latin America, 1.7 million in Africa, 1.5 million in Afghanistan, and about 10 million victims of the international communist movement and non-governing communist party system". Thus whirlpools of the struggle for a "bright communist tomorrow" took about a hundred million lives.

The 1917 Bolshevik revolution led by V. Lenin occurred in a Russia worn out by World War I. The Bolsheviks wanted to establish their government according to the Marxist theory of class warfare – the dictatorship of the proletariat. For that purpose, they strove to destroy the rising Russian manufacturers, successful merchants, landowners, and clergy. They branded these representatives of the wealthier classes as bourgeoisie, capitalists, counter revolutionaries, and anti-soviet elements, taking everything that they had, killing some, and imprisoning others in labor camps. During the period ending in 1953, the Soviet Union built a giant gulag system consisting of 476 forced labor camps. Eighteen million innocent people spent time in these camps.

Called the years of the Great Terror, 1937 to 1938 was a most tragic period in the Soviet Union, when 1,575,000 persons were imprisoned. Of these, 681,692 persons were condemned to death; 115,000 persons died from starvation, dangerous and overwhelming work, horrible living conditions, and torture. Those who suffered the most were military officers, clergy, and scholars. Great numbers of people perished during two periods of mass starvation. An artificially created famine in the Ukraine in the years 1930–1932 caused the deaths of six million people.

As a result of these terrible events – famine, cruel terror, imprisonment – there were many children left without parents, seeking food, clothing, and shelter. These children often ended up in the criminal system. To manage these young homeless persons, the Soviet Union established a system of juvenile "work colonies" in 1935. In 1936 these colonies processed 125,000 children. Youths twelve to sixteen years old were sentenced for as many as twenty years and could even be condemned to death.

In 1945 there were eight such children's colonies in the Ukraine alone. There was a children's camp established in the far North, at the Norilsk labor camp. The children at these camps were treated the same as adult prisoners. They were humiliated by their keepers and interrogated at night; they did hard labor, suffered hunger, cold, and miserable living conditions.

Not all the children in the camps were caught on the streets. Women with small children and newborn infants were also imprisoned in the labor camps. In 1948, the GULAG contained 500,000 women, 22,815 children up to the age of four, and 9,300 pregnant women who gave birth there.

In the Communist eagerness to build after World War II and occupy new territories, large numbers of people were exiled to Siberia, northern Russia, and the sparsely inhabited steppes of Kazakhstan. About six million people from the Ukraine, Poland, Lithuania, Latvia, Estonia, Moldovia, Crimea, and the Caucasus were deported without trial or investigation. Among the exiles were Cossacks from the Don, Chechens, Germans from the region of the Volga River, and other nationalities. Although the deportees were not surrounded by barbed wire, they were not permitted to leave their place of exile. They were forced into hard labor, insulted, humiliated, and starved while living in dire circumstances. Approximately forty to fifty percent of the exiles were children up to the age of sixteen. Of the 89,000 children deported to Kazakhstan, only 12,000 attended school. Lessons were taught only in the Russian language.

In 1940, when the Soviet Union occupied Lithuania, the same procedures took place there and the same laws were implemented. People were imprisoned, sent to the GULAG, exiled to Siberia, and killed. Lithuania's civil servants, safety and defense workers, military officers, members of various organizations, teachers, farmers, and all the more wealthy residents became "socially dangerous elements." Their children, born or yet unborn, were also guilty just because they belonged to these categories of families.

During the years 1940 to 1957 in Lithuania, 24,303 people were murdered: soldiers, national guard, local defense, partisans, and other members of the resistance movement and their families. The largest mass grave with the remains of 724 victims was found at the Tuskulėnai estate in Vilnius. During the years 1940 to 1953 in Lithuania, 198,367 people were imprisoned. Of these, 20,000 perished in prisons and labor camps. Some died from starvation, unbearable cold, and hard labor. Others were tortured to death or shot.

127,000 Lithuanians were deported to various locations in the Soviet Union. Of these, 55,350 were children up to sixteen years of age, who were exiled with their parents. 28,000 persons perished, and among them were 2,047 children. In 1948 one of the largest groups sent into exile included 12,271 children. 18,306 Lithuanian children were born in exile.

The most cruel fate befell Lithuanians who were deported in 1941. During the night of June 13 and the next four days, the occupiers surged through Lithuania. They barged into houses, broke down doors, dragged infants and children out of their beds. Innocent people, with no understanding of what was happening, were taken from their homes and seated in trucks which drove them to railroad stations. Rows of cattle cars stood surrounded by armed soldiers. People were shoved onto trains, often with almost no food or extra clothing. In Naujoji Vilnia, adult men were separated from their families and transported in separate convoys to the GULAG slave labor camps in Siberia. Most of them died there from starvation, bitter cold, dangerous hard labor, and untreated illnesses. Some were shot. Women, old men, and children were transported to the Altai region in Siberia and other locations in the Soviet Union. 18,500 people were exiled from Lithuania in 1941. Of these, 4,913 were children. In the summer of 1942, those taken to the Altai region were transported to the far North.

Over several centuries, various countries—Norway, Holland, Russia, and others—took an interest in the Arctic. They organized expeditions manned by strong, healthy men, able to tolerate the Arctic climatic conditions. Even though they were well equipped and had adequate supplies of food, many perished. Lost in snow drifts or trapped in ice, members of these expeditions often died from illness, hunger, and unbearable cold.

In the summer of 1942, steamboats pulling barges, filled with women, children, infants, and old people, traversed the Lena River across Siberia's expanse. These poorly fed people, dressed in summer clothing, were transported to catch fish from beneath polar ice to feed soldiers at the front—as if they were Arctic fishermen! 2,795 Lithuanians, including 1,004 children up to the age of sixteen, were transported far beyond the Arctic Circle to the Laptev Sea by the Arctic Ocean. Some of them were left at the Lena Delta on permafrost islands and peninsulas, others by the Jana River. People were left at isolated locations unsuited for human habitation. The exiles had to build shelter for themselves. With logs dragged out of the Lena River and meager building implements brought on the barges, they built barracks. There was a shortage of food and no suitable clothing or shoes for the Arctic conditions. People were sent to die, which was the predominant outcome during their first polar winter.

This kind of "expedition" had never been experienced in world history. There was no precedent for this kind of treatment of civilians in an occupied country. Moreover, there was a cynical rumor that the people were being taken to America.

And so Lithuania's children were scattered throughout the Soviet empire. Hungry, ragged, lice-infested, and sick, they worked in logging camps, grain storage, and collective farms, or fished in the Arctic. They suffered persistent hunger. Their backs were bent under the load of hard labor. They had sores that never healed.

As did the adults, the children sought ways to survive their most painful experiences. Some tried to become hidden and blend in with the local children. They played the same games, wore similar clothing. The girls braided their hair in a similar style. They danced and sang the same as the locals. Others had their secret memories that consoled them in their difficult hours. They had their Lithuania smelling of apple trees. And this single hope – to return to their homeland – no one could take from them.

This book, *Children in Siberia*, is a collection of the memories of sixteen Lithuanians who were exiled to Siberia in their infancy or childhood. Some parts were written earlier and have been published previously. Those authors kindly permitted use of excerpts from their copyrighted material. Other parts were written for this book.

The first part, "HUNGRY AND HUMILIATED," contains the memories of children exiled to various parts of the Soviet Union during the years 1941 to 1951.

The second part, "CHILDREN ON ICE," contains the memories of children exiled beyond the Arctic Circle by the Laptev Sea.

More than half a century has passed since those horrible events. Very few survivors remain of the GULAG prisoners or the adult exiles of those years. The number of child exiles who still call themselves "Siberians" is also decreasing each year.

The Lithuanian patriarch Dr. Jonas Basanavičius said, "A nation that forgets its past has no future." The Lithuanian Parliament has designated 2011 as the Year of Defending Freedom and Remembering Our Great Loss.

Irena Kurtinaitytė Aras

Translated by Vita Milaknis Markevicius

References

Anušauskas, Arvydas. *Teroras ir nusikaltimai žmoniškumui. Pirmoji sovietinė okupacija* ("Terror and Crimes against Humanity. The First Soviet Occupation"). Vilnius: „Margi raštai", 2006.

Applebaum, Anne. *Gulago istorija* (*Gulag: A History*). Vilnius: „Baltos lankos", 2009.

Courtois, Stéphane, Nicolas Werth, Jean-Louis Panné, Andrzej Paczkowski, Karel Bartosek, and Jean-Louis Margolin. *Juodoji komunizmo knyga* (*The Black Book of Communism*). Vilnius: „Vaga", 2000.

Data about victims of the Soviets' genocide of the Lithuanian nation are taken from the Memorial to Lithuania's Suffering ("Lietuvos Kančių Memorialas"), Petrašiūnai Cemetery, Kaunas.

Data from the Research Center of the Genocide of Lithuania's Population and the Resistance Movement, 2010.

Vaitiekus, Severinas. *Tuskulėnai: egzekucijų aukos ir budeliai (1944–1947)* ("Tuskulėnai: victims of execution and executioners," 1944–1947). Vilnius: LGRTC ir VSD, 2006.

HUNGRY AND HUMILIATED

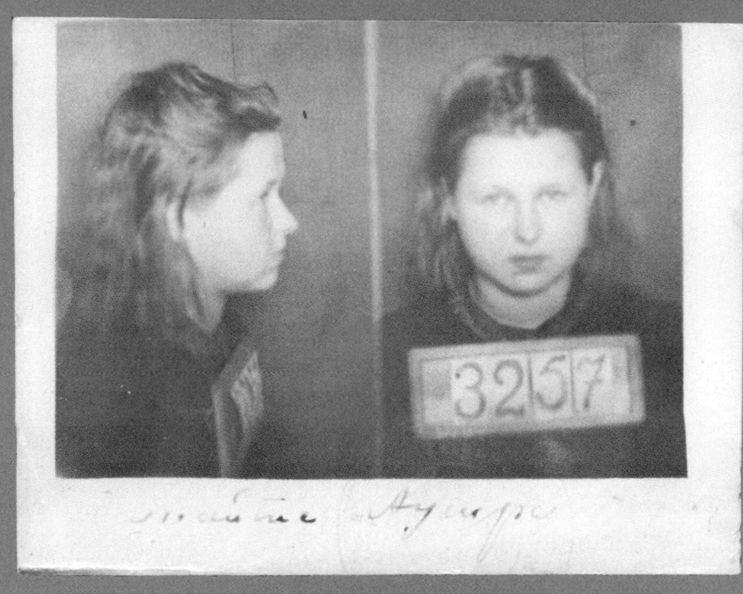

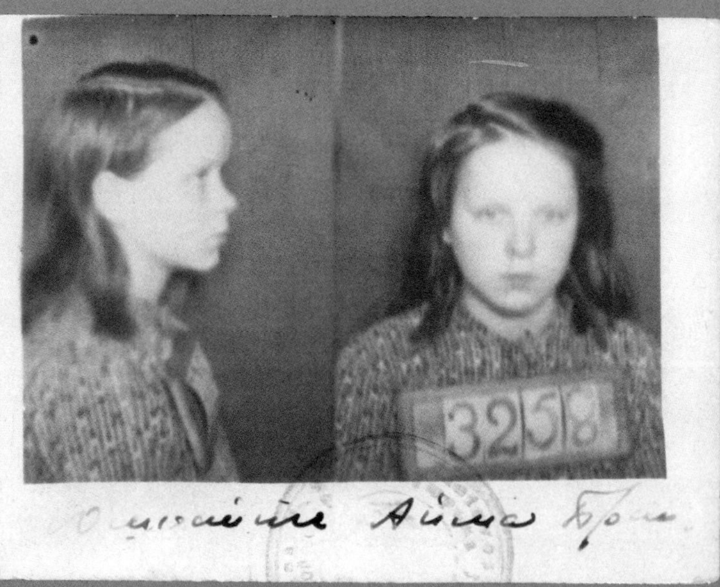

"Criminals" – thirteen-year-old Aušra Juškaitė (above) and her fourteen-year-old cousin Laima Juškaitė in the Raseiniai prison, March 1949.

Aušra Juškaitė-Vilkienė

On June 14, 1941, five-year-old Aušra Juškaitė was exiled from Šiluva to Komi, along with her father, Rapolas Juška, and mother, Kotryna Žemaitytė-Juškienė (sister of General Jonas Žemaitis and a teacher), her four-year-old brother, Ramojus, and two-year-old sister, Rūta.

In 1947 Aušra returned to Lithuania illegally, without her parents, and attended high school in Šiluva. In the spring of 1949 she was arrested and, together with her cousin Laimutė Juškaitė, detained in several prisons en route to her former site of exile in Komi. Aušra was then thirteen years old; Laimutė, fourteen.

Our childhood was cut short on June 14, 1941—and there were over five thousand of us, under the age of fourteen, exiled from Lithuania that day.

I remember our parents waking us up at night (my two-year-old sister Rūta, four-year-old brother Ramojus, and me, the eldest, age five). They brought us to the living room, where we saw two Soviet officers (*chekists*),* conversing in Russian, and a family acquaintance from Raseiniai, who said they were going to take us to Raseiniai. When I broke into tears, protesting, one of the men took pity on me and suggested that I bring along a favorite toy. For some reason, I took my plain butterfly, not the beautiful doll that my godfather, Uncle Jonas Žemaitis, had brought me from France. (Later in exile mother regretted my choice because we might have bartered the doll for food.) The officers led us outside and began to seat us—my parents, us children, and one piece of luggage—in an automobile standing in the yard.

* ***chekist*** *– formerly an official of Cheka (1917–1921), the All-Russian Special Commission for Combating Counter-Revolution and Sabotage; in the World War II era, the title for a security officer or one employed by the Ministry of National Security (MGB).*

Sensing misfortune, I bolted in the direction of town and the home of my dear godmother, the teacher Antanina Berzinienė. One of the officers caught up with me, grabbed me, and returned me to the vehicle. Then we were driven to the train station at Lyduvėnai.

At the station, we were the first to board our train car, or rather freight car. Later we were joined by my aunt Elžbieta Juškienė's family, with three-month-old Vytukas and my cousins Antanas and Laimutė—whom I was childishly very glad to see. New arrivals were loaded onto the train car until it was crowded with both familiar and unfamiliar faces. Toward evening, the train must have reached Naujoji Vilnia (near Vilnius) when *chekists* read off the names of three men in our compartment and ordered them to prepare for exit. We said our good-byes to Daddy and went to sleep. What joy it was to see him still with us when we woke up! Our parents could not understand whether the bullies overlooked him in the rush or simply did not get around to the men in our train car.

Aušrelė in Lithuania with the doll from her godfather, Uncle Jonas Žemaitis

After a long, difficult journey, we found ourselves in a forest in the Kortkeros region of Komi, ATSR (Autonomous Soviet Socialist Republic), at the site of the Second *Uchastok* (literally "lot"), surrounded by high wire fences and studded by watch towers from a former prison camp, twelve kilometers away from other lots. There were twelve to fifteen barracks on our lot, each housing numerous people within its bunk-lined walls. The barracks were infested with bedbugs, lingering from previous prison camps. In summer there were hordes of mosquitoes about and masses of miniature flies (*moshkara*); later, infestations of lice. We were left to our own devices of defense from these pests and bloodsuckers.

Deportees with families lived under horrible conditions and had no rights whatsoever. Everyone was forced to work at clearing woods and felling trees, whether they were fit for the task or not. People did not have adequate clothing or footwear for this kind of work. I remember everyone returning from work in cold, wet clothing, ragged, angry, and tired. The forest clearing sites were five to six kilometers away, and workers had to walk the distance back and forth, despite the bad weather. After work, parents queued up for bread, then got their ration of warm broth in the kitchen. To increase the amount of this broth, in summertime they added boiled sorrel, nettle, or other herbs. (Unfortunately, these delicious herbs did not grow in the vicinity of our lot.) On their return from work in winter, the adults brought along wood blocks from the trunks of young pines. When these blocks thawed, they shaved the brown part of the bark, peeled off the layer of white bark underneath, sliced it like bacon, and boiled it a long while. The resulting brown stew, mixed with broth gotten from the kitchen, made for our supper, and we savored it. Nevertheless, we were always hungry. A day's ration for children was 300 grams of bread, and my brother, Ramojus, would devour it instantly. My sister, Rūta, would hide a piece of bread under her pillow and eat it in the morning—brave girl! I tried and failed to store bread for tomorrow, for I couldn't fall asleep until I had soothed my hunger somewhat.

One day a kerosene lamp fell into the pot of soup in the kitchen. They decided to serve this "kerosene soup" to the children instead of rationing it. We kept running to the kitchen to ask for soup while the grown-ups were hard at work, starving.

Workers usually took no time off for illness; they would fall dead on their way from work or expire while sitting. There was no doctor or medical assistant at our living quarters. Occasionally, with the commander's permission, workers who were ill walked twelve kilometers, if they could, to see a doctor at the regional hospital. Once our mother, feeling ill, obtained permission to see a doctor and set off for Kortkeros by herself. The day was very cold and school had been cancelled. At about noon, my father returned from work in tears and told us that we had lost our mother—she died. I remember how I cried, how everyone in the barrack tried to comfort me. Daddy said that he had received the message from the commander, was dismissed from work early and allotted potatoes for the funeral. He changed and left for Kortkeros in order to retrieve her body and make arrangements for the funeral.

Winter afternoons were dark in Komi. On his way to town, father glimpsed a human silhouette in the distance and, getting closer, realized that he beheld our dear mother! Boundless joy! When they returned, mother related that someone had actually passed away in the hospital reception room. As there was no telephone service at our *Uchastok*, the commander had apparently received an erroneous report of mother's death from some passer-by. I remember people in our barrack commenting that Kotryna Juškienė would have a long life after this incident.

Our miserable life at the Second *Uchastok* wore on. My father, Rapolas Juška, had worked as a forest guard in Šiluva, so he was accustomed to forest clearing, but my mother, a certified teacher with twenty-two years' teaching experience in Lithuania, could not fell trees.[1] Father had to do the work of two in order to obtain their daily bread ration (500 grams). Mother would help him shovel snow around the trees, pile branches, and perform other lighter tasks. For two years, father persevered in the herculean labor, but one evening we received word from another worker that Juška had a fall on his way back from work. Mother and I hurried to the store, obtained father's bread ration, and with it, I ran looking for father. I found him by the wayside, about two or three kilometers from our lot, sitting alone, numb, with a bloody face. He managed to eat the bread I gave him and, barely audibly, asked for water. This I found in a muddy puddle further in the woods. He drank a little, rested a few more moments, and slowly we made our way back to the barracks. Thereafter, father was considered *dokhodyaga* ("barely alive") and was no longer assigned to forest work.

Now I'll turn to my memories of kindergarten in exile. As no one had birth certificates during the war years, most parents tried to keep their children in preschool as long as possible, for there they were fed, if poorly, three times a day. The kindergarten was comprised of one group of about twenty children of various ages, from one to eight or nine, or rather to an age measured approximately by a child's height. No one took care of us there. Our teacher and the preschool director used to spend day after day in their room, scraping each other's heads with a knife, picking off lice. Meanwhile, the older boys, particularly the Beryozov brothers, organized a racket.

On one's first day in preschool, a child would be accosted by these boys in the teacher's absence, beaten, and bullied, so as "not to tell their parents or the teacher." We were all terrified of these older boys. And now it seems incredible to me that none of us who could speak at the time informed on them or complained of their wrongdoing. Their racket was tough with its tacit rules: whenever we got some bread, or maybe a biscuit, with soup at lunch or supper, four fists on the table meant that we had better surrender the bread or the biscuit to them while the teacher was not watching. The brothers would eat some of the booty and take the rest home with them.

During 1942–1943, in the midst of famine, starving Chinese women (of the upper class, as I understand now) used to come around to our preschool. They would show us their mutilated little feet, and for this, our "rich racketeers" would treat them to some bread. I know that all those Chinese women eventually died of hunger because they were unable to work and even had difficulty walking on their tiny feet.

In 1943, I entered first grade. There was only one teacher at the *Uchastok*, so four grades were accommodated in one room. We had neither books nor notebooks; we wrote on old newspaper sheets. Somehow my father procured a set of sturdy red book covers to bind my essays and compositions. One day, as I was packing my sheets of newspaper into those covers, the teacher approached and yanked them from me, yelling, "Where did you get these?" I was frightened and felt guilty; the book covers were confiscated as proof of my wrong-doing. I could read then, so I remember the name *Mikh. Zoshchenko* inscribed on the front cover, but fifty years passed before I learned that this was the name of an author censored and suppressed in the Soviet Union. Now I'm ashamed to admit that I haven't yet read any of his works.

My second encounter with literature occurred in second or third grade. Our new teacher used to read a page of *Gulliver's Travels* for us after lessons every day. This adventure seemed like a miracle to us. We would eagerly anticipate story time throughout the four regular lessons and thus patiently endure them each day. I didn't read or hear of any other books in elementary school because there were none at hand. However, I do not recall wanting to read, for all I wanted at the time was food.

We did not have any meals in elementary school, contrary to preschool, where my younger sister and brother were being fed on a regular basis. My parents did what they could to provide me with an extra potato, or two small ones, to sustain me after school. They carefully secured these provisions in a little coffer to ensure the next day's ration. I used to grate their offerings of unpeeled potatoes, add lots of water to increase the mush, and boil a kind of glop. Once, when school was cancelled due to freezing weather, I had my usual meal but hardly satisfied my hunger. My eyes wandered instinctively to the little coffer—and it was unlocked! (My parents must have overlooked it in the morning rush.) Finding a kettleful of potatoes, I could not restrain the temptation: I grated them one by one and soon finished off the whole bundle. God knows how I dreaded my parents' return from work… but neither that evening, nor later, did they ever refer to my transgression. Thank you, my dear parents!

Our exile would not have been so difficult and miserable would we have had at least a little more to eat. As it were, the whole experience of exile is memorable as persistent, gnawing hunger.

I recall a day when Rūta and Ramojus stayed home from preschool. We were alone, had nothing to eat, and talked of nothing but bread. Suddenly, Rūta announced, "I'll bring you some bread." Soon we looked out the window and there she was, carrying a loaf under her arm! Were we delighted! But when she entered the barrack, we saw that the "loaf" she carried was a plain brown brick. We were so deeply disappointed that to this day it pains me to remember my sister's innocent joke.

Yet another sad incident from the time of famine is engraved on my mind. On a few extremely cold days, some other children and I stayed home from school without providing a written explanation for our absence. On the third day of our delinquency, father was denied my ration of 300 grams of bread at the store, according to the teacher's instructions. A mighty argument between my father and the teacher came to no avail; such was the Soviet teacher's pedagogical practice.

I have more cheerful memories as well. We lived for a time at the First *Uchastok*, where O. Stulginskienė, the wife of former President of Lithuania A. Stulginskis, worked as housekeeper and cleaning woman for the commander of the lot. She had to clean, cook, and tend the wood-burning stove. Whenever hunger totally got us down, my brother and I would run to the commander's house and cleverly ask, "Mrs. Stulginskienė, may we bring you some wood?" Now I understand that she didn't need our help with the wood, for she gathered it herself. However, at the sight of starving children, she would comply. We used to fetch some firewood for her and she, dear heart, would furtively bring us a bundle of potato peelings from the commander's kitchen. Among the peelings we would always find some potatoes. To be sure, such dealings were risky. If discovered, they might have cost Mrs. Stulginskienė her position, or worse. Thank God, neither she nor we were caught. If there were more such benefactors in hard times, the world would be brighter!

Toward the end of the war, I had worn out all the clothes I had from home; I was taller and had nothing to wear. Somewhere, Daddy found a burlap bag, from which Mrs. Alminienė (now deceased) made me a dress, embellished with embroidery at the collar and hemline. I was very happy and proud of this garment. The dress must have been pretty (or so it seemed to us), for after many years my sister often remembered it, saying, "How beautiful it was!"

In the course of our childhood we often saw our parents humbled and humiliated. The supervisors of forest work areas treated families like slaves, transferring them to other sites without previous notice—to Poztykeres, Sobino, the First *Uchastok*, or elsewhere. They drove our family back and forth to the First *Uchastok* several times.

On one occasion the commander of our barracks at the Second *Uchastok* ordered the German and Lithuanian deportees to sign a document stating that they were exiled *navechno* ("forever"). Everyone signed, including my father; however, my mother refused to sign, commenting that nothing was "forever" in this life. Returning to our barrack, father fretted nervously about the consequences of not signing. But there were no consequences. Now I think that the commander himself must have signed for Kotryna Juškienė.

In the fall, when exiles were sent to dig potatoes in the fields, my father once remarked to the

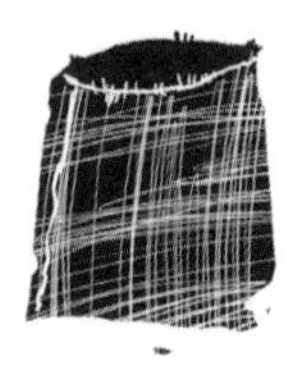

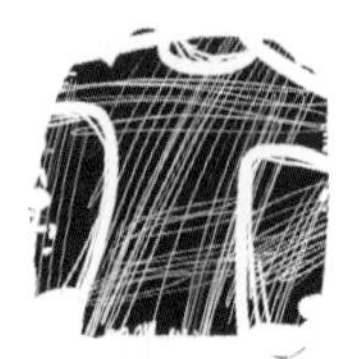

supervisor that furrows were tilled with ploughs in Lithuania. Though taken by surprise, the supervisor let my father harness a horse to a plough, and he, with experience in cultivating land, plowed alternate furrows in the field. When the boss inquired why only every other furrow, my father explained that he would plow the others after the potatoes were gathered from the tilled rows. One of the other workers, eager to ingratiate himself with the supervisor, shouted, "Juška wants to keep every other furrow for himself!" Incensed, the supervisor spat in father's face while we children stood there and shared in the humiliation. Father wiped the spittle off his face, unharnessed the horse, and proceeded to work obediently.

In 1947, I completed four grades of elementary school. (I had earned fine marks, with only one "four"—good—among "fives"—excellent.) During that year, driven by hunger, exiles began to escape surreptitiously to Lithuania. Some succeeded in the attempt; others were caught and returned to their site of exile. Our family decided that I should risk the long journey home. Later my parents regretted letting me go because the famine subsided at the end of that year. Ration cards were terminated, and bread could be bought for money.

My parents befriended a free Byelorussian family, who agreed to escort me and the sisters Vanda and Halina Bytautaitė to the railroad station at Lyda; from there to Lithuania we would be on our own. I remember a long, miserable journey. We were constantly hungry and anxious about the next inspection of documents. I had only a certificate for the completion of four grades of elementary school. Fortunately, none of the officials asked us young, tired girls for our ID's. Eventually, at the end of September or the beginning of October, 1947, I found myself in Šiluva, sheltered by the kindly Berzinas family.

Lithuania seemed like paradise to my twelve-year-old eyes. I was well fed and dressed; I enjoyed attendance at the Ib class at Šiluva High School. On weekends, my mother's long-time friend and fellow teacher Kotryna Teišerskienė used to take me to her farm at Leonava, where I spent happy, carefree days with her children, especially Danutė.

Of course, I did not know at the time that I would be watched by Soviet agents and returned to Komi in another year and a half; or that my stay in Lithuania would cause hardship for my guardians, the Berzinas family—who were, in fact, obligated to leave Šiluva after my arrest. However, the year and a half in Lithuania was invaluable for me: I learned to read and write in Lithuanian, improved my speech, and assimilated to local customs and manners. At home, I was tutored by Antanina Berzinienė and Emilija Kačarauskaitė, teachers who were close to me. I grew fond of my teachers at the high school: Julija Burneckienė, who taught Lithuanian; Mr. Burneckis, the Jankūnaitė sisters, the math teacher Mr. Tautkus, Miss Vyšniauskaitė, and the Ib homeroom teacher, A. Kairytė. By their efforts and other teachers' at Šiluva High School (whose names I cannot remember), I soon caught up with my classmates and completed the first year of high school successfully. Throughout the imminent calamities, imprisonment, and second tour of exile until the present day, I've treasured my homeroom teacher's graduation gift: M. Valančius' novella *Juzė of Palanga* (*"Palangos Juzė"*), inscribed "To Aušra Juškaitė, second student of the Ib class at Šiluva High School, from the teacher, Alf. Kairytė, 06.20.1948."

During the summer vacation of 1948 I visited my grandparents Petronelė and Jonas Žemaitis. They had been ousted from their farm in Kiaulininkai; their handsome house was demolished. The elderly couple went into hiding for a while. When their resources were depleted, one of their acquaintances managed to place them in an old folks' home near Gargždai-Laugaliai. Upon arrival at this home, I learned that my grandfather had assumed a different surname. I found my grandmother—dear "*mamaitė*" of our childhood—in another room, curled up in her chair, her head tied with gauze, anticipating the return of her son Jonukas (the partisan leader General Jonas Žemaitis). She neither recognized me nor remembered me.

I teared up and departed. Both grandparents passed away in this wretched asylum, in utter poverty.

That summer I also visited my grandfather's brother, Uncle Antanas Žemaitis. Having lost his home, like my grandparents, he lived with his good neighbors, the Šimkus family. On the second day of my visit, the Šimkus' son, a teacher, and his wife came to Kiaulininkai with an assignment from the MGB (R. *Ministerstvo Gosudarstvenoy Bezopasnosti*, "Ministry of National Security"), as I understand now. In the course of conversation, they questioned me at length about my relations, activities, and whereabouts. They were particularly interested in knowing whether I had had occasion to see my uncle Jonas Žemaitis*—and thank God that I had not. If I had met with my uncle, I would probably have answered truthfully and remained guilty, like the hero of V. V. Landsbergis' film *When I Was a Partisan*. When independence was restored to Lithuania (1990), a report by agent Mikutaitis (the teacher Šimkus), dated June 14, 1948, was available at the MGB Archive, stating that Aušra Juškaitė had no communication with Jonas Žemaitis; that her grandparents resided at the nursing home at Laugaliai; and that Aušra, having returned from exile illegally, lived with A. Berzinienė, a teacher.[2]

On the morning of March 10, 1949, as I was preparing for school, a pale-faced Mrs. Berzinienė rushed into my room, saying that a *stribas*** (literally "exterminator") had come to see me. I was arrested and taken by the armed *stribas* to the military station in Šiluva. A while later, my cousin Laimutė Juškaitė, also arrested, was brought to the station. We were both extensively interrogated at the station by officer Pigaryov. After 1990, when I researched my cou-

---

* ***Jonas Žemaitis*** *was the organizer and leader of Lithuanian freedom fighters' (partisans') armed forces and coordinator of the resistance to Lithuania's occupation. (b. 1919 – executed in Moscow, 1954).*

** ***stribas*** *(from the Russian* ***istrebytel****, "destroyer, exterminator") – a member of a group of armed civilians employed by the Soviet government, 1944-1954, to carry out repressive measures. The term stribas acquired connotations of disdain and contempt, for it was associated with collaborators and traitors.*

sin's and my case No. 13668 in the Archives of the Ministry of Internal Affairs, I was surprised to read that our interrogation had proceeded in the presence of J. Dogelis, High School Director in Šiluva. We know now that, by law, a representative of the community has to participate in the interrogation of minors; however, there had been no trace of J. Dogelis at the station. The High School Director must have signed the interrogation record after the event.

When school was out that day (March 10), high school students gathered round the military station, filling the entire street. When ordered to disperse by an officer, no one budged. In late afternoon, Laimutė and I were seated in the back of a truck and guarded by four armed *stribai*; their leader took a seat in the cabin. Meanwhile, high school students surrounded the truck, attempting to give us whatever they had: money, bread, or bacon. My schoolmates in the IIb class had collected two hundred rubles for us (then a huge sum of money). When the motor started, there was a commotion. Some of my schoolmates were crying; others shouted, "Where are you taking these youngsters?" (I was thirteen; Laimutė, fourteen years old.)

Only now, sixty years later, do I have a chance to thank those schoolmates who remember me, or their families: "I am so thankful for your generosity, your kindness, sincerity, and your courage that day!"

So, for the second time, we were driven from Šiluva. The *stribai* took us to the KPZ (R. *Kamera predvaritelnogo zaderzhaniya*, "preliminary detainment ward") in Raseiniai, where my cousin and I spent four days amongst scampering rats. This experience was a terrible trial for us. We were both constantly in a state of fear. At night we could hear the *stribai* swearing as they dragged detainees from the interrogation chamber to their cells. While some of them were quiet, probably unconscious, we could hear others moaning or shouting. We were interrogated, but not beaten at the KPZ. Nevertheless, we were traumatized when they took us to an interrogation room in the basement one day. The interrogator recorded some information and ordered us to hold out our hands with fingers stretched. We thought they were about to prick beneath our fingernails with needles, but they only took our fingerprints that day.

When all the "procedures" at the KPZ were completed, we were transferred to the prison in Raseiniai. Here we were thoroughly searched and deprived of all our metal and paper belongings. According to the record of this search, I had to relinquish the following items:

1. an old brown leather briefcase
2. ten notebooks
3. a book (*Juzė of Palanga*)
4. a prayer book
5. a cross, black with little white stones
6. a fastener, of yellow metal with three stones
7. a brown leather wallet
8. thread of various colors.

Such were my riches (and later they were returned to me). I was allowed to take the food I had to my cell.

We were held in cell no. 39 at the prison in Raseiniai for about two months. We spent day after day doing nothing but sitting, for they had taken away our books and sewing gear. We were not allowed to sleep during the day. During those two months, the prison librarian once brought us a book about Sigutė, which we learned by heart. There were no other children's or teenagers' books in the prison library.

While Laimutė and I were together, none of the guards dared say "*Ruki nazad!*" ("Hands behind your back!") as they led us to interrogation, to the toilet, or the daily walk. I was the taller and larger (though younger); Laimutė, the smaller and shorter of us two girlish inmates. An experienced woman warden at the prison once asked us in Russian, "What are you girls here for?" We replied, "for escaping from exile to Lithuania," but she seemed not to understand our crime.

Eventually we were transferred to the ward for minor refugees, no. 37, where we found Mrs. Botyrienė, Regina Botyriūtė, Aldona Navickaitė, Maryte Avižienytė, and another girl whose name I do not remember. Life became more interesting. Mrs. Botyrienė used to tell us about the books she had read and the plays she had seen at the theater in Syktyvkar (the capital of Komi). Aldona Navickaitė would cheer us by enacting her imminent release from prison: she would throw a knapsack on her back and happily stride homeward. (In fact, she and her brother were soon released because they were truly orphans.) With lots of time on our hands, we used to sit around inventing nicknames for the wardens, like *Shtik* ("bayonet"), Grasshopper (for a good one), Wolf, and others.

There were certain regulations in the prison. When we were taken to the bath, we had to bring along all our clothes, to be heated and so rid of lice. We had to leave our food in the cell. While prisoners bathed, the wardens inspected their cells, looking for needles, safety pins, hair pins, and other forbidden items. Back in the KPZ in Raseiniai, I had stowed my needles in the wadding of my winter coat. Most of them were found by the wardens, but some escaped their nimble fingers. If we needed a needle and searched my coat carefully, we usually found one or two. I can't remember which one of us hid a safety pin in the bacon. Upon returning from the bath one day, we

noticed that our slab of bacon had dwindled. We surmised that our wardens "borrowed some bacon for a snack" and chuckled, wondering whether the warden who swallowed a particular part of it choked, for the piece that was taken contained the hidden safety pin.

Laimutė and I gained courage in the company of other teenage girls (though now we had to hold our hands behind our backs on the various perambulations). Occasionally, we dared look through the fissure in our cell window (which was against the rules) and observed other prisoners taking their daily walk. One day I recognized Antanas Babenskas, an elementary school teacher in Šiluva, who had often visited with the Berzinas family. Mr. Babenskas had been arrested in the teachers' room at school on January 16, 1949, for supporting partisans (Lithuanian freedom fighters); later he was sentenced to twenty-five years in a concentration camp.[3] When he saw my face in the window, he appeared agitated and inquired in sign language why I had been arrested. I tried to express "escaping from exile" with my hands; I don't know whether he understood.

In 1970, having finally returned to Lithuania, I heard that Antanas Babenskas had passed away at the camp in Magadan.

Our routine existence in prison dragged on. In the quiet of night we could hear the sound of beatings and prisoners moaning. One night, perhaps after a session of interrogation, an inmate shouted, "They're killing people in prison!" The ensuing disturbance, with wardens running about, frightened us and deprived us of sleep. Next day, Regina Botyriūtė wept continually, murmuring that we would all be murdered. Neither her mother nor we could placate her. A warden brought the prison doctor, who examined Regina and told her that the guards must have been joking around last night. He gave her some valerian drops and deemed the cure complete.

Laimutė and I were regularly led to interrogation together. During one session, they pinned numbers on us—no. 3257 on me and no. 3258 on Laimutė—and photographed us with these numbers. The photos in our dual case No. 13668 accompanied us throughout the stages of our deportation to the former site of exile.

Transportation was arranged at the end of June, and we—Regina Botyriūtė, Laimutė Juškaitė, and I, along with other prisoners—were driven by truck from Raseiniai to a prison on Mickevičius Street in Kaunas. Soon thereafter we were driven to a transfer prison in Vilnius, and from there we were taken by train to Leningrad. Our wardens had some difficulties on my account in this Russian metropolis: officials who were acquainted with the law refused to admit a girl under the age of fourteen to prison; according to regulations, I had to be held in an institution for minor convicts. However, one of the superiors relented, commenting that criminal minors might devour us. So, with a few detours to other prisons, we were placed temporarily in a women's prison. As soon as transport was available, we were driven to the transfer prison in Vologda.

To this day I remember a large prison cell lined with bunks, its walls sputtering red when teeming with bugs in the evening. The three of us were settled on the upper bunks, next to prisoners who spent their time tattooing one another. I still don't understand how we escaped their tattoos; God's blessings must have protected us. One day at exercise our cowering threesome met with some brave young women from Lithuania. They had been signalers for the freedom fighters and were now on their way to concentration camps in the north. Next day, they presented us with little black ribbons they had sewn and embroidered with the yellow, green, and red colors of the Lithuanian flag. I regret that I no longer have my ribbon; nor have I seen any one of those fine women in Lithuania since my return.

From Vologda we were driven to the prison in Syktyvkar. With us in the truck was a convicted signaler and her baby girl, born in prison. Since the baby was being breast-fed, it was not separated from her mother. When we stopped and the woman took her child out for some fresh air, the baby extended her arms to the uniformed guards but not the wardens in civilian clothes. Such was her early conditioning in prison surroundings. Being much older, we felt guilty.

In my case No. 13668, I found the minutes of my interrogation of March 14, 1949, where I signed a statement to the effect that I was guilty of all accusations against me. The indictment, signed by Lieutenant Kalinin of the militia in Raseiniai and Major Kachyusov of the MVD (*Ministerstvo vnutrennikh del*, "Ministry of Internal Affairs") division in Raseiniai, recommended sentencing me—a thirteen-year-old girl—to two years of concentration camp and at the end of this term, sending me back to Komi. The indictment also recommended forwarding my criminal case to the Ministry of Internal Affairs, USSR, for resolution by special consultation (*na rassmotreniye Osobogo soveshchaniya pri MVD SSSR*). Of what cruelty were the Soviet officials possessed when they delivered such sentences to innocent, underage children?

According to the verdict of April 11, 1949, I had committed a crime, that is, I had fled from exile while under fourteen years of age (in September 1947, I was only twelve years old!); therefore, I was not punishable by criminal law. Via prison No. 9 in Raseiniai I would be returned in stages to my former place of exile and to the authority of the Ministry of Internal Affairs in Komi, ATSR (Autonomous Soviet Socialist Republic). They kept to their word.

On August 31, 1949, after two months' travel with our bags and knapsacks (I, still clutching the old brown leather briefcase gifted by my grandfather J. Žemaitis), Laimutė and I were brought to Kortkeros. My father was summoned from the Second *Uchastok*; Laimutė's mother from the First *Uchastok*. We were turned over to our parents in order to submit again to the slavery of exile. My family's exile lasted until June 29, 1957. During this time, twice a month and later once a month, we were obligated to register with the commander of the site.

After my return to exile in Komi, I attended sixth and seventh grade at the middle school in Kortkeros. Throughout the school year we could attend classes in Kortkeros without the commander's permission, but during summer vacation we were supposed to obtain permission to trek the twelve kilometers to town. One early summer day, I set off for Kortkeros with a German woman, Ms. Faifert, for a reason I cannot remember. We were found with no permits, arrested, and taken to the military station. The military officers conversed in their Komi language, saying that they would dismiss the old woman; the young one (referring to me) would have ten days to clean the entire station building (which had just undergone extensive repairs). I understood Komi well enough to gather the plan for my ten-day detention; therefore, when the military supervisor arrived for work, I told him that I had gone to the school in Kortkeros to pick up my sixth grade certificate. They let me go that time.

When independence was restored to Lithuania, I could examine my case at the Archives. I wanted to know who those officials were who had written up the orders for our arrest and the records of our detention; who interrogated us, convicted us, and fabricated our case. Where had all those merciless officials come from? Had they no children of their own, nor conscience, that they could calmly perpetrate the genocide of exiled children?

In Laimutė's and my case No. 13668, the perpetrators were Soviet officials (*chekists*) in Raseiniai—Kalinin, Pigaryov, Kachyusov, Yurov; the public prosecutor Molchyanov; and officials of the Ministry of National Security (MGB) in the Soviet Socialist Republic of Lithuania—Lisenko, Semidyakin, Novikov.

May the Lord forgive them, though they knew what they were doing....

Aušra Vilkienė, Kaunas, 2009

[1, 3] A. Vaišvila, "Šiluvos apšvieta" ("The Enlightenment of Šiluva"), Publishing Center of the Lithuanian Law Academy, 1999: 309, 267.

[2] N. Gaškaitė-Žemaitienė, "Žuvusiųjų prezidentas" ("President of Those Who Died"), Genocide and Resistance Research Center of Lithuania, 2005: 161.

In 1951 Aušra Juškaitė enrolled in the trade school in Syktyvkar. While studying there, she met her future husband, Henrikas Vilkas.

Henrikas had also been exiled from Lithuania in 1941, at age thirteen, together with his sisters, Viktorija and Elena, and his mother, Elena Vilkienė. His mother died in exile in 1942. His father, formerly vicemayor of Telšiai, passed on at the concentration camp in Reshoty in 1943. In 1947 Henrikas and his sister Elena returned to Lithuania illegally. In 1949 he was arrested, imprisoned for three years in Ustvymlag, then sent back to the site of his previous exile.

In 1970 Aušra and Henrikas Vilkas, with their daughters, Elena and Marija, finally returned to Lithuania. They settled and worked in Kaunas, where they still reside today. They have five grandchildren and one great grandchild. Now retired, they enjoy life in independent Lithuania as well as the achievements of their children and grandchildren.

Elena Laskevičienė with her children, Birutė and Algirdas, in Siberia, 1947.

The „zemlyanka" ("earth-house") which Algirdas built. It housed five people.

Algirdas Laskevičius

On June 14, 1941, nine-year-old Algirdas Laskevičius, his mother, Elena Laskevičienė, and his sister, Birutė, were exiled from Kaunas to the Novosibirsk region. In 1947, they returned to Lithuania illegally, but in 1949, they were arrested and exiled again. Algirdas, a minor, was deported to their former site of exile; his sister and mother were sentenced to three years in a concentration camp and then exiled to their former location in Novosibirsk.

Algirdas' father, Bonaventūras Laskevičius, the supervisor of a police station, was separated from the family and deported to a concentration camp in Arkhangelsk, where he died in 1944.

How many of them there were in the yard and around the house, I don't know; inside, there were four: three soldiers and one military officer. They seated all of us—my father, mother, mother's stepmother (who was about seventy years old), and my sister—in one room and ordered us to stay put and be quiet. They spoke Russian, so I didn't understand what they were saying. The military officer sat with us while the soldiers searched the entire house. My mother's stepmother would not be leaving with us because her name was not included in the list of deportees. The military officer, evidently a good-natured person, knew of our approximate destination and advised us what to pack: warm clothing and food, for the journey might be long, a month or more. He also informed us that father would be travelling separately because men and women were segregated in the train cars. So we packed our things. Father took two large suitcases; mother had one and another bundle. We children were also given something to carry. Upon leaving, the officer said my mother's stepmother would keep the house and safeguard the rest of our belongings until we returned home. Then we departed in a truck.

We were driven to a freight station by the metal factory in Šančiai. A long line of boxcars (freight cars) was standing there, and numerous trucks were arriving with people and soldiers. My mother, sister, and I were loaded onto one of the boxcars while father was led further, we knew not where. They only said we would travel separately and meet later on. My father had taken the heaviest pieces of luggage to ease mother's journey with us children. The caravan stood in Šančiai all day, until all the cars were filled with deportees.

The two-axle freight car was specially prepared for deportation. Looking to both sides of the door, the car was fitted at each end with bunks, or boards, the width of the car, about two meters. The door on the opposite side was boarded, as were the windows. On the side through which we entered, the miniature windows were railed. There was an aperture in the floor for a toilet.

How many "passengers" there were in our car, I couldn't say exactly, but it felt tight. There were a number of Jews among the Lithuanian exiles. Weaker passengers and mothers with babies took turns standing by the little grated windows to breathe fresh air, for the atmosphere in the boxcar soon felt heavy. Once we were on our way, some people arranged an enclosure of draped spreads around the "toilet"; our group included several men as well as women and children.

After two or three days of travel, we were standing in the Smolensk station on reserve railways, opposite another train like ours. Peering out the little windows, women began to inquire where that other train was from and who was in it. Finding that it was the men's echelon, they tried to look for their husbands. Serendipitously, it turned out that my father was in the boxcar directly opposite to ours in the men's train. When our turn came to look out the window, we children had a chance to see father. But even in daytime, with meager light from the miniature windows, the cars were dark. I saw father for the last time that day because our routes diverged beyond Smolensk: we were going beyond the Ural Mountains whereas the men were heading north to concentration camps in Arkhangelsk.

Our train frequently stopped at by-stations along the way. Once a day the boxcar door was opened at one of those stations and people were let off two at a time to get water and soup. Hardly soup, it was more like watery cabbage glop. At the beginning of our journey, one woman who had gotten her ration of soup and tasted it poured the liquid mess out the window, hitting a guard on the head. (Whenever the train stopped, the guards who travelled with us kept walking back and forth alongside the boxcar.) We were all punished for the incident: we were deprived of water for three days and soup for a week.

In a week's time, our train was somewhere beyond Moscow. We heard that the war had begun from outfitted soldiers in trains going in the opposite direction. From then on, our train stopped at by-stations for longer hours, standing on reserve rails until army trains travelling westward had passed. We travelled about four weeks. Our journey and that of three or four other boxcars ended in the Karasuk station in western Siberia. We were let off the cars by causeways and allowed to drink our fill of water. Then we were seated, one, two or three families together, in wagons sent to shuttle us to our destinations. As we heard later, all the Jewish people remained in the town of Karasuk.

Our family and a few others were taken eighteen kilometers from Karasuk to the third farm, or village, in a soviet farm called Dzerzhinsky. The farm was surrounded by plains and steppe, here and there some woods with birches and asps. The village itself consisted of one street, lined with houses on both sides (about forty houses in all). The houses were 1.8 to two meters high on the outside, their walls made of turf, at least a half meter thick. The ceilings and roofs were also turfy. The houses were about three meters wide, with beams through the center, just above the side walls, supported by poles in the rooms. Every thirty to forty centimeters on those beams and the walls, there were laths blanketed by brushwood. The brushwood was covered with reeds, and these with a layer of turf plastered on top with a mixture of clay and cow dung. The ceiling-roof was about forty centimeters thick. The windows were tiny, seventy by forty centimeters, and

the height of the door about 1.5 meters. (Windows and doors were made small to keep in more warmth.) The houses, about six meters in length, were partitioned in half, making for one room and a kitchen with a large Russian stove, which served as a bed for two or three people. Larger houses, about nine meters long, had two rooms in addition to the kitchen. These houses were locally called *zemlyankas* ("earth-houses" or dugouts).

Wood was scarce in that area of Siberia, so the cross beams were thin; to support the weight of the roof, they were set on poles in the rooms. These poles were studded with nails for hanging clothes. There were no closets, and in fact these were unnecessary because the local people were very poor and had very little clothing. Their furniture consisted of a table with legs constructed crosswise, a similarly constructed bed or bunk, and a bench. On the kitchen wall they had a few shelves to store dishes and pots, but they didn't have much to store. Families shared one bowl at meal time and ate with wooden spoons. They had never seen forks.

The day after our arrival and settlement in some of those houses, women were assigned to work in the fields or on the farm with livestock. It was exhausting physical labor, to which the women were totally unaccustomed because they were all from the city. We chil-

dren stayed at home by ourselves because we didn't speak Russian and could not communicate with local children. Moreover, local inhabitants avoided us at first because they had been advised that the exiles were "enemies of the people."

The soil there was fertile and used mainly for wheat fields. Later, in Khrushchev's time, newly plowed lots, including those in our region, could be privatized. But in 1940 there was a severe drought in the area and the harvest was meager. With the onset of war, local people had almost nothing to eat; they had only the bread they could get with coupons. They also kept cows, which were a source of food and their salvation. We used to buy milk from them or get some in exchange for items of clothing.

As it turned out, our suitcase contained mostly father's clothes while father had taken most of the children's wear. However, this happenstance proved to be partly an advantage in the battle for survival: we could exchange father's clothes for grain from the Kazakhs whereas children's clothing was not very useful in bartering for food.

Days passed in our new environment and we children were eager for a trek beyond the village, but we were afraid to leave the house unlocked. We thought we might borrow a padlock from the neighbors, so we all gathered together to decide who would ask them and how to ask for a padlock. My sister, who was two years older than me and had completed four years of primary school in Lithuania, knew two words in Russian. These words, *chyort* (devil) and *devchyonka* (lassie) wouldn't be of much help. Naujokienė's daughter, Violeta, was smarter, for older, and seemed very knowledgeable to us. So our council managed to chart a request and chose delegates to communicate it. The sentence was: *Odolzhite nam spinu**. When we asked this of our neighbors, they were greatly humored, for no one could lend us a "back." We clarified our request with sign language, and they let us borrow a padlock. Thus we gradually began to relate to the local people and speak their language. I must say, the villagers were good people and understood us exiles. Apparently, they had also suffered from Stalin's repressive measures in one way or another. Their living conditions hardly differed from ours, except that they had cows, and they were used to living in poverty.

The first winter was hard for lack of food, warm clothing, and fuel. We kindled fires with branches, that is, brushwood we brought or dragged from the woods, called *okolki*, in the vicinity. The nearest wood was three to four kilometers from the village. We used to go there, gather brushwood, tie it in bundles, and drag these by a rope thrown over a shoulder. That was children's work: gathering firewood and heating our homes.

The local inhabitants prepared fuel in the summer. The fuel, called *kizyak*, was produced as follows. In the winter, when cows were kept in the barns, cow dung was taken outside every day or every other day and piled up. The pile froze before spring. When the weather grew warmer, the dung was diluted with some water and mixed with straw, making for a sticky, clay-like substance. Women and children kneaded it with their bare feet. Then they pressed the mixture into molds about the size of two bricks, tread on it again, and removed the molds. When the *kizyaks* dried out some, they

* ***Spinu*** *is the Russian objective case for* ***spina****, meaning "padlock" in Lithuanian and "back" in Russian, making for "Lend us a back."*

were turned over to dry thoroughly and then piled in stacks. This fuel was very good; it burned hot and long. We didn't have the raw material to produce *kizyaks*, but we improvised. In summer, when cows were grazing in the fields, we used to collect piles of dry, thick dung, pack as many as we could carry in bags, and take them home. So we also had reserves of fuel for the winter.

Winters were very cold, with temperatures dipping to –50° C (–58° F). Fierce winds came with the snow. Our house used to be covered with snowdrifts until springtime. Beneath such blanketing, insulation of sorts, we needed less fuel to heat our little cottage.

Every house had an annex, a little corridor where cows were kept by one wall and fuel stored by the other. (Hay for the cows was stored outside.) The door of the corridor always opened to the inside of the house; otherwise it would likely be blocked by snow. After blizzards, the villagers shoveled paths to the houses for one another. The upper layer of snow used to be padded so thick and hard that it supported horses and sleds as well as human weight. People rode on those snow banks in winter.

After the first year of war, there were very few horses left on the farm—lame, blind, or old ones. Horses, like able men, had been taken to the front. Farm work was done with oxen. My mother and one other woman used to transport straw from the fields to the farm with two oxen harnessed to a sled. The animals were trained for their tasks in wintertime. I, too, participated in their training. Women cooperated in the task of harnessing the oxen; then we children, usually in pairs, sat down on the sleds and rode across the steppe. The oxen would pull with all their might, trying to break away from their harnesses, so our challenge was to stay on the sled. When the animals tired, they slowed down. In four or five days, they became obedient and fit for work.

When we were settled in the village, the women began to search for their husbands and sons. They wrote inquiries to all the concentration camps in the Soviet Union. In a year's time, we received a message from my father and began corresponding. All letters to and from the concentration camp were censored, so they had to be positive and politically correct. But the corps of censors must have included inmates because we received various kinds of letters. For example, my father wrote that he had become close with his best friend, Hunger, and never parted with him. So we found out a little about the men's predicament.

During the first two winters in exile, we also experienced hunger and a whiff of starvation. First the legs would swell from starvation, then the arms, and finally the face. A face would swell beyond recognition. Once the face swelled, the stricken person was unlikely to survive; death came four or five days after the onset of swelling in the face. At one time, we suffered swelling in the legs and arms.

We used to get food for coupons. Initially, a worker received 150 grams of bread per day; a dependent, 50 grams. (A 50-gram piece of bread was the size of a match box.) My sister, Birutė, used to divide her little piece of bread into three parts for breakfast, lunch, and supper. I used to eat all of mine right away. When Birutė ate, I used to escape to a corner of the house or outside, so that I wouldn't see her eating. Mother tried to give us her ration, but we resisted as best we could because we knew that she worked and if she couldn't work, we would all starve. We used to make the rounds of trash bins and gather peelings or other scraps of refuse, only to avoid death by starvation.

There was also a lack of fodder, and animals began to fall off from starvation. When an ox or cow died, all the villagers went to the farm for meat. To prevent illness from the carrion, they began to douse it with some kind of foul-smelling liquid and take it away by sled to a burial ground about three kilometers from the village. Whenever a dead beast was being transported, a procession of villagers followed as if in a funeral. Some came with sleds, others with bags, to bring home whatever they could get. That meat had to be cooked a long time until the stench evaporated. Then we would eat our fill.

In early spring we used to go to the potato fields, where potatoes had been planted the previous year, to dig them up before they thawed. Those potatoes made for a delicacy because frozen potatoes are sweet. Their sweetness might even turn bitter.

While we still had clothing to spare, we used to exchange items for wheat. We crushed the wheat in a mortar, which we borrowed from neighbors; then we made wheat porridge. Eventually, I replicated a little grain mill someone had. The mill, or grinder, was based on a meter-length board. On one end, I secured a peg, about twenty-five centimeters high and eight centimeters in diameter, bound on the outside by tin (from an old pail) with numerous holes punched outward, as in a grater. On this "grater" I set another one, five centimeters higher and wider in diameter, made to turn around the inner peg by a handle (a little board or stick) fastened to an edge. Then, sitting on the board, which I set on a bench, I poured in grain and

turned the outer grater by the handle until the grain went through the graters and ground before settling at the bottom. For finer grain, I repeated the process. Later, I produced many of these little mills for people in our village and others. I used to get grain as reimbursement. Then we had flour and bran, and we could vary our diet.

There was a lake about two kilometers from our village, and we—everyone who didn't have to work—used to go fishing in wintertime. The ice was apt to be about a meter and a half thick, so we fished through the same ice holes throughout the season. Everyone had ice holes of their own; I had three of them. For warmth and a windbreaker, we used to build little snow walls around the ice holes, with doorways for entrance. We made hooks from needles by heating them above an oil lamp and then bending them. For fishing-line, we used bristles from horses' tails, so a few horses on the farm would be seen without tails in spring. For bait, we used insects gotten from other villages and sold in glass jars, as there were none in the lake. I used to keep the jar of insects in the cellar; while fishing, I kept it close to my chest, so the insects wouldn't freeze. If they froze, I would stick one into my mouth to thaw out, so I could get it on the hook. We caught perch for the most part. There were good days when I caught a hundred or more, and bad days, when I returned home with but a few. We used to stay on the ice all day, hungry, in about – 40° C weather, so it wasn't fun; it was work. We used to boil the fish and make soup. We fried the fish bones to dry and crushed them in a mortar, producing flour. We ate everything and wasted nothing.

Once we received news of father's whereabouts, we sent him everything we could produce and spare. We made cheese if we could buy separated milk on the farm. When we had grain, we baked bread and dried it for croutons. During harvest in fall, we children secretly gathered ears of wheat; women would be arrested and imprisoned for doing so.

In the second year of exile, my mother's health deteriorated. Her frail constitution could not withstand the hunger, cold, and exhausting physical labor. She came down with a heart ailment, *angina pectoris*, or as they called it, *grudnaya zhaba*. When she suffered heart attacks, we called on the neighbors for help. What else could we children do? There was no medication. With time, we learned to apply cold compresses to her chest and rub her hands, arms, and temples until she recuperated. Even though she was ill, she had to proceed with the same physical labor, like all other women.

Before the snow came in late autumn, my mother and a Polish woman who lived with us obtained a wagon with a few oxen from the farm supervisor to bring in some firewood. After work, as it was getting dark, the women and I drove about seven kilometers to the woods. We unharnessed the oxen and tied them to a tree. We split branches, gathered brushwood, and loaded it on the wagon. By then it was totally dark. We had loaded about half the cart when we noticed that we were surrounded by wolves—many of them, about ten, for we could see their eyes shining in the dark. Sensing wolves, the oxen became restless and began to fling about. Luckily, my mother had some matches. We set some hay on fire by the wagon while the Polish woman banged her ax against the wagon wheels to make noise. (They say that wolves are afraid of noise and fire.) The wolves scattered; their shiny eyes disappeared from sight, but the wagon and surrounding brush caught fire. That wagon must have been used to transport fuel to the tractors because it was saturated with oil. We managed to unload the firewood and hastened to quell the flames by tossing and rubbing chunks of frozen sod on parts of the wagon. By the time we extinguished the flames, the wagon was scorched. Meanwhile, the oxen had broken loose, and we had to wander around to find them. We returned with very little firewood and a burnt wagon.

My mother was convicted for ruining the wagon. The trial took place three days later, with all administrators of the soviet farm and all village women in attendance. Mother had many supporters, who begged the judges for leniency and pity on the children. Indeed, they were lenient. They did not send mother to prison but fined her for the cost of repairing the wagon.

We spent three winters preserving ourselves from cold and starvation. Mother's health got worse and her heart attacks more frequent. At the time, 1943, disabled soldiers were returning from the war. In the town of Karasuk, they established an "artel of invalids" [a workers' cooperative], where veterans and other people unfit for physical labor could work. There was shoe repair, basket weaving, knitting, and sewing at the artel. My mother knew how to sew. She and some other Lithuanians repeatedly sought permission to move to town and work at the artel. Finally, when mother was too weak to continue with farm work or forestry, she was granted permission to leave for Karasuk. That was in April, 1943. There was still plenty of snow, and we departed on a sled. In Karasuk, we rented a room from local people. It was about seven square meters in size, with a stove for heating and cooking.

By day mother worked as a seamstress at the artel; at home, she knitted scarves, socks, trousers, and whatever else people needed. Birutė also knitted. Even I learned to knit and spin yarn from wool on a little stick called *veretyoshka*. I did pretty well, but I was the slowest knitter, so I had to assume other tasks: heating the stove and preparing meals. With the milk and potatoes gotten in exchange for knitting, we had more food. Once I boiled some potatoes and, after straining them, added a few cloves of finely chopped garlic. The taste was beyond description! It seemed we were eating the best of sausage with the potatoes. After that meal, I often dreamed of potatoes seasoned with garlic.

There were many other Lithuanians in town, including numerous Jews from Lithuania. We all got along very well and helped one another. In 1943 and 1944, when Russia and the United Stated became allies, the Jews located relatives in the U.S.A. They received care packages and aided Lithuanians who were experiencing hardship. Among the Lithuanians in Karasuk, our family was closest to Naujokienė and her daughter Violeta, the Žvirgždinas family with two children, old Rubavičienė, Čivilienė with her son, and some others. Žvirgždinienė was a doctor, and her husband, a chemical engineer, worked in a brick factory. Naujokienė also worked in the brick factory.

We knew of the Gudaitis family with two children, Juozukas and Laimutė. Gudaitienė took up fortune-telling with cards as a defense against starvation. She used to get milk or other products in return for her services. She had many clients because all the women wanted to know whether their husbands or sons were still alive at the front. Gudaitienė must have become overly daring in her predictions or spoken too freely for the ears of local authorities: she was arrested, sentenced, and deported to a concentration camp. Mr. Gudaitis and the children lived wretchedly. Gudaitis worked in a meat processing plant and fended as best he could for the children, but he died of starvation in 1944. The children were supposedly sent to an orphanage. We never saw or heard of them again.

We continually corresponded with father and sent him packages. The letters were all very similar. Father asked mother not to send him packages but rather to see that we children would not go hungry. However, he had apparently grown very weak and exhausted himself. He died on March 27, 1944, when the hardest times had passed. We received a death certificate to the effect that Bonaventūras Laskevičius, son of Juozas, born in 1900, died of cardiac attack in the region of Arkhangelsk.

<…>

When the front moved westward and the Russian army reached the Baltic countries and Germany, soldiers began sending packages to their families back home. Then we could buy needles, thread, matches, salt, and other items we had constantly lacked. (When we had no matches, we used to keep the fire until morning by lightly covering the live embers with ashes, so we might blow on them and rekindle the fire.) Local people received all kinds of fabrics and clothes in those packages and began to call on mother for sewing or alterations. They didn't know how to use some of the clothing they got, for instance, women wore nightgowns as dresses. But they were totally innocent, having lived in poverty and seen very little throughout their lives. They hadn't seen watches until these came in packages from the soldiers. A bicycle was a rare luxury, a great "car," and there were maybe two of them in the town.

While we lived in Karasuk, mother became acquainted with a local woman who had three sons and a daughter, and plenty to eat. Her husband worked as a senior accountant in a grain elevator; he was lame, so he hadn't gone to war. This woman often brought something for mother to sew or alter. For lack of a sewing machine, mother sewed by hand. When we became friendly with the family, mother was invited to sew at their home with the manual machine they had. Moreover, they used to treat us to delicious rolls and breads they baked with the grain and flour they accessed somehow. The woman and her children were extremely generous and warm-hearted.

In 1945, at harvest time, Birutė obtained work as a laboratory assistant in the grain elevator, thanks to the accountant. She took samples of grain to determine their grade and moisture before the grain was accepted. The delivery trucks were unloaded by so-called *vizirovshchiks* ("grain samplers"), who recorded the number of a truck, took grain from various parts and layers of the tailgate load, put it into containers, and brought these to the lab. I became employed as one of those *vizirovshchiks*. I was thirteen years old at the time; Birutė was fifteen. Now we all received workers' bread rations and were better off. While working with grain, we were also allowed to taste and eat it. Nevertheless, one day after several weeks' work at the grain elevator, I stole a few kilograms of wheat and took it home. I thought I would delight my family, but I was mistaken. Seeing the booty, my mother was terrified. She scolded me severely and even whacked me. In tears, she pleaded with me never to steal again, for it would be the end of us. If she were caught carrying a kilogram of grain, she would be sentenced to ten years in a concentration camp. That sufficed: I pilfered no more grain.

The lab was open throughout the year, so Birutė remained at her job. My work ended with the last of the grain deliveries. Having tasted a worker's bread ration (400 grams, as opposed to a dependent's 150 grams), I wanted to go on working. Again, thanks to our friend the accountant, I was employed for a time as a yard laborer at the grain elevator. For about three months I worked in the granary with a women's brigade. We transferred loads of grain with wooden shovels from one end of the storehouse to the other, so the grain would air out and not overheat. The storage rooms were large, about fifteen meters wide and a hundred meters long; the grain stacks, about four meters high. I shoveled from morning to evening, wading in grain and chewing on grain as I worked. It was not a bad job. When it was cold outside, in the granary our feet were warmed by grain, and of course we warmed up from the physical work.

Algirdas at a work bench, 1952.

Later I was assigned to transport coal to the boiler-house. I was equipped with a two-wheeled cart and a mature ox to pull it. I had to shovel coal into a box-like cart, drive it to the boiler-house (on the grounds of the grain elevator), and unload the coal. The cart held about one cubic meter of coal, and I had to transport eight to ten cartloads per day. It was very hard, tiring work. Eventually, I made a tip-lorry of the cart. Thereafter, I only had to unfasten the latch on the end of the cart: the box tipped over and the coal spilled out. This made the job much easier. I transported coal throughout the winter. Between rounds, I used to get some grain from Birutė in the lab. I would fill my pockets with it, take it to the boiler room, where stokers baked it in a tin, and snack on the "granola" all day. It tasted very good.

When spring came, there was no need for coal in the boiler room. Another job turned up: repairing granary roofs. The granaries were huge and there were many of them, so there was enough work for the whole summer. A brigade of teenagers like me, thirteen to fourteen years old, was organized for this work. We had to replace the torn and rotted slivers of boards in the roofing with new ones. I enjoyed the views while working high up on the roofs. The downside was that I used to wear out my trousers within a month of roof repair. We were given burlap bags to sew new ones. I had some trousers made from nice-looking, thick yellow bags, which seemed too good for work wear; they served initially as holiday attire. The supply of bags must have dwindled toward the end of the summer. We didn't get any for a few months, and we were ragged. I pushed for the six of us to go to the director and ask for more bags. We all went to his office with our request. First of all, the director inquired whether we had our bread cards with us; then he collected them and said, "You may go free. I don't need any striking workers." There were many tears, and I went home crying. But again, through mother's efforts and the helpful accountant's mediation, we were pardoned and re-employed. We had to apologize to the director, and he returned our bread cards. We continued to repair roofs and were often given bags for new trousers.

Next winter we loaded grain from the granaries onto wagons. That was hard labor for women and children! We would fill a bag with grain and then help one another get it on the shoulders—not any which way but vertically, for the bag was untied. Once we got the knack of it, the bag stayed put as if glued to the back. We proceeded from the granary upward on a ladder, poured grain through the wagon door, and went back again. Meanwhile others were filling bags with grain. It was very difficult at the beginning: the bag of grain tipped; the legs gave in. When we got used to the work, it wasn't so bad, though our legs felt numb toward evening. We didn't watch the time while loading those wagons....

Algirdas Laskevičius, Kaunas, 1985
Text received from the family archive.

In 1957 Algirdas Laskevičius returned to Lithuania, along with his mother and his sister's family—Birutė, her husband, and their three-year-old daughter. They stayed with their uncle Jeronimas Laskevičius in Kaunas; however, settling in Lithuania proved to be very difficult. Algirdas and his mother could not register as citizens for six months, so they could not obtain work. Eventually, Algirdas found employment at the electric power station in Petrašiūnai, where he worked for thirty years. While working full-time, he attended and graduated from the polytechnical school in Kaunas.

In 1963 Algirdas married. He raised two daughters, Rasa and Dalia, and enjoyed four grandchildren. In 1983 Algirdas suffered a stroke and thirteen years later, another one. He died in 1997. He was buried at the cemetery in Petrašiūnai beside his mother, who passed on in 1972. His father's, Bonaventūras Laskevičius', burial place is unknown: a city covers the site of the Arkhangelsk concentration camp as well as the bones of those who perished there.

Birutė raised a daughter, Ina, and a son, Alius. She has two grandchildren and resides in Kaunas.

A facsimile of Marija Beleckaitė's fifth grade arithmetic notebook made from newspaper sheets.

Marija Beleckaitė-Rimkevičienė

On June 14, 1941, six-year-old Marija Beleckaitė and her mother, Ona Gaigalaitė-Beleckienė, were exiled from Kaunas to the Altai region in Russia. Her father, Povilas Beleckas, a military officer, was separated from the family and deported to a concentration camp in the northern Urals, where he was executed on September 18, 1942.

LIFE IN THE ALTAI REGION

After eighteen days of travel, the train began to stop at larger railroad stations, leaving a few carloads of people at each one. Our turn came when the train stopped in the town of Troitsk.... We were driven from the station to a market square, where we were lined up next to our belongings and surrounded by guards. If we moved even a meter from our places in line, the guards would immediately order us back. There was a sudden downpour of Altai summer rain and nowhere to hide; everyone and their bundles were soaked. Mother held me close, with her back to the rain, while I gasped for breath from an asthma attack. We sought cover under our carpet, but it was drenched along with everything else. The rain soon gave way to searing rays of sunlight. We stood in the open square as if in a medieval slave market shown in motion pictures. Walking around the new assembly of twentieth-century slaves were communist party officials and supervisors of collective farms, soviet farms, and forest farms, looking for a labor force. No one selected us. Who needed a conspicuously over-dressed, educated woman with a sickly child in her arms? The slave traders sorted out stronger women with adolescent children until the square was almost empty. We stood there until sunset.

We were put up in an abandoned, windowless building for the night. Next morning there were wagons outside the door, sent from the village of Yuzhakovo, forty kilometers from the regional cen-

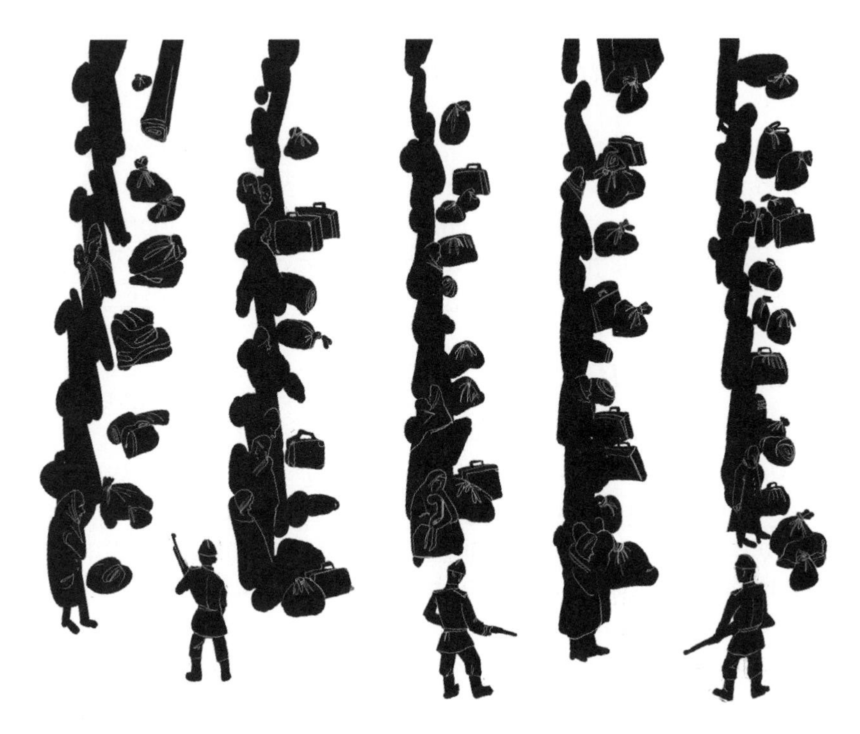

ter. They loaded our belongings and laid me down on top of them. Mother had to walk alongside all the way, like those tired cart drivers who answer only "yes" or "no" when spoken to. After another asthma attack, I fell asleep, rocked by the wagon's motion. I woke up in the evening when we were approaching the village.

Yuzhakovo was situated on the shore of a river flowing from the Altai mountains. The settlement was flanked on one side by vast steppe, overgrown with sagebrush; on the other, by dark taiga, dense with windfallen trees and huge ferns. Our wagons stopped at a solid-looking, empty log house with no doors or windows. It had been forcibly taken from wealthy farmers (*kulaks*) at the time of collectivization, when entire families, dispossessed of their property, were killed on the spot. We were moved into this house. The stoves were wrecked; the wells were blocked up with dirt. People in neighboring houses observed us through cracks in their fences. Otherwise, they stayed at home and remained aloof. They had been advised to keep their children indoors and lock their gates and wells, for the newcomers were fascist families and capitalist bloodsuckers, to be avoided. Passers-by were chased away by guards voicing curses and threats.

Four families settled in the same house: Starkienė's, Kubilienė's, and Beleckienė's in one room, and Ratkelienė's in the other one. We laid our bedding in the corners of the room, on a seemingly new floor of unplaned boards. We took our bundles outside to dry, but the commandant intercepted, saying that we were arousing the local people's curiosity.

We were constantly subjected to searches. The agents were supposedly looking for weapons, but they were really interested in jewelry. They always conducted searches at night, when we had just fallen asleep. In the morning, the mothers were driven to forest work, ten to twelve kilometers away. They had to clear huge piles of decaying, moss-covered wood from trees felled long ago. With no appropriate work clothes or footwear, nor experience in forest work, they had to fell young pine trees, up to 1.5 meters thick, with dull saws and axes. Then they had to split off branches, saw meter-length logs, and stack them up in piles. If they didn't achieve a day's work norm, they wouldn't get coupons for bread. However, those coupons were useless for exiles because there was usually no bread in the store after work hours. There was none because it was sold out, or they didn't bake any, or no flour had been delivered.... That's the way it was throughout the war years. If there were harvested crops in the fields, they were taken to the "front."

The soil in Siberia was dark and fertile. Later, when we had a garden, we just turned sod over with a shovel, planted a seed, weeded, and one potato eye would yield a bucketful of potatoes. But that was later, after two years of illness and hunger.

The beginning was very difficult. We had no stove, fuel, pots or water–no way to prepare food. We were not allowed to go anywhere beyond the lot of the house. There was a river about two hundred meters away. The turbid runoff from melting snow in spring became a muddy, greenish, stagnant stream in summer. Cows stood up to their knees in the deeper parts, defending themselves against stinging flies. The water we brought from the stream and let settle overnight was clear only at the top of the bucket. One day mother borrowed a pail from Ratkelienė, uttering, "What will be, will be," and went to ask for water at the neighboring yard, surrounded by a high wooden fence. No one let her in. Both the gate and the well were chained and padlocked. A woman's silhouette appeared in the window, motioning to mother to go away.

Later, that neighboring landlady, Mariya Fyodorovna Shakhova, told us that they had been ordered to have no relations with the bourgeois newcomers: not to give or sell them anything, nor to converse or let them into their houses.... "We observed them furtively and thought, these attractive women and children, dressed in clothing we'd never seen before, do not look like criminals. They're more like fish thrown out of water" They took pity on us and, in the early morning quiet, set two buckets of water by our door.

Eager for friendship with children, I was the first to try to communicate with the neighbor's daughter, Natasha Shakhova, who was about my age. Waving my hands, I tried to invite her over to play. She looked at us through a crack in the fence without a word. I went closer and handed her a doll I had brought from Lithuania. Natasha wouldn't take it at first and ran away laughing. After a while, perched on the pantry roof, she beckoned to me: "*Idi syuda*" ("Come here"). I didn't understand and ran to ask mother. Mrs. Starkienė explained that the girl was inviting me over to her house. Later we used to squeeze through an opening in the fence to play with each other. During the summer, Natasha taught Sigita and me to speak Russian. Only my mother was slow, perhaps unwilling, to speak the local language.

We built a firepit a short distance from the house. The boys brought some stones from the river shore and dug a hollow, which they filled with twigs and driftwood. Our mothers would set a pot on the hot stones and embers to cook barley or fry bacon they had brought from Lithuania. Mother and I had neither bowl nor spoon, so we' d wait for the others to finish eating and offer us theirs.

The outhouse was a deep pit amidst tall mountain sage, covered with a board. Further into the sagebrush, there was an old, dilapidated wooden outhouse from the time of the *kulaks*, to which I once ventured. I tripped on the old boards and one of my shoes fell into the "gold pit." I went crying to mother. She tried but could not retrieve my shoe. A group of children gathered 'round. They fished out my shoe with a long pole and, holding it high, marched down the village street singing *Za rodinu, za Stalina, za Kolku Kanina* ("For our country, for Stalin, for Kolka Kanin"). Kanin was a very active, fierce party official, a persecutor of local farmers (*kulaks*), and terror of exiles. Our mothers were frightened by the demonstration and feared negative consequences; however, those singing children were local Pioneers,* so there were no complications.

In the fall, Mrs. Starkienė registered Sigita for first grade in the Russian school. Kęstutis and Jurgis were already enrolled in higher grades. My mother argued with Uršulė Starkienė as to whether attending the Russian school was worthwhile. My mother thought the war would end soon, we' d return home, and the children would be able to study in their native language. In Starkienė's opinion, all education was beneficial and learning Russian was a necessity. Mother said, tearfully, that she would not let me attend school; besides, I was only six years old. But when Sigita left for school, I ran after her, shouting; when we reached the school, I sat down beside her on the same bench. The teacher let me stay if I wanted to, even though I was too little. Thus I began to attend school. About a month later, the teacher told us about Little Octobrists, "Lenin's grandchildren".

---

* ***Pioneers and Little Octobrists****: a massive political organizations for school-age children in the USSR, intended to indoctrinate communist ideology in the context of various activities.*

They sing, dance, and play together; in the winter, they decorate a fir tree and get presents. "Raise your hand if you want to join them," she said. Everyone raised their hands and I, foolish girl, did too. Sigita leaned over and whispered, "Take your hand down!" I wouldn't. She slapped my hand and I slapped her back. Then, pointing to Stalin's portrait on the wall, she asked, "Do you want to serve the dictator who is persecuting your father?" I lowered my hand. At home that evening, when our mothers returned from work, Sigita told them about my intent to join the Little Octobrists. My mother spanked me with a switch, crying and lamenting that her daughter behaved so foolishly. Uršulė consoled her. Then I understood that I could not trust those who had unjustly punished my father. Sigita had given me a good lesson in politics that day.

At school during intermissions, a group of older Russian boys began to push me around and bully me. The teacher protected me in school, but on the way home, the whole gang, lurking by the wayside and yelling *fashistka*! ("fascist!"), showered me with stones. Sigita was ill at home at the time. One day Kęstutis saw the boys victimizing me, chased them away, and told his mother about it. Mrs. Starkienė went to the school to investigate the problem. It turned out that the boys had taken an ornamental starburst embroidered on my knit hat for a swastika—a fascist sign—and decided to get me. My mother removed the ornament from my hat, but traces of its color remained after washing; she had to find dye to re-color the hat. After all this and a talking-to by the teacher, the youngsters left me alone.

My memories of that first summer in Siberia are replete with romantic images. We children did not feel the humiliation of exile, the loss of husbands, and uncertainty concerning their fate that our mothers suffered. We didn't experience the exhausting physical labor. We lived enveloped by motherly love, defended against evil and the specter of starvation. I recall how mother, having exchanged an item of clothing for food or bought some milk, potatoes, or millet, used to feed me first and not eat herself until I was satiated. "Mummy dearest, eat at least a little yourself," I might have said, but I came to understand her motherly sacrifice only in adulthood. My mother was resolved first of all to sustain her child.

After a very hard and cold winter of semi-starvation, we found ourselves covered with festering boils. Mother had a particularly painful sore inside her ear. She lay half-conscious on a thinly blanketed freezing floor, by frosty walls and ice-covered windows—with a forty-degree fever and no doctor's aid. The Shakhovs took me into their part of the house, warmed by a huge Russian stove. While most of the family slept on top of this stove, I shared a bed with their daughter, Natasha, on a sideboard secured high up on a wall. At night, the Shakhovs would check us for an overdose of fumes from the stove and see whether mother was still breathing. But they did not let me go near her. I overheard their muted conversations: "She' s bound to die, and we'll keep the girl, such a good friend to Natasha." Starkienė and her children often came over to visit mother, helping as they could with a warm bowl of soup, nursing, and sympathy. There was no medication or medical assistance. The nearest village was thirty kilometers away; the regional center, forty kilometers away, and the roads were covered with snow.

I was told to behave and pray for mother's recovery. I remember lying on that high, fume-soaked sideboard while a Siberian blizzard raged outside, crying quietly and whispering a prayer I had learned back in Kaunas. I thought I would only ask the Virgin Mary and surely, tomorrow mother would get up feeling better; my sore-ravaged legs would heal as well. Natasha complained that I was keeping her awake, so I would cease praying and go to sleep, curled up in a ball. Upon waking one day, I saw a blue light outside the frosty window: morning! Maria Fiodorovna was kindling a fire in the stove and mixing a batter of barley flour and water for pancakes. She greased the pan with bacon rind, poured in some batter, and held the frying pan to the fire. The pancakes were singed, but their smell was delicious!

Overnight, mother's sore suppurated through her ear. She lay still, as if sleeping, but also looking at me silently. Tearfully, I offered her the pancake I had, but she kept her silence. Mrs. Starkienė and Sigita came over, bringing milk. While Starkienė tended mother, Sigita persuaded her to let us go outside for a sleigh ride. After the blizzard, there were mountains of snow everywhere, larger than the village houses, and children on top of them. The cold was bearable, only about twenty degrees. They wrapped me in a scarf, seated me on the sled Sigita brought, and we were on our way. Natasha was skiing with the wind, snowdrift to snowdrift, while I sped downhill on the sled and—oh horror!—it turned over.... I was shrieking from pain as several boils on my legs burst open. Worried, Sigita quickly pulled me home and inside the house. Mother attempted to get up, but Starkienė wouldn't let her and came to my aid herself. She carefully bandaged my bloody, pus-covered legs with shreds of old linen. Even now, in my old age, I have ugly scars from those boils, mementos of our first winter in Siberia.

That winter our mothers were not forced to do physical labor. All physically able men had been drafted into the army; only invalids, women, and children remained in the village. Spring was a season of dire want. People ate buds off the trees and peeled bark for sustenance. If anyone had potatoes, they ate them whole, saving only the eyes for planting. Anyone with a cow was considered rich.

Our mothers were obliged to knit socks, hats, and gloves for soldiers at the front. For lack of heated community facilities, they brought their work home. They also taught us girls to knit. Sigita and I had to knit a sweater per month, work for which we'd receive a liter of milk each day. I was very eager to begin. Our knitting needles consisted of twigs, and thread was gotten from the coarse, rough wool of local sheep. The women expressed pity at seeing me—the youngest and weakest child, plagued with asthma, my little bony hands and transparent fingers pecking at my needlework, stitching away. But I enjoyed it immensely and, most important, I was working! I was helping mother.... She once remarked that she had noticed my inclination to do something useful early on, in Kaunas. Seeing me at play with my toys, she asked me what I was doing. I replied that I was "working bread," recapitulating phrases I had heard from mother. She used to explain that father left for work each day because he had to "earn bread" for us. Those words reverberated throughout my life.

I remember moving when my mother and Starkienė decided to rent a little one-room house with a large stove and a small plot for a garden. We had to carry our things from one end of the village to the other, about two kilometers. We could barely drag our feet with all those bundles. I can still see Kęstutis Starkus, clutching the briefcase gifted by his father and staggering as he walked. Later, in exchange for some things, our mothers rented a cart, *telega*, with which they brought logs and poles from the woods for bunk beds. They constructed bunks high up on logs. With some board ends, they hammered together a little table, which they covered with pieces of cardboard boxes they found by the store. All our belongings

were piled on the bunks, where we also slept, did our homework, and knitted while singing or chanting.

At bedtime, our mothers covered us with their hand-made quilts, and we all kneeled down to say a prayer in words of our own: "Thank You, Lord, for sustaining us today. Watch over us at night. Grant us health and tenacity; protect us from errors and temptations. Keep our fathers and husbands alive and healthy and let them return to their families. Watch over our brothers and sisters. Have mercy on all Lithuanians, suffering at home and in Siberia, and show us the way back to our homeland. Lord, be merciful; do not punish us for our sins. Lord, grant eternal peace to our deceased fathers, brothers, sisters, and Lithuanians in all parts of the world." Later, we used to add, "to Kęstutis, to Zigmas…." We said this prayer from the bottom of our hearts, with passion, believing in our words

Ona Beleckienė with her daughter, Marija.

and trusting that our pleas would reach the good Lord. We just had to wait a while and be patient. Then our mothers crossed us and we snuggled into bedding that had been warmed by the stove. After many years, I repeated this prayer by Sigita's and her mother's grave sites in Lithuania when I, who had been the smallest and weakest among exiles, was the only one of us still living. There will be no one left to say it at my grave.

In the spring, we dug furrows for garden beds in our little yard. The shovel was gotten from local people in exchange for some personal belongings. Our mothers, semi-starved throughout the winter, had no strength, but they stubbornly persisted in the task. They would turn some sod over with the shovel, then sit down to rest, covered with perspiration. Sigita and I were given a patch of our own. We planted potato eyes, pumpkins, squash, beets, carrots, beans, and melons. We seeded a few square meters with millet. The soil was black and fertile but also conducive to weeds. Sigita and I weeded the garden all summer. Every day each of us was supposed to weed one garden bed. I did this quickly whereas Sigita would come to in late afternoon, after running around all day, and ask me to help her before our moms returned from work. Of course I used to help her and not tell, as I was asked. Such were our mischievous collaborations.... We also had to gather firewood for the evening. We could find it everywhere—by the farms, the sawmill, the river—because the village was in the taiga.

Our relentless efforts bore fruit but incurred another misfortune: we were dispossessed of our property and deported a second time. We had too large a crop of potatoes in the fall; we had dared to raise a heifer and a sheep. Jealous neighbors had apparently complained to the authorities. They came at night and ordered us to pack our things; they took us to a soviet farm in arid steppe. This happened in the spring of 1944.

Our last year in Yuzhakovo, when we had a garden and raised animals, was the most prosperous. In addition to knitting our quota

for the soldiers, we also sold some of our handiwork. Local women liked to wear large, soft scarves with designs and fringes, with which they wrapped themselves head to waist. They didn't know how to knit, or maybe didn't want to, so they commissioned our mothers to knit scarves, reimbursing them with milk, flour, grain, or potatoes. In our house we had only one light: an oil (tallow) lamp with a wick of twisted linen, which gave off fumes and an unpleasant odor while it burned. I often remember Mrs. Starkienė by that light, bent over with her knitting. I was often ill with asthma and mother, though exhausted and weary, used to carry me around our little cottage in the evenings: a few steps forward and a few steps back…. Nestling up to mother in almost vertical position, I breathed more easily. My lungs wheezed like an harmonica and I gasped for air while mother kept moving, stumbling, and praying. Mrs. Starkienė knitted to the grating sounds of villagers squabbling outside. Meanwhile Sigita slept peacefully.

Mother used to rise very early in winter, to heat the stove and prepare food. She'd make millet and potato, carrot, or beet soup, mixed with some milk, or simply bake a panful of unpeeled potatoes. When the stove was hot, she used to bake pumpkin, round and large as a tire, filled with guilder-rose berries. While baking, those berries gave off a foul smell, but their taste was delicious. Later, in Lithuania, when Sigita and I had our own families, we used to get together and reminisce about those days. Sigita said she grew pumpkins in her garden outside Vilnius and baked them. While her family made sour faces, she enjoyed eating them. Yet the taste was not quite the same….

In winter, blizzards used to cover, indeed bury, our little cottage in blankets of snow. We shoveled a path to the door so we could bring in water and fuel, and children might go to school. We kept a heifer in a shed by the house throughout the winter. We stored hay and beets in the cellar. Our cottage was warm inside when ensconced in snowdrifts up to the chimney. Besides the stove, there was an iron furnace (*burzhuyka*). In severe cold, we'd let our heifer,

Milka, inside. She liked to keep her snout above the furnace while we kept close to the stove.

In summer, we used to let the heifer out to pasture in the fields beyond the village. Come evening, my mother, taking a bucket of water with slices of potato or a handful of barley, went out to the edge of the fields and called, "Milka, Milka!" The sun was setting, the day's heat subsiding, and suddenly in the stillness we'd hear mother's thin, wistful voice: "Milka, Milka!" It sounded like a lament or a longing, or the soul's cry, drowned in everyday reality. I can hear that voice now when the sun sets and the day's bustle gives way to evening's calm. It is so touching and so painful.... Milka would come mooing out of dense sagebrush, covered with straw and burrs, bitten up by gad-flies. We took Milka along when we were deported again in 1944. She grew up a good cow but also required lots of care. In the new location, Sigita and I joined other shepherds, mainly Volga Kalmucks, and took Milka to graze in luxuriant ravines about twenty kilometers away from the farm. There we also gathered basketfuls of fragrant wild strawberries.

Our schooling

Sigita and I attended the Yuzhakovo school and sat next to each other on the same bench. Classes were large, comprising children of various nationalities, for the most part exiles. Of course, everything was taught in Russian: reading, writing, arithmetic. We had no books or notebooks. We wrote on anything at hand, mostly old newspapers or the pages of old books; if we were lucky, pieces of cardboard or wooden boards. We wrote with pencils we moistened with saliva, forming large letters and numbers between lines of printed text. (Chemical pencils could be obtained only in the marketplaces of big cities like Barnaul or Biysk.) My mother safeguarded a notebook I had made for arithmetic in fifth grade and brought it back to Lithuania. It consisted of pages of a newspaper *Tarybų Lietuva* (*Soviet Lithuania* of May 26, 1945) relatives had sent us, folded in the shape of a notebook, with title and purpose noted and glued on the "cover."

The basics of writing and arithmetic which I learned at the Russian school have stayed with me throughout the years. Even today, when I have to compute numbers quickly, I figure in Russian: *pyatyu pyat = dvadcat pyat* ("five times five is twenty-five").

Sigita and I were both eager to study. However, Sigita's grades were much better than mine because I was often ill and missed lessons. During the cold spells and blizzards of winter we sometimes stayed home for weeks. Once, on the way to school, we were caught in a fierce storm that knocked us off our feet and almost buried us in snow. Sigita told me to follow her, holding on to the belt of her coat. Unable to see the path in front of us, we faltered from snowdrift to snowdrift. Suddenly we tripped and fell onto something like a log—but it turned out to be a corpse outside a Kalmuck barrack. We found ourselves at a building away from the road and went inside through a corridor. An old Kalmuck woman with disheveled grey hair beckoned us inside the room. It was permeated by foul odor. The woman, smoking a long pipe, offered us cups of tea enriched with sheep tallow; in fact, she ordered us to drink it lest we die without ever seeing our mothers again. Sigita merely sipped it while I, closely watched by the "witch," drank it all. Then she beamed a toothless smile and seated us by the barely smoldering fire burning on an earthen floor. Smoke rose upward through a hole in the ceiling. Blizzards sometimes raged for days, but luckily this one subsided as quickly as it had struck. We waded home through deep snow, missing school that day. Our moms were in a fright, especially mine, who fretted that I would suffer another asthma attack. The day's stressful adventure did not aggravate my condition. It seemed that God protected us in all calamities.

In the evenings, our mothers taught us Lithuanian reading and writing, as well as songs and hymns. Mrs. Starkienė taught us some German. I can still remember a children's poem she recited to us in

German, though I do not read or write that language. Many years later, when we celebrated Mrs. Starkienė's 100th birthday, I recited the first few lines of the poem and she continued the playful verse to the end. Mrs. Starkienė and Sigita had beautiful, strong voices. Starkienė taught us about a hundred folk songs, which I recorded on sheets of paper. We used to sing while knitting in the evening. I tuned in with my thin voice while Sigita carried the melody with her sonorous, rich alto:

Leiskit į tėvynę, leiskit pas savus,
Ten pradžiugs krūtinė,
Atgaivins jausmus…

(Let us back to our homeland, let us back to our loved ones, where our hearts will rejoice and revive our feelings…)

or

Šešias lentas kai išpjaus,
Juodą grabą kai sukals,
Tai tada, motinėle,
Aš pas tave sugrįšiu.

(When they hew six boards and build a black coffin, then, dear mother, I will return to you.)

My mother usually broke down in tears while Mrs. Starkienė stoically encouraged us: "Very good, girls. Now let's try this one…." Local Russians who passed by the house and heard us sing used to say, *Litovki molyatsa* ("Lithuanian women are praying"). We had neither prayer books nor rosaries. Everything had been confiscated by NKVD agents in the course of searches. Our mothers tried to revive some of the litanies from memory. When I returned to Lithuania in 1946 and lived in the country with my aunt, we used to frequent the neighbors on May evenings, chanting *mojavas* (prayers or hymns to the Virgin Mary). I knew most of the hymns by heart, and everyone wondered where and how I had learned them.

At school, Sigita was my best friend. Natasha was in a higher grade and in another building. However, I always sought the company of other children. During intermissions I would get together with the Russian girls to chat. After such intimacies, I often came home with lice. My mother had to inspect my head, shampoo my hair, and wash my underwear with soap from lye and ashes. Whenever Sigita saw me rubbing shoulders with other girls, she would call on my mother when she came home from school: "Mrs. Beleckienė, Marytė has been chummy again; you must inspect her hair." Even the teachers were lice-ridden. Those parasites were a part of everyday life in Siberia, but not everyone battled them as persistently as our mothers did. Our household was cleaner than most.

When I was in third grade, there was a new physical education teacher, who had returned from the front with an amputated arm and a face disfigured by scars. The malicious man vented his anger by yelling at us, especially at exiles' children. We all feared him. During one of his lessons, he had us line up in military fashion and began commanding us: "left, right, about face." I understood "left" and "right" but kept turning around by the wrong shoulder. He noticed my error immediately, called me to the front of the class, and ordered me to keep turning about face. I couldn't understand what he expected of me, and he waxed angrier, accusing me of irritating him on purpose. "You spawn of the bourgeois, I'll show you!," he yelled. But he didn't show me anything; he kept ordering me about. I started crying and gasping for breath from the stress and a sudden feeling of weakness. He persisted, foaming at the mouth. Finally, when the whole class became restless, he ordered me back to my place in line and continued drilling us. When I turned the wrong way again, a Russian girl tapped me on the shoulder, saying, "Turn this way." I understood and carried out the rest of the commands correctly. "See how I've taught this saboteuse," the teacher remarked to the class. After that lesson, I was ill and stayed home from school for a long time.

I have no happy memories of school in Siberia. Most of the teachers were elderly, enervated women, who had graduated from tenth grade long ago. They were living on the brink of starvation and were constantly anticipating or, in fact, receiving news of their husband's or son's death at the front. They did not hurt us exiles but kept aloof. They were frequently prepped in political dogma by visiting regional inspectors. These officials inquired about the subject matter of dictations and pupils' knowledge of Lenin's and Stalin's childhoods, education, etc. I don't recall reading any Russian classics, except for Krylov's fables about an animal orchestra and a bitch that barked at an elephant. We didn't celebrate any holidays during the war years. Instead, there were incomprehensible lectures about the October Revolution or the first of May. The school children were assembled in a long corridor, where we had to stand, crowded together, for hours while teachers and representatives of the regional administration spoke. The physical education teacher would demonstratively wave his one hand, shouting, *My pobedim, nashe dyelo pravoye! Ura!* ("We will win, we are right! Hurray!") Everyone had to clap, shout "hurray," and throw their caps up in the air. The New Year was not celebrated, nor fir trees decorated. Besides, there were no fir trees in our vicinity.

Sigita and I used to decorate a pine branch or a stalk of sage with paper ornaments for Christmas Eve. At Christmas Eve supper we used to have oatmeal wafers, baked pumpkin, and sour cranberry juice (for we had no sugar). At school, we all had to learn a poem about a fir tree: *V lesu rodilas yolochka…* ("A fir tree was born in the forest…"). I remember reciting this poem eloquently in front of the class and receiving a compliment from the teacher.

Marija Beleckaitė-Rimkevičienė, Aldona Starkutė-Šmatavičienė, Birutė Starkutė-Pratašiene. *Pelynų metai* ("Sagebrush Years"). Kaunas: Naujasis lankas, 2010.

Marija Beleckaitė returned to Lithuania with orphaned children of exiles in 1946. She stayed with her aunt Teodora Krumplienė's (her father's sister's) family in Linkuva, where she graduated from middle school. Then she attended and graduated from the Agricultural Academy; she wrote a dissertation, which was certified as a Ph.D. degree in the Republic of Lithuania. In later years, she worked at the Agricultural University in Kaunas. She raised a son, Rimvydas, and a daughter, Lina. Marija Beleckaitė-Rimkevičienė died in 2009. She was buried at the cemetery in Karmėlava next to her mother, Ona Beleckienė, who died in 1989. Ona Beleckienė had returned to Lithuania in 1956.

Sigita Starkutė returned to Lithuania illegally in 1947. In 1950, at age sixteen, she was arrested and taken back, in stages, to exile in Altai. Finally, Sigita and her mother, Uršulė Starkienė, returned to Lithuania in 1955. Sigita Starkutė-Umbrasienė died in 1994; Uršulė Starkienė, in 1997.

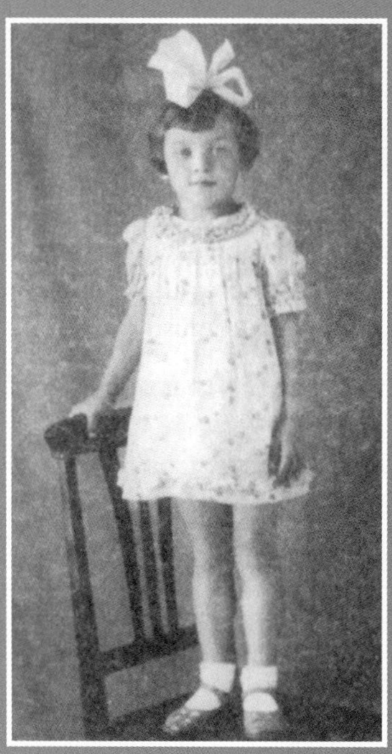

Dainora Tamošiūnaitė, 1938

Valerija Tamošiūnienė with her son Arutis, 1940

Valerija and Juozas Tamošiūnas with their daughter Dainora, 1937

Dainora Tamošiūnaitė-Urbonienė

On June 14, 1941, nine-year-old Dainora Tamošiūnaitė, her mother, Valerija Tamošiūnienė, a teacher, and one-year-old brother, Arutis, were exiled from the town of Raguva in the district of Panevėžys to the Altai region of the Russia. Her father, Juozas Tamošiūnas, also a teacher, was separated from the family and imprisoned at the concentration camp in Reshoty, where he died in 1942.

D. Tamošiūnaitė-Urbonienė's daughter, Rasa Juknevičienė, is one of the signers of Lithuania's Declaration of Independence in 1990; she is a former Minister of Defense in the Republic of Lithuania.

ARUTIS

At the end of November we were taken by truck from Barnaul* to a railroad station. The weather was stormy. Sitting in the open truck, exposed to wind and snow, we were soaked. We were chilled to the bone when we got off in the snow, beyond the station. Fortunately, we had our winter clothing, but it hardly protected us from the cold.

Before long we boarded a train. We rode most of the day until we reached Talmenka in the late afternoon and were ordered to disembark. We were taken to some field where no one met us or guided us; we were simply shown where to set down our baggage. So we sat, cold, wet, and sleepless, on our bags. The three of us huddled together, mother and I sheltering Arutis as best we could.

Late in the evening, someone directed us to a barn nearby. Inside it was a little furnace, leaking fumes so badly when it was lit that we were soon gasping for breath. Arutis slumbered, pale-faced. He would not eat. In Barnaul, mother had provided food for our journey by bartering or selling something. We had boiled potatoes, pickled cabbage, biscuits, some flour, groats, and bread. We had prepared some porridge beforehand and taken it along in a small army mess pot.

---

* ***Barnaul*** *is the capital city of the Altai region in Russia.*

Word spread that they would be taking us to Shipicino in the morning. However, morning came and we were not going anywhere; we were still freezing in the barn. At noon we saw several carts and one open truck outside. Women and children were told to pile their bags on the carts and get on the truck. Mother worried about losing her belongings, but she calmed down when Konstancija Banionienė, a teacher whom she knew from Panevėžys, offered to keep an eye on our bags. We boarded the truck. Sofija Gruzdienė, a teacher and wife of the Traupis elementary school principal Antanas Gruzdys, and her children soon seated themselves next to us.

The journey was utterly miserable. We shivered from the cold because our clothes had not dried overnight. Nestling close to each other on the floor of the truck, we tried to protect Arutis from the wind and dozed. At sundown we saw village lights in the distance. Then the truck stopped and the driver came around to tell us the motor had broken down: we would have to walk to the village (*selo*) or wait there for the wagons with our belongings.

The travelers did not understand everything the driver said in Russian. They translated for each other and conferred as to what to do. Some women with older children set off for the village, but we waited on the spot. The snow and wind subsided. We all got off the truck. Mother suggested I warm myself by running around while she tried to feed and entertain Arutis. Awakening from sleep, he felt very well, ate plentifully, and laughed. But I was beginning to feel sick; I felt chilled and wanted to lie down somewhere to sleep.

Eventually the wagons arrived, and we found the one with our belongings. We children were seated in the wagons while the women had to walk alongside them. I remember mother asking me constantly how I felt, checking my forehead for fever. I dozed most of the way, however long or short it was. Then I remember being lifted from the wagon and walking beside mother, with Arutis in her arms, to a shelter, perhaps a school building, where mattresses were scattered on the floor.

I was very drowsy, but mother wanted me to eat before going to sleep and to wait for the milk that someone was distributing. I felt as if I were in a fog. I heard them saying Dainutė was sick. A Russian woman offered me herbal tea, milk, and bread. I drank some tea and fell asleep.

When I woke up, everyone was preparing for further travel. Mother was glad to see that I felt better and asked if I could walk to the wagon. The Russian woman appeared again, saying something I could not understand. She gave me more tea and warm milk to drink and handed mother some herbs. Then she gave me a slice of bread with cheese on it, saying, "*Kushay, vkusno, brinza*" ("Eat, it tastes good, brinza"). I didn't understand *brinza*. Mother said it was a name for the cheese.

As I was about to get up, we heard that a few wagons had already left, and we would be departing later. I was happy to lie still a while longer. Everyone felt better here, warmed and refreshed by food and rest. However, we had to leave at noon. The three of us got into a cart and sat down on our bags, but the driver signaled angrily to mother to get off. A few more children were seated beside me and Arutis.

At first the journey was tolerable. Arutis played and laughed as we looked around at the scenery. Mother seemed more cheerful as she conversed with other women. Then I saw her sitting down in another wagon, apparently one with a nicer driver. In a while she returned for Arutis and told me to walk in order to warm up. So we travelled, taking turns holding Arutis.

Toward evening the air turned cold. When the drivers stopped for a break, mother searched her bundles for the scarf she had kept for winter and wrapped it round Arutis. We spent the night in some kind of barrack in the woods, with another smoking furnace. The building resembled a barn. There were no bunks or cots, only mattresses strewn along the walls—some of them torn and rotting, merely lumps of discolored wadding. The tired travelers competed for a better spot in the room, for everyone wanted to be further from the door, in the middle by the furnace. Though it gave off fumes, it did produce heat. We settled far in a corner by a frosty wall, which began to leak water when the room warmed up. In our attempt to move to another part of the room, we found ourselves in the middle. As she laid Arutis down, mother remarked that bugs would be torturing us again. They did, indeed, but we must have become accustomed to those bugs or indifferent to them on account of fatigue.

All the barracks we saw on that wretched journey were similar to this one: old, rotting, and drafty. An old man sitting by the furnace in the evening said that these barracks were built to provide temporary shelter for exiles and prisoners who were transported to their destinations in stages (R. *etapy*). While some travelers stayed a night, others inhabited the barracks for a longer time. One of the children asked what a "stage" was. The old man replied that all of us were now being driven in stages from one place to another. We did not know where we would be exiled for the long term.

I could not relate the entire journey from Barnaul today, but one of its stages—the last one—I'll remember to the end of my days. The events of that stage are vivid in my memory as though they happened yesterday, with no intervening passage of time. Various distinct images come readily to mind.

On a cold late afternoon my brother and I are sitting on our bags. A pony is straining to pull our sled, but the angry driver keeps urging the weary animal forward. Whenever the horse slackens its pace, the driver swears and brandishes his whip, hitting me and Arutis in the process. I am afraid as I try to shield Arutis but do not say anything. I cannot complain to my mother that the whip end with its knot hits my forehead, for she appears to be very tired and sad walking alongside the sled. Ahead of us and in back is a caravan of carts with old folks and pale-faced children shivering from the cold, and beside them, women trudging, barely dragging their feet. It seems that road will never end, and we will be travelling on it forever.

I doze off and on, but the whip wakens me, and I watch Arutis. He is very quiet this evening, asleep most of the time. I peek under the scarf and see that the handsome fellow is pale. When I talk to him, he opens his eyes and looks at me but does not smile. Fear sweeps over me. For some reason it occurs to me that we may all die on this road in the woods. Such a thought had never before crossed my mind. I may have been affected by grown-ups' conversations and recent talk that old Aleknavičienė, former landlady of a manor in Pušalotas, was dying. "An old woman but very beautiful," I thought when I first saw her in Panevėžys. She rode in the train car next to ours; we used to see her at resting stops—in a fancy dress, wide-brimmed hat, and high-heeled shoes adorned with glittering buttons. I liked her clothes, but the women wondered why she was dressed that way. In Barnaul I used to see her dressed differently, in a quilted jacket and comfortable shoes. Later we heard that she hadn't been permitted to pack any other clothes or belongings; she was taken from her home in the fancy dress, with a light cloak on her arm. Her clothes were getting shabby and her shoes worn out, so others came to her rescue as best they could. But without winter clothing, she was very cold on this journey. Now, hearing of her illness and, possibly, impending death, I also feared for Arutis.

I called mother and told her Arutis looked very pale. She asked the driver to stop, got into the wagon and took Arutis in her arms. Observing his face intently, she teared up and said, "Arutis is sick." I nestled close and embraced them silently, looking at the sun as it set slowly beyond the gloomy forest. While many things and events have escaped my memory, that dim, lowering Siberian sun returns to mind. Even now, when it's freezing cold, the winter sun reminds me of that journey, sending chills down my spine.

It was getting dark. The driver said that we had arrived at the 60th block and were approaching the barrack. It was another huge, cold one, lined with bunks, with a wood-burning stove (*burzhuyka*) in the center. While mother sought a place close to the stove, there were others who were ill and interested in the warmth of the central area. We had to settle on the periphery, far from the fire.

Late that evening old Aleknavičienė passed away. Her body was laid close to the door. Some men went out to find a burial site and agreed to dig the grave the next morning. A candle shone by the head of the deceased, and people took turns keeping watch.

The stove in our barrack emitted no fumes, but its heat melted the frost on our walls, and the room felt humid. The sick child had no choice but to imbibe this atmosphere. When mother inquired whether there was a doctor in the vicinity, she was informed that there was a nurse in the nearest village and a doctor's assistant about twenty-five kilometers away. Someone promised to ask if the forest workers could bring the doctor's assistant on a tractor. Meanwhile, mother prepared some of the herbal tea gotten from the Russian woman when I was sick. Arutis drank it as he dozed but did not seem any better for it. He tossed about in his slumber, throwing off the scarf that covered him, wanting something. Mother kept tending the fire. Neither of us slept much.

In the morning we were visited by a woman in a white smock. She was more likely the nurse than the doctor's assistant because she didn't diagnose Arutis' illness. She left some powdered medication, saw a few other patients, and left. Arutis drank the medication and slept calmly, breathing more lightly for a while. Mother and I also fell asleep. We woke up to talk of Aleknavičienė's burial. Mother told me to stay with Arutis while she attended the funeral. I sat there, moistening Arutis' fragile lips with tea, talking gently. Once in a while he opened his eyes, seeming to light a smile and attempt to say something, then shut his eyes again.

Everyone was quiet and sad upon returning from the funeral. Someone commented, "The 60th block will be our cemetery" and broke into tears. Back at Arutis' side, mother wept, lamenting the lack of a doctor and treatment for her sick child. I comforted her, reporting that Arutis had woken up, smiled, and tried communicating with me. Gladdened, she went to the stove to prepare some porridge. When she brought the meal, Arutis woke up, looked at us and lifted himself, asking for "opa." We understood his wish but, seeing him in a sweat, were reluctant to carry him about in the cold barrack. Instead, we seated him and offered him the warm porridge. He took a few spoonfuls, sat up a few minutes, and lay down again, looking around and pointing at something. We gave him more medication, and he fell asleep. We felt appeased. Mother slumbered beside Arutis, and I sat next to them, assured that Arutis was getting better, until I fell asleep.

When I awoke, I saw mother at the stove, conversing with other women and boiling potatoes. We hadn't eaten all day; we only drank some boiled water in the morning. Mother served us the potatoes, first Arutis, who was up again. He ate a few mouthfuls, sitting up and saying, "Dai" and "mee." Some women who observed the feeding ritual were delighted to see that the child was getting better and would certainly be well again.

However, later in the afternoon Arutis began to toss about, cry, and moan as if he were in pain. Mother changed his clothes, though others scolded her and advised her not to move him or expose him to cold air. But the baby needed to be cleaned up and changed. Dressed in dry clothing, he settled down and dozed off. Soon he awakened, sat up, and asked to be carried around. Mother wrapped him in a blanket and took him in her arms. She walked about and entertained him, but he closed his eyes and moaned. In the evening, Arutis got worse. He kept crying in a strange, wheezing voice. He calmed down when we took him in our arms. Then he lay quietly for a while, looking around. I lay down beside him, amusing him and expecting him to laugh. But I heard no more laughter.

At midnight everyone was asleep in the barrack. Mother went to kindle the fire. Arutis slumbered, sighing. When, for a moment, I saw him opening his little eyes and looking at me, I addressed him cheerfully, but he squalled in a strange way, obviously agitated and breathing heavily. Mother hurried back, took him in her arms, and carried him around. I walked beside them, holding his tiny hand and kissing him, all the while believing that he would calm down, go to sleep, and soon mend. My hopes were shattered by mother's sudden shriek. I felt Arutis' hand growing heavy in mine… Mother sat down on the bed, bursting into tears. I was about to say that Arutis was looking at us—his eyes were open—but I fell silent. Arutis was looking at mother, strangely tranquil, and the little hand I held was growing colder. Then both of us bent down to kiss his cold little body.

People were getting up. Someone lit a candle. They tried to comfort mother and gently patted me on the head. I was in a state of disbelief until Vygandėlis (who was sick but had gotten up to console us) approached me and took my hand. I gave a start—his hand was so warm, unlike Arutis'…. Recalling my little sister's, Gražytė's, cold hand, I understood that I had lost my little brother. I knelt by Arutis and cried a long while. Then I saw mother lying in the next bed, with eyes closed, looking very pale. She was given some pills. It occurred to me that she was also dying. I bolted in her direction, but Vygandėlis' mother held me back. She embraced me and held me tightly in her arms, saying, "Your mother feels ill; let her rest. Vygandėlis also has to lie down, for he is very sick." His sister, Aldutė, kissed me and led her little brother to bed.

When mother got up, we both knelt by Arutis, stroking him gently, gazing at him. People gathered round and prayed. Still, at moments I wondered whether my little brother had really died.

I heard women asking mother how she would dress Arutis. She chose the finest clothing she had carefully packed away: a white shirt and blue suit. So outfitted, Arutis was laid on the bed. We stayed beside him all night, kneeling or sitting, while others joined in the vigil. I patted his cold little hands and ceased to fear the coldness; on the contrary, they seemed to grow warm from my touch.

I looked at his little face with anticipation, for it seemed to me that he might smile, open his mouth, and say "Dai" or "Nutė" [Dainutė] or ask for something. Mother may have seconded my thoughts; she was calm now as she observed Arutis.

In the morning some men brought in a little wooden coffin they had constructed. The trough seemed ugly to me. I burst into tears, thinking they would now carry out Arutis. But they didn't. They lined the coffin with white fabric and inserted a little pillow, which someone must have sewn that day; then they laid Arutis in the coffin. With the blue suit on white fabric, the little fellow looked even more handsome. I asked mother if they would now carry him out. Not yet, she said. There was talk about digging a grave. However, the coffin cover standing against the wall looked ominous to me.

For some reason, I don't remember a particular incident which mother related to me later. While we were keeping vigil over Arutis' body, a local Russian woman, tired and ragged-looking, entered our barrack. Seeing my mother in tears, she said to the other women, "Why is she crying? I have six children but no food for them, so I would be glad if at least one of them died. And why bury such beautiful clothes? She might have sold them or given them to my half-naked children." She stood there a few moments and left with a wave of her hand. Mother commented that the woman's appearance and words caused anxiety in the barrack: they indicated the utter poverty of the region to which all of us were exiled.

Everyone chanted hymns and prayed, as they did when old Aleknavičienė passed on. After the prayers and hymns, they covered the deceased, closed the coffin, and carried it out from the barrack. Nor had I forgotten the funeral of my sister, Gražytė, in Raguva, especially the terrible moment when they covered her. The little coffin was beautiful, lined with glistening silk and a little silk pillow, and filled with flowers and wreaths.

I kept glancing at the door lest they came for the coffin. This I feared most of all. I was anxious as I hovered over Arutis and stroked him. Mother wept, resting her head on the coffin, or looked sadly, lovingly at her son. Then she embraced me and held me tight. She must have dreaded the imminent closing of the coffin, much as I did.

Nevertheless, the time came, unexpectedly. The door opened, and we saw the men who had been digging the grave. Everyone began to stir and surround us. They knelt and chanted again. And then.... someone was approaching Arutis with headboard in hand. Mother and I leaped forward, embracing each other over the coffin, but they raised us up. Mother, then I, planted kisses over Arutis, his very cold yet beautiful little body. That is how I remember him. They covered the coffin and nailed it down. (I don't remember who helped us dress or how we left the barrack.)

The grave was beside Aleknavičienė's: a shallow one, lined with fir branches; across it were two boards, on which they set the little coffin. The service that followed was like a dream. There were prayers and hymns again. They told us to scatter three handfuls of sand over the coffin. We did so, mother and I. Then the hollow sound of clods of earth against the ground and wooden coffin, ever lighter and less audible. Mother and I stood holding each other, quietly shedding tears, until the grave was filled with sod and a miniature mound molded above it, marked with the shape of a cross. (Later, a wooden cross was erected by the mound.) We were the last to leave the gravesite.

In the barrack, we sat down on our bed, the one Arutis had been lying on so recently, and cried a long while. I guess I fell asleep sitting there. When I woke up during the night, I found myself lying down, covered, but mother was no longer beside me. I sat up anxiously and looked around: she was sitting by Vygandėlis, talking to his mother and sister, Aldutė.They came over to comfort me, laid me down again, and told me to rest so as not to get sick from fatigue. They said Vygandėlis was very weak. He wanted to see me very much but could not get out of bed (therefore he did not attend Arutis' funeral), so I should visit him in the morning. Mother and

I lay down. Before sleep overtook me, I kept thinking how awful it would be to lose a friend as well as a brother.

In the morning, I hurried to the side of the little patient, Vygandėlis. It pained me to look at him, pale and exhausted, definitely changed during the days when I had been nursing Arutis and hadn't seen him. He took my hand and said how sorry he was about Arutis.

In the next few days, mother and I were either at Arutis' grave or the bedside of Vygandėlis, who was gradually weakening. When his spirits lifted, we talked and reminisced about our mutual experiences in Barnaul. But he would easily tire, cease talking, close his eyes, and lie still. One evening I heard Aldutė's and her mother's crying—Vygandėlis had lost consciousness. Mother and sister patted him and spoke to him, but he was silent. When I came up to his bed, I was glad to feel the warmth of his hand and told Aldutė this was a good sign. She embraced me gently, saying nothing. We conversed later. I learned that Arutis had been ill with the measles, and Vygandėlis had scarlet fever. I registered those two illnesses as the very worst ones.

Vygandėlis did not regain consciousness as he lay there a few more days. I attempted conversation with him, feeling the warmth of his hand—surely a sign of vitality. I expected him to open his eyes and say something, but he was silent. He would only sigh, turn

about, and calm down again. I can't say exactly when Vygandėlis passed away; I only remember the sudden sound of grief at his bedside. Then I saw him lying quiet and stiff. His hands were cold now, like Arutis.... I knew what would follow: they would dress him handsomely, construct a coffin from white wood; after chants and prayers, they would close the coffin with that dreadful lid, carry it out by Arutis' gravesite, and cover it with cold sod. That is what happened, except that Vygandėlis was buried on the other side of Aleknavičienė, not by Arutis. I was disappointed because I wanted the two boys resting next to each other.

Many people were ill in our barrack, including mother and myself. We suffered coughing fits, even shortness of breath. Mother would get up and boil some water, for drinking hot liquid soothed the cough. We would fall asleep but soon be roused by another coughing bout. When my cough kept me awake, I thought about the burials and gravesites, fearing that mother might also pass on. I would cuddle close to her and sometimes hear the muffled sound of her sobbing into a pillow.

Our barrack was indeed ill-fated and miserable; yet we were saddened by the news that we would be moving on. We would have to leave Arutis' grave in the middle of the woods, and no one would tend to it. While most people in the barrack were preparing for travel, we sat despondent; likewise Vygandėlis' mother and sister.

On the day the wagons came, the four of us loaded our things and went to visit the grave sites for the last time. We were pleased to see fences around the graves, the handiwork of some good Samaritans. We stood there as if tied to the spot. The drivers were calling us angrily, cursing and waving at us, but we couldn't walk away. Finally, a few women came for us, saying the Russian drivers would leave us and take our belongings. Gripping mother's hand, I strode back to the wagon.

This time they seated only small children and sick people, apparently on account of the emaciated horses, which had difficulty pulling even an empty cart. Adults and older children had to walk alongside the caravan. And so we departed from the 60th block, continually glancing back to the gravesites until, with a turn of the road, they disappeared from view.

Urged by some instinct, I suddenly sprang out of line and, turning backward, ran through snowdrifts past the wagons behind us. Mother ran after me. There was shouting in Russian. Then one of the men caught me, carried me back to our wagon, and seated me down. Mother soon joined me, breathless from the chase. The driver was heard swearing and muttering for a while, but other women also seated themselves while men and teenage girls continued walking alongside the wagons. The travelers had evidently rebelled and insisted that the drivers had no right to force them to walk. We settled ourselves less fearfully; however, we soon felt chilled and irritated by cough. We walked to warm up, then sat down to rest, and so altered our mode of travel.

Our emotional state was worse than the cold. We couldn't imagine living without Arutis. Sometimes, when I dozed off in the wagon and mother wakened me lest I freeze, I would look about and succumb to fear when I saw no little brother on my lap—only the scarf in which he had been wrapped and carried. Just a short while ago we had been talking to him, feeding him, sheltering him from the elements.... Other children had befriended me, but I was content with only mother and Arutis. When my brother died, I feared losing my mother and would not let her out of my sight. I often saw her crying or gazing sadly into the distance, as if I were not there. I would nestle close to her, and then she would embrace me without a word.

FAMINE

We were brought to the 82nd block and told we would be settling here. We looked around. The area was surrounded by woods, with a few structures in the clearing. Upon closer view, these buildings appeared different from the others we had inhabited. They were houses rather than barns; the doorway was in back, opening to a long corridor with rooms on both sides.

Two or three families settled in each of the rooms. That first winter we had a series of roommates: Licienė, Mozūraitienė, and Konstancija Banionienė. I hardly remember the first one, who was exiled alone, without her family, from Suvalkija [southwestern Lithuania]. We knew Elžbieta Mozūraitienė from Barnaul. She was also exiled from Suvalkija and had to leave behind her husband and son, Matas. She used to worry especially about her son, whom she called "Matelis," anxiously asking herself, "Were they still alive?" She was about sixty-five years old. Konstancija Banionienė stayed in our room very briefly. She and mother used to converse about teachers they had both known and Lithuania in general. I also became friends with her, especially during the journey from Barnaul. In this barrack, I used to await her return from work because she was always cheerful, and she entertained us with anecdotes.

When Konstancija Banionienė was assigned work at another site and left, mother and I were given a very small room for the two of us. It had two narrow beds along the walls, a rickety, slanted table by the window, and a small gas stove with a shelf above it by the door.

All the while we could not forget Arutis. We entertained thoughts of returning to the 60th block to visit his grave, at least briefly. But how could we walk that far in the middle of winter, snowdrifts and raging blizzards? We postponed this trek until summer and, for the time being, often talked about Arutis. It was a very sad time for us. Arutis never left our thoughts, but we had to forge on and attend to our own survival. We were not the only ones grieving over the loss of a loved one. We began to participate in the community affairs of our block, along with everyone else.

Mother was sent to work just a few days after we arrived here. Whenever she was taken to work sites far from our block, she returned exhausted. She suffered back pains at night and groaned in her sleep.

Our chief administrator was someone by the name Kiselyov, who came around from Shipicino occasionally. It seemed that his most important duty was to keep count of the number of exiles who had died. Upon arrival at the 82nd block, he used to call an assembly in the dining hall, which was also a club room, explain some matter at hand and take notes. Whenever we saw him in our block, we children used to spread the message, "Kiselyov has arrived." We also had a commander, Timin, who lived in our block. We called him *pozharnik* ("fireman") for some reason. Maybe he was responsible for preventing and putting out fires in the barracks and surrounding woods.

When mother showed her certificate from Barnaul to both Kiselyov and Timin, they told her to negotiate with the brigade leader, Lapkovsky, who allocated and supervised work. He, like Timin, lived in our block but in a separate little house, not a barrack. At first Lapkovsky refused to look at mother's certificate, but after she collapsed from pain at work one day, he gave her a month's leave from hard labor. She was assigned work in the vicinity of the barracks.

Working exiles used to get a bowl of soup in the dining hall, where daily bread rations were also distributed. Mother could pick up both our bread rations, but she used to ask me to come to the dining hall at dinner time in case she could get enough soup for both of us. However, they didn't always oblige her request for another ladle of soup. When she was served only her portion of *rasolnik* (cucumber soup) or *shchi* (cabbage soup), she would share it with me. I felt bad because I knew that mother was no less hungry than I was.

Early on, when we had some groats and flour, we used to prepare a thin soup that was very tasty with bread. But our food reserves soon dwindled. When mother worked, she received 400 grams of bread. When she was assigned lighter work or didn't work, her bread ration was reduced to 150 grams, like mine; so we had to buy additional bread. Workers were paid very little, just enough to buy bread. When mother didn't work and received no pay, we got by with the money we had brought with us from Barnaul.

Finally our reserves of food were used up. When we got our bread ration, we would decide how much of it we should eat that day. Mother would spread our little table with two scarves we had from Raguva. In one of them, she tied up part of our loaf of bread and set it on the shelf; the other served as a table cloth. She tried to slice the bread very carefully so that it would not crumble. But how could she slice it neatly? The bread was usually damp and apt to crumble. When crumbs scattered over the table cloth, I used to moisten my finger and collect them from the cloth, suck on them, and swallow. When I lay down at night, I tried not to think of the bread and to forget where it was stored. But sometimes my willpower failed me, and I asked for at least a tiny piece. If we had more bread, mother would give me a piece, but if we had only a few extra slices, she would boil some water for both of us to drink. Thus appeasing our hunger, often chatting about Arutis and father, we would eventually fall asleep.

Women undertook treks to Shipicino, ten kilometers away, to trade clothing for food. Mother also prepared for this venture. First she had to decide which clothes to take, so we pulled our bundles from under the bed and spread out our "riches." The various baby clothes triggered memories of Arutis when he was healthy, cheerful… and deceased. We remembered the good times we had while taking care of him and delighting in his unique language. After some reverie and thought, mother surmised, "Maybe I should take these first." Then she quickly put away Arutis' things, tied the bundle, and looked for other clothes. There was not much choice, for we had only the clothing we needed. We treasured our winter clothing most of all, as did everyone else. But now mother took out her winter coat and announced that she would sell it: it was warm and beautiful, so it might fetch money as well as food.

I thought it would be a pity to sell the coat and tried to dissuade her from this plan. At the same time, a neighbor, Verutė Sinkevičienė, came by and advised mother to keep her coat and take Arutis' clothes first. Hearing this, I started crying and expressed some petulance toward the woman. She consoled me and tried to explain that we could not bring Arutis back; we had to think of our own survival. I calmed down. Mother agreed and took out Arutis' clothes again. She put aside some pieces as keepsakes (a little cap, trousers, and something else), saying she would never sell these, and then packed the others in the bag she had sewn herself back in Barnaul.

Mother left for Shipicino with two other women, one of whom was Gontautienė, as I recall. She had gotten up very early, while it was still dark. I had woken up as well, anxious about her journey and afraid of being alone. Who knew what might befall mother on the way? But I did not voice my qualms. After mother kissed me good-bye and departed, I sat in bed for a long while, wanting neither to get up nor go back to sleep. I thought of our days in Barnaul: whenever mother went somewhere, I used to stay with Arutis, and Vygandėlis used to come over to be with us.

I felt worse when I got up. Although mother said she would return in the evening, I started fretting at noon. I set off on the path to Shipicino with some other children a few times, expecting to meet her on the way. I was thoroughly upset by signs of a blizzard in the afternoon and went back to our room. There was enough food—some bread and soup that mother had prepared last night—but my anxiety got the better of my appetite all day.

In the evening, I was overwhelmed by fear. I would fall asleep and awaken fitfully. When, finally, I heard mother entering the room, I asked her why she hadn't returned all night. She said it was still evening in a strange whisper and, taking a load off her shoulders, sat down on the bed. She was very tired and tearful. Despite my bewilderment, I had sense enough to prepare some hot tea for her. She drank it eagerly, warming her hands as she clasped the cup. I offered her a slice of bread, but she shook her head, finished the tea, and told me to open the load.

I untied the frozen string with some effort and looked inside: it was packed with food! On top were two frozen chunks I soon recognized as milk. (I remembered seeing this kind of milk on our previous journey. Someone had procured it for Arutis; when it thawed, we fed it to him in spoonfuls.) I was about to chat with mother when I saw her resting her head on a pillow, asleep. I took off her shoes and lifted her feet onto the bed. As I was undoing her quilted jacket, she awoke and sat up; then she changed her clothing, asked for a warmer cover, and went back to sleep. I knelt down beside her and pressed my ear to her chest to check her breathing. I felt the warmth of her hand and calmed down. I covered her with the winter coat. Whenever it was cold, she used this coat as a blanket and covered me with the scarf she had wrapped around Arutis on our travels.

We had two blankets, worn and threadbare, so hardly a source of warmth. The mattresses, like those in other barracks, were decrepit, with pieces of wadding falling out of them. The window frame, marked by cracks and seams, was an effective conduit of drafts and gusts of wind, especially during blizzards. We tried to fill the cracks with rags and stuff, but the effort was futile. Our only comfort in this dwelling was the wood-burning stove, which we tended all day. We kept a pile of firewood, for resources were plentiful in the forest surrounding us. It was certainly difficult to gather the wood, to saw it and chop it to pieces, but first mother, then I, became proficient at this task.

As I tucked mother in, I felt chilled myself—the fire was out. I was glad we had an ample supply of firewood. I thought of the lack of firewood in Barnaul, where we had settled in a basement and rarely had sufficient fuel for heat. There was a sawmill nearby with lots of scraps of lumber scattered about—not only chips but stumps and butt ends. Trespassing and taking these was, of course, prohibited, but we children managed to carry off the scraps secretly. Vygandėlis and I used to collect a considerable amount of fuel this way. We feared the dogs on our path most of all. On one escapade, we had to drop some boards in order to get out of a soldier's sight as fast as we could. We were often scared, but next day we would resume the risky venture.

Warmed by the fire, I continued to unpack the load of food and put everything away in order. I licked the milk and set it on the windowsill so that it wouldn't thaw. The groats belonged on the shelf; the potatoes, in an aperture beneath the gas stove, where they would not freeze. Deeper in the bag I found a few skeins of yarn and knitting needles, thick ones and thin ones. I set these on our little table, wondering why mother bought these instead of more food. Though I felt sleepy, I tried to stay awake to tend the fire a while longer. (Mother said that we must not go off to sleep with the fire burning.) Watching the embers flicker out, I finally closed the latch, lay down, and went to sleep.

<…>

Next morning, mother was at the stove, cooking, when I got up. I asked if she'd caught a cold. No, she said; she was happy about the bartering she had done with the baby clothes though she had brought some of them back to keep for the next trip to town. She had gotten money as well as food for the clothes because the Russian women liked the outfits very much. There wasn't much to buy with money, except for an occasional bowl of soup in the dining hall. "It might come in handy in the future. I can buy our ration of bread with it if I'm not working," she said, putting the little satchel in a drawer. She was especially pleased with the yarn the Russian women had given her, asking that she knit some scarves for them. Only then did she relate what happened on the way back from Shipicino.

Toward evening, as they were approaching the 82nd block, a blizzard befell them. It was difficult to walk with the weight of the bag on her shoulders, and soon she found herself sitting in a snowdrift, hardly aware that she had slumped down. The snow had a pleasant, soporific effect on her—she felt good and sleepy. Women walking ahead noticed her absence among them and called to her, but she did not respond. She told them she just wanted to be left in the snow. They had to shake her firmly to get her up and persuade her to walk on; they even scolded her. Recovering herself, she realized that she might die there in the snow. She had heard of people freezing to death this way in Siberian forests. Thinking of me, she made her way back along with the other women. I was terrified as I listened to this story.

Mother's second journey to town was easier because the weather was better. Again, she returned with food. The Russian women were pleased with the scarves she knitted, and she had new orders. But when she finished the new set of scarves, she could not deliver them. It was March perhaps, and we were looking forward to spring, but instead, there was heavy snowfall. Neither horses nor tractors could reach the dining hall, so bread was not delivered to our block. Women conferred as to what to do and whether they could reach Shipicino. Some tried walking but did not get far on the snow-covered path.

Meanwhile, our food supply was dwindling. We had mainly potatoes and, not knowing how long the bad weather would last, we had to ration them. I volunteered to count them and determine how many we could eat per day. At first, mother was amused by this plan, but she soon joined in the conscientious effort of counting and rationing. I pulled the bag of potatoes from under the gas stove and counted them carefully: we had sixty-three potatoes. While we still had a loaf of bread, we decided to eat three potatoes a day. After we finished off the bread, we boiled four and sometimes, when we couldn't endure the hunger, five potatoes. We understood that our potatoes would soon come to an end. And so they did. We had no more food, only water. To be sure, we had set aside some potato pieces with shoots for planting in the spring. We looked these over but found nothing substantial to spare, just some peelings, which we boiled for a semblance of soup. When there was nothing left to peel, we drank only water. We tried to limit our movements and spent more time lying down, dozing or talking. We became so weak that even starting a fire in the stove was a challenge.

I remember that hunger so well. We survived on water for about a week, maybe five days. As I slumbered, I used to think we would never return to Lithuania, and I wouldn't have a chance to attend school. Closing my eyes, I used to envision the school in Raguva: my class, schoolmates, books, and notebooks. Then everything would get mixed up and Arutis would take a seat next to me.... When I told mother about my dreams or worries about returning to Lithuania, she would allay my fears or say nothing, as if in deep thought herself; more likely she was dozing off, too weak to speak. At one point, she remarked, "We are already swollen. Another few days of starvation and things will get worse." I don't know if I was swollen, but I definitely noticed a change in mother's appearance.

One day, in our exhausted state we heard the drone of a tractor. We went outside and there it was, arriving with a load of bread for the block. We felt energized at the sight. But when I ran up to the wagon, the fragrance of the bread wafting from the open door made me dizzy and unsteady on my feet. Caught in the queue of people pushing each other around, I found myself near the cart. Then I noticed a board missing in the floor of the cart and a loaf of bread fallen into the hole. I could not take my eyes off that loaf, nor could other children around me. I could not resist the temptation: I got down on my knees, crawled toward the loose board, and pulled out the loaf. I cannot remember clearly with whom I shared the bread, how I ran home, set a piece of the loaf on the table for mother; how I returned to the queue and stood next to mother with shaking legs.... The episode was dream-like.

Back in our room, surprised to see another piece of bread on the table, mother asked who had given it to me. I told her the truth, and she waxed angry. Pulling me roughly by the hand, she sat me down on the bed; then, sitting opposite me, she covered her face with her hands and burst into tears. I was dumbfounded. In a while, looking me in the face, she asked, "What would father say to you?" Only then did I realize what I had done. I felt blood rushing to my ears and a shiver through my body. Mother evidently took pity on me, starved and swollen as I was. She sat down beside me and related some kind of story, attempting an explanation or analogy, patting my head all the while. But in the course of all that talk, the question "What would father say to you?" reverberated in my ears. I didn't say a word. When mother beckoned me to eat, I came to the table.

I was upset for quite a while. Lying in bed at night, I used to wonder whether I was indeed very bad; whether father would ever love me again if he found out about this incident sometime when we were reunited with him. We did not discuss the matter further with mother, but henceforth I always made sure I was standing beside her in the queue for bread.

We didn't get very much bread, but still, it was something. Eating it in small portions with hot water, we soothed our hunger and anticipated the early Siberian mushrooms, which were supposed to flourish once the snow melted. Russians called them *smorchki* (which we pronounced *shmorkshtay*). I have yet to find the Lithuanian name for them. Some call them *bobausiai*; others use other names. We children were the first to search for these mushrooms. Each morning we would find increasing numbers of little black patches on the ground. Ignoring mothers' warnings, we used to run far into the woods, expecting to find at least one long-sought-after mushroom.

They sprouted quite unexpectedly around the barracks. At first women doubted they were edible, but they stood the test of eating and proved to be our salvation, those *shmorkshtay*. Soon there were all kinds of herbs in the area—more than we were able to gather and cook. We were not satiated by this diet, but we were no longer starving.

One spring day mother set out for Shipicino, alone for the first time. I worried, but she insisted that she had to deliver the knitted scarves; she would get food in exchange for them. We needed food because the mushroom season was short-lived, and we were subsisting merely on herbs. Mother left early in the morning and returned at dusk, tired but cheerful. The Russian women liked her scarves and asked for more. She brought back some milk, a small cube of cottage cheese, millet, and several potatoes.

It was a few days later that she told me about a frightful experience she had on her way to town. As she set foot on a little bridge, she confronted a swarm of snakes—lots of them, sprawling, coiling, raising their heads. How could she pass over the bridge? What could she do? She balked and turned homeward but then returned to the bridge. She found a long stick and attempted to ward off the snakes. This worked: the snakes wiggled away and disappeared in the bushes. She walked onward with trembling legs. Even as she was walking around Shipicino, she worried about passing that bridge on her way home. Fortunately, the bridge was clear of snakes on her way back.

I had already encountered a snake. I remember, the weather had warmed up, women were sitting near the barrack, and children were running about when a beautiful flower caught my eye. I ran toward it and leaned over to pick it when, suddenly, I screamed, stepping backward—there was a huge, fat snake coiled round the stem of the flower! In another instant I was by mother's side, trembling, my teeth chattering. I was given some medication. I heard women talking of burning incense for me lest I become epileptic from the scare. I don't remember any incense; nor did I become ill with epilepsy. But the fright affected me: I began to stutter.

It was embarrassing to stammer or stop short in the middle of a word. This rarely happened when I was talking to mother, but I had difficulty conversing with other children. I would be saying something and falter suddenly, unable to pronounce a sound. The first time this happened, children began laughing, but later they ceased to poke fun at me; perhaps they understood that I had a problem. I had most trouble calling on neighbors with some errand. I would become nervous at the door, afraid that I would be unable to communicate a message. Several times I had to return home and try to deliver the message later. This went on for about a month. Then V. Sinkevičienė, a dentist, came to my aid. When I stammered and started crying in her presence, she sat me down beside her and told me to calm myself. She said that my stuttering was an illness, but a curable one, because I developed it from sudden fright; I wasn't born with a stutter. It should pass. She spoke with my mother, who worried about my problem, and suggested I visit her everyday to practice speaking.

Her counsel was very helpful. She told me first of all to conquer my fear. She advised me to take a deep breath before uttering a word and to convince myself that I could say the word. My speech improved gradually because I made the effort. I calmed down and learned to speak more slowly. Nevertheless, the stuttering or some kind of faltering persisted for a long time.

I was terribly afraid of snakes, but I had to overcome the aversion. If I wanted to eat, I had to go looking for berries or mushrooms. Besides, other children just ignored those reptiles.

SCARVES

Although mother's account of the incident on the bridge horrified me, a few weeks passed and I begged her to take me along on the next journey to Shipicino. Mother agreed. Last time, she had been invited to a meal with a local Russian woman, who served her cabbage soup with potatoes, tea, and two miniature cakes, which mother brought home for both of us to share. She would bring me along now with the hope that I might experience such hospitality. I happily anticipated our journey, despite my fear of seeing those repugnant reptiles on the bridge. Luckily, there were no snakes on the bridge, nor did we see any others on the way to Shipicino. We sat down to rest a few times, and I scouted around, feeling like a bunny rabbit. There were no berries yet, except for unripe wild strawberries. We snacked on these together with the bread we had.

Shipicino appeared very strange to me. It was dotted with little wooden houses, surrounded by high blue fences. Each of these featured a large gate with a small entry door. There were benches here and there along the fences. The streets were very dusty, and in the middle of the village was a little pond, or perhaps a huge puddle.

We entered one of the yards. Upon opening the door of the house, the smell of food tickled our noses. Inside, the house was spacious and clean. There was a shining white stove on the side of the room and in back, several people were seated at a table, eating. I felt hungry. Remembering mother's tale of hospitality, I expected to be served dinner immediately. However, no one got up from the table. A woman came in from an adjoining room, took the knitted scarf from mother's hands, and, draping it round her shoulders, displayed it by the table. She was saying something as she pointed to mother and called her Valya.

I was still waiting for an invitation to dinner, but this was evidently not their intention. On the contrary, an older boy got up from the table and, pointing at us standing by the door, said something to a girl of about my age. She snickered, and others joined in the laughter. I didn't know what they were laughing about. Perhaps my ragged shoes seemed funny to them, or my dress, patched and altered for growth. The dress was from Raguva; mother had sewn some material onto the hemline and sleeves in order to lengthen them. I felt embarrassed, standing by the threshold. But that wasn't the end of it. The Russian boy, still looking at us and laughing, took a large potato from the table and, holding it up in front of him, started peeling it; when he finished peeling it, he stuffed it into his mouth and glanced back at me. I felt I would burst into tears any minute. I clutched mother's hand and asked if we could leave now. She was upset as well but asked me to persevere until she was reimbursed for the scarf. The woman finally gave her some money. Mother commented, speaking Russian with difficulty. I understood the words *malo, moloko, kartoshka* (little, milk, potato). But the woman shook her head and went back to the table, saying something to her kin. Everyone laughed. The boy took the half-eaten potato from his mouth and threw it at our feet. I heard the word *nemci* (Germans). The woman scolded the urchin and smacked him on the head. Mother took me by the hand, and we left. When we were at the gate, that boy came running out of the house, picked up a stone, and threw it at us (but his missed). Mother told me to keep quiet and not to look back, then hastily led me down the dusty street.

I was very hungry. Mother led me to a store, *lavka*, as written above the door. However, on the shelf inside we saw only a few containers of preserves and some kind of flour in a tin bowl. Mother checked the price of the preserves and said the money she had gotten for the scarf would not suffice—we could not buy them. Beneath the flour, she read, "*Prodayutsa po talonam*" ("Sold for coupons"). So we left. My hunger was unbearable. We had eaten one cold potato each and a slice of bread on our ten-kilometer trek that day.

I walked down-hearted toward another house, though mother said the people there were nicer. Upon entering, we found a woman whitewashing the stove. Seeing us, she put away her brush, wiped her hands on her apron, and said "Valya" with a smile. She took the scarf mother offered her and, like the other woman, wrapped it round her shoulders, then stroked it, saying "*krasivaya*" ("beautiful"). Looking at me, she asked if I were the daughter. Then she left the room and returned with two potatoes, which she gave me as she led us to the table. Seeing me swallow a potato instantly, the Russian woman must have understood how hungry I was. She pulled a pot out of the oven, poured large bowls full of fragrant, steaming cabbage soup for mother and me, and served us more potatoes. It was all extraordinarily delicious. She also brought payment for the scarf: groats, potatoes, and a large chunk of tallow.

Dainora Urbonienė. *Sibiras vaiko akimis* ("Siberia through a Child's Eyes"). Panevėžys: UAB Panevėžio spaustuvė, 2003.

In 1946, Dainora Tamošiūnaitė was sent back to Lithuania with seventy-two other orphaned children of exiles. That same year, her mother, Valerija Tamošiūnienė, returned to Lithuania illegally. In 1956, while studying at Vilnius University, Dainora married her classmate Eugenijus Urbonas. They raised a daughter and two sons; they now have four grandchildren. After graduating from Vilnius University in 1958 Dainora taught in the city and environs of Panevėžys.

Her mother, Valerija Tamošiūnienė, died in 1999.

At present, Dainora Urbonienė is retired, living in Panevėžys.

Romualdas Zubinas, May 2, 1939

Jonas Zubinas, May 10, 1939

A photo from J. Zubinas' case No. 1811

Romualdas Zubinas

On June 14, 1941, three-year-old Romualdas Zubinas, with his mother, Elžbieta Zubinienė, and brothers—five-year-old Algimantas and one-year-old Vytautas—were exiled from the district of Mažeikiai to the Altai region of Russia.

His father, Jonas Zubinas, a border police officer, was arrested and imprisoned on June 18, 1941. In 1942 he was executed in the prison at Novosibirsk.

The Summer of 1944

That summer we knew that we would attend school in the fall. My brother Algis and I were registered for the same first grade. In fact, all the children in our village, irrespective of their age, nationality, or social status, would be attending school—first grade—for the first time in their lives. It did not matter that I was only six years old and did not speak Russian well, or that the schoolmate next to me on the bench might be a boy or girl twice my age. We all felt equal then. The prospect of school attendance also resolved the childcare problem that often troubled mother: she could rest assured that we would be supervised in some way.

The school was supposed to provide all the necessary supplies. We were told that we would be given textbooks, notebooks, pencils, pens, nibs, and even ink—but only one of each of these items, excepting notebooks for each subject. If anyone needed additional supplies for any reason, they would be left to their own resources. So I was enrolled in first grade!

Everyone who was registered for school was obliged to work a certain number of hours in State fields that summer. We already had our first teacher, Lyubov Petrovna. As I found out later, her fiancé had died at the very end of the war; however, we never saw any changes in her mien or facial expression. She was always cheerful though she had to work under very difficult circumstances both in the fields and at school. Our first task for the benefit of the State was to weed an oat field. We all lined up with our teacher in front of us and, irrespective of age, were all assigned similar tracts in the field, which we were to clear of every last weed. As luck would have it, the sun was especially hot that day. To shield myself from its burning rays, I took off my shirt and used it to cover my head. Thistles, like nettles, stung our hands because no one had given us gloves or any other kind of hand protection. My hands suffered terribly that day, but leaving the field was not an option; abandoning a work site would be considered an action against the State. Yet all this was bearable. The worst of it was that we had no drinking water—in a region where, a few hundred meters away, there was a mighty river of potable water flowing down a mountainside. I was so thirsty that I had to hide behind the nearest bush, pee into my hands, and drink my urine.

Of course, no one cared at the time whether working children were fed. The farm manager and the brigade leader were concerned only with a timely, high-quality weeding of the State's oat field, designated for the feeding of steeds raised for the army's front lines. We accomplished the task successfully.

The Fall of 1944

<...> Our barrack did not offer favorable conditions for reading and writing. There was one table and fifteen to twenty school children.

I can see it now: most everyone in the barrack is asleep while Algis and I are sitting by the stove and the light of a burning wood torch, trying to memorize a Russian poem, the meaning of which eludes me. First of all, the poem was overly politicized. Second, when I heard Algis read it, I didn't see the punctuation or versification, so it was just a stream of words to my ears. I gathered the meaning of this poem the following year, when I had a chance to read it myself. It was verse of praise for the "homeland" and boundless gratitude to the communist government for a happy childhood. Wasn't it a paradox? While Algis and I were memorizing the poem by the dim light of the torch, my brother was also busy sticking potato peelings he had salvaged somewhere onto the heated stove door. After frying these peelings, eating them, and studying the poem of praise a while longer, we lay down to sleep. Mother had not returned yet. She must have gone to Jelo to beg for food.

I received a "2" [a failing grade] for the poem, but that did not depress me. With renewed energy, however much of it I had at the time, I tried to comprehend what the teacher said and assigned for homework. However, I was not doing very well in school. Seeing this, my mother did not press or scold me. She was content to know that I was attending school regularly and was making an effort in my studies. Then came the winter of my first school year.

Winter of 1944–1945

This winter, much like earlier ones, was marred by hunger. Nothing had changed in our life. Mother was still sawing and splitting wood by the smithy. Vytukas was attending kindergarden. Algis and I were trying to excel in our studies.

We used up our ink quickly and had to produce some ourselves. We made it from soot that we scraped from the stove chimney. Although it wasn't good quality ink, we could write with it if need be. When one of us lost a pen, we improvised one with a little stick. The teacher gave us a nib, which we bound to the stick with some string. The resulting instrument was quite handy. By the middle of the school year I had filled my notebook for penmanship.... Some Russian boys, who had piles of newspapers, came to my rescue. Boris Nekrasov gave me a newspaper, from which I made a notebook. I hardly needed to line its pages, except for the spaces with pictures, which were most useful for writing. Ironically, the first picture on which I did some homework was a portrait of Lavrenti Beriya, chief of the NKVD* and terror of exiles. Word of my blunder soon reached the Administrative Center, and a representative was immediately dispatched to pay us a visit.

I must note that no representative came out when twelve-year-old Algimantas Žąsinas died, nor on the occasion of the opening of our school. And now we had the honor.... I trembled like an aspen leaf. Mother was called from work for this meeting. But fortunately, there were some reasonable people even among employees of the NKVD. The teacher was commended for her vigilance as well as her loyalty to the communist party and homeland; mother was instructed to maintain strict control of my activities in order to avoid a recurrence of such a blunder. Needless to say, the representative from the Center did not provide me with a new notebook for penmanship.

After this incident, I did not write over pictures of communist leaders, but misfortune comes unexpectedly. While we were doing our homework in the barrack, some mischievous children accidentally pushed the table, and ink spilled on my notebook—on the side of a page featuring a portrait of Stalin, "our leader." Stalin's face was covered with the ink we had produced from soot. This time mother resolved the case herself with wisdom worthy of Solomon, namely a plan of default: I was to stay home from school next day and not show my notebook to the teacher or anyone else. She threw my newspaper pages into the stove and so "extinguished an impending

---

* ***NKVD*** *– (acronym for Narodniy komisariat vnutrennich del, "People's commisariat for internal affairs") was the Soviet Union's department of repression, officially claiming to uphold order and fight crime. The NKVD combined the functions of interior ministry and security police: on the one hand, administration of transportation, firefighting, census, collective farms, and border patrol; on the other, suppression of anti-Soviet activities and supervision of ethnic cleansing, genocide, deportations, prisons, and concentration camps.*

political fire." We dealt with the resulting need for another notebook on our own, without the intercession of the teacher and representative from the Center.

Spring of 1945

This spring was special, for the end of the war was in sight. The faces of local people were lit with smiles although there wasn't a family among them that hadn't suffered the loss of a loved one. Some families had lost a few or even all of their men. We rejoiced about the end of the war in general rather than anyone's victory or defeat. The loudspeaker in the village blared ever more loudly. Survivors of the war from our village began to return home. Few returned, so all were welcomed home as heroes. But there weren't any who were not crippled or injured in one way or another.

The school year ended on the first of May. Soon we were informed of our final grades and decisions as to whether we would be promoted. Algis was among those promoted to second grade. I was held back to repeat the first grade curriculum. So I was destined to sit in the same row of seats next year while Algis would be sitting in the second row. That was quite an accomplishment on his part. Consequently, he rose in stature in our eyes.

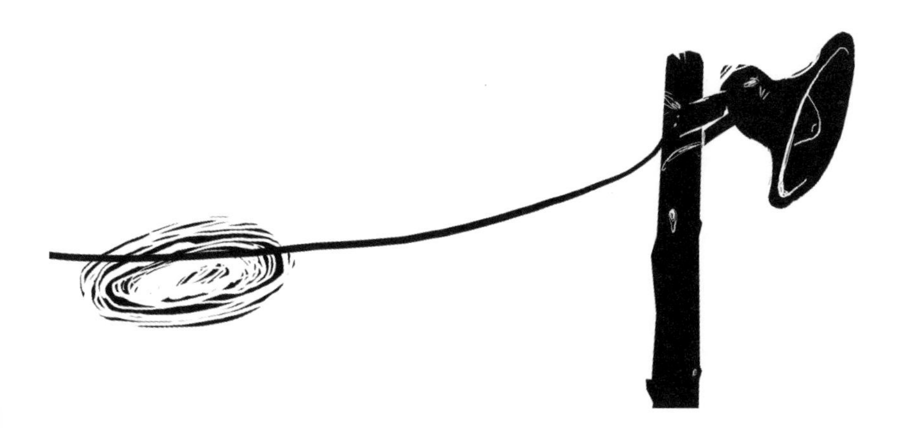

<...>

Summer of 1945

When school was out, we were immediately sent to weed the oat field. Again, I was working together with Algis, and again we met up with thistles. The heat was unbearable.

Mother told us to wear our knitted winter caps and quilted jackets, though these were in tatters after the winter season. Local Altaic people dressed that way to protect themselves from both cold and heat. We also learned from experience how to deal with very high and very low temperatures. We brought along some winter gloves and a glass container with a stopper, a *chetvert*, of water. This held a fourth (*chetvert*) of a bucket, in other words, three liters of liquid. We had used this container almost every week after school to bring whey or, if we lucked out, buttermilk from Yelo.

Of course we always walked. There was no regular transportation between our barracks and Yelo; had there been any, we wouldn't have had money to pay the fare. In the village of Yelo, there was a small dairy which produced cheese and cottage cheese. We were not allowed inside, so we used to stand at the gate, hoping to attract the workers' attention. At first, when the workers or guards noticed us, they asked why we were standing there. We answered straightforwardly: to get at least something! They usually poured some whey into our glass container, but occasionally they gave us some buttermilk. This made for a celebration. One time Algis and I tasted away most of the *chetvert* of buttermilk, bringing home only about a liter. We were not highly praised by mother that time.

When we returned from Yelo, mother used to send us to the hills to look for rhubarbs. So we made our rounds like scurrying squirrels. We used to go barefoot to the hills, though the hillsides teemed with snakes. Once we got there, we had some fun. We would send a hefty rock down a hillside and watch it roll, catching on other stones, sometimes creating a cascade of falling rocks. We often happened upon snake matings and marveled at the unique spectacle of the swarms and their energy—though we tried not to linger at the scene.

That summer we were initiated in the work of harvest and haymaking. We rode to the field on horse carts. They used to seat us on some old nag, fitted with a collar on which they tied a device for catching hay (Lith. *valkšna*), a thick birch pole with little birches set into a series of notches. We had to transport piles of hay caught on this device to the main stack, which often weathered winter snow and lasted until the following spring. When the hay was unloaded at the stack, the process had to be repeated. This gathering and unloading continued for days until the end of harvest, actually until the beginning of the next school year. The downside was that we exiles were always left with the weakest, most emaciated horses. It was uncomfortable to sit on the horse's withers (the crest near the neck), so we aimed to sit on its croup (back end). Local Russian boys were permitted to choose their horses in the stables. Exiles' horses stayed in the area of harvest, where they could graze and rest overnight under our watch.

Since we did not have saddles, we had to use some old, worn woolen mat instead, or our quilted jackets, which didn't help much because they were apt to be ragged and always slipped from beneath us. Consequently, our bottoms used to be covered with sores. When we returned to school, if we didn't pad the bench with something soft, we could not sit for a long time.

There was yet another source of discomfort during harvest: gadflies, which we called *bimbalai*. On hot summer days, they used to attack our old nags like hornets going for honey. Of course we suffered from those gadflies no less than the horses. Our bodies were speckled throughout from their stings because we usually dressed lightly in summertime.

Algis met with some extra bad luck that summer. He was given an old nag blind in the left eye, so he always had to mount it from the right side. This move was unusual for both riders and steeds, but this old nag had grown accustomed to it. One day Algis tried to mount it from the left, and he was thrown—naturally, for the horse couldn't see who was getting on it. Algis was scared more than he was hurt by the fall, and he would not try to mount the nag again that day. As the brigade leader did not have a spare horse or a substitute worker for Algis, and the work of harvest had to proceed, my brother and I rode to the farm on the same horse. Once we got there, Algis was given a better horse.

Incidentally, we had no problem with footwear during harvest. The soles of our feet had grown so thick and hardy that we didn't even feel them. We used to go barefoot from early spring until snow came in the fall. We roamed the hills and ran about dirt roads and stubble-fields on bare feet.

How our work was reckoned I couldn't really say. Keeping track of it was our mothers' responsibility. But did they always know where, when, and how long we worked? My brother and I worked far off in the fields while mother usually cut and split wood in the vicinity of the barracks. As we stayed in the area of harvesting overnight, we didn't have a chance to converse with mother in the evenings and tell her where we had been working, what we had been doing, and how much we had accomplished.

Although we spent the entire summer working in the oat fields or harvesting, we found time for treks to the hills. Our little brother, Vytukas, was still too weak for these hikes. The sun-drenched southern slopes yielded only shrubs and rhubarb while the northern slope was luxuriant with vegetation: red and black currants as well as cedars. We frequented these hillsides with the specific errand of bringing home rhubarb, currants, or cedar nuts. We picked rhubarb between spring and summer. Red and black currants ripened in late summer. However, we went berrypicking whenever we had the time and energy. We used to pick huge clusters of currants like grapes and load them in a pail. Cedar nuts ripened toward fall, so we used to go nutting at the beginning of the school year.

Fall of 1945

The main difficulty was carrying the berries home. We used to pick berries in *Shebalik*, a section of the taiga razed by fire in the northern slope, seven kilometers from our village. Large black currants grew there, juicy as grapes. We used to fill a metal pail with them in about an hour, but we exhausted ourselves by the time we brought it home. When a group of us boys set out for berry picking, Algis often found a good excuse to prevent his coming along; then I joined the group by myself. We were often accompanied by local Russian women, whose songs and talk made our treks more enjoyable and seemingly shorter. In their presence even the pail of berries seemed lighter as I shifted it from one shoulder to the other. Sometimes, when we stopped to rest, they treated me to a slice of bread or a potato.

We never planted potatoes ourselves because we couldn't obtain seeds or shoots. Whenever mother got some potatoes, we immediately boiled and ate them. But why mention boiled potatoes if we boys, like boars, used to burrow stealthily in local gardens in the fall, root up potatoes, and eat them raw? We also helped ourselves to others' peas, green beans, carrots, and radishes in those gardens. Fortunately, I was never caught red-handed. Or perhaps the women who owned and tended the vegetable gardens overlooked me intentionally. After all, they suffered but small losses on account of me and other children.

Even if we had planted potatoes, we wouldn't have had a place to store them in winter. It was impossible to keep anything in the barrack basement that was shared by everyone; somehow, everything disappeared from its premises. Last winter Mileškienė found that even the carcass of her young calf was missing.

Our basement was very insecure, and one could not keep anything valuable there. Moreover, it was often inspected by committees, which evidently looked for and found not only oats but other products. Therefore, we tried to eat the berries we picked as quickly as possible, so they would not fall into the wrong hands. Besides, we could not make any jams or preserves because we had no sugar, nor pots for this purpose. So we did not produce any food supplies for winter. Like bears and other wild animals, we ate everything we had without anticipating winter or other deadlines. Our bodies accumulated reserves of vitamins needed for the winter season. These had to suffice until next spring despite recurrent hunger.

Finally, the new school year came around.

Winter of 1945–1946

How I dreaded school! I would have to repeat everything I studied last year and be embarrassed to face the new first graders. But mother was categorical and would not consider any reservations or stipulations. I walked to school with my head down. There, a new teacher, Zinaida Pavlovna, awaited the first graders; Lyubov Petrovna worked with the older pupils, who were divided into second and third graders. The older children attended the morning shift while we first graders were allowed to sleep in and come in the afternoon. Algis and I now attended school at different hours. Vytas was still in kindergarden. The burden of housekeeping remained on Algis' and my shoulders: gathering rhubarb, making trips to Jelo, and other tasks, which proliferated even in our small household. Vytelis was able to perform a number of these quite easily. Indeed, when I was his age, I had also done many chores.

Mother worked every day, as usual; after working hours, she made trips to the village or neighboring settlements. I understood her very well and I constantly felt sorry for her. She was still in the dark about father's fate and other loved ones' predicaments. She often reminisced about father, life before the war, Lithuania, and being exiled from home. Therefore, I dared not oppose or gainsay her, though I used to get angry at Algis for his cleverness at making excuses and evading trouble. Occasionally, his cleverness made for comedy, such as the following incident.

We had kept hens for a few years, so we could often improve rhubarb or goose-foot soup with an egg. At one time, however, Algis and I could not find any eggs in our hen-coop for several days, and we could not keep this a secret from mother. Then one day, instead of eggs, mother found Algis in the hen-house and knew right away who the culprit was in the case of disappearing eggs. Grabbing a switch, she intended to flog Algis on the spot. But my brother did not lose his bearings. He knelt down on the ground covered with chicken droppings, set his palms for prayer, and, looking skyward, implored, "Dear mother, please do not beat me. I will never do that again; I'll go straight to heaven!" How could mother's heart not tremble in the face of such sincere repentance and noble resolve? She returned to the barrack in a lighter mood and, chuckling, told everyone what happened. The folks in the barrack had a good laugh. However, such outbursts of good humor were very rare in those days.

We've digressed from the topic of school, which was my main concern in those days. Come what may, I had to overcome the barrier posed by the first grade curriculum and be promoted this year. I attended school with this goal in mind. Again, they distributed writing utensils, notebooks, and books, but I was not given the latter because I had last year's books and notebooks. I now had to read and complete all the assignments on my own. We were again assigned the poem of boundless praise for the "homeland" with which I had struggled unsuccessfully last year. As I read this poem, I tried to understand its meaning, paying attention to every word. I asked mother to help me. After reading the poem and reflecting, she said, "You must do your best in memorizing this poem and recite it in class as loud as you can!" I did as I was told. I was amazed when when Zinaida Pavlovna complimented me and evaluated my recitation with a "5" ["excellent"], for nothing of the sort had occurred during the previous school year. I then felt great respect for mother and henceforth asked for her advice more often. I realized that she was a very good psychologist.

After a few months of diligent studying, I was out of notebooks and ink. Then I wrote between the lines of last year's notebooks. When I filled these, I had to look for more newspapers from which to construct notebooks. I now knew how to treat pictures of various national leaders and chiefs of the communist party.

The ink we produced from soot had a certain defect: the soot quickly settled at the bottom of the bottle, so we had to whisk the ink frequently. This procedure came with the risk of spilling ink, which often caused trouble and annoyance for me and everyone around me. Eventually, a Russian boy brought me a small red beet, suggesting I make ink from its red juice. He also advised me to add a little sugar to the beet juice for this purpose. I was grateful to him for a long time because he helped me solve a seemingly unsolvable problem. The ink made from beets turned out very well. Besides, it was red, so my assignments were clearly visible in the old notebooks and pages of newspaper, and they were also in accord with the spirit of the times [the red banners and other red insignia of communism].

That winter I wore out almost all my clothes. Even the outfits mother had knitted did not last until the end of the season. I wore out my shoes as well. I used to run to school barefoot through deep snow, with only trousers on me. As the school was heated, I used to warm up quickly once I got there. But there were other difficulties related to my clothing. The teacher noticed that my trousers were held up merely by a string, and one day during intermission she intimated to her little sister-in-law, who was also a first grader, the notion of pulling on that string. Why, I had nothing on beneath my trousers.... I had to exert myself to escape from the girl and prevent the devilish mischief. I ran around the school as well as the classroom more than once or twice that day. While my schoolmates and the teacher had some fun, I did not!

Spring of 1946

The snow melted and the earth warmed up.... At sowing time, mother was again called to work the treadle of a seeding machine. On the other treadle of the same machine was Ališauskienė, while Mockienė and Danutė Mileškaitė worked on another seeding machine. As in previous years, the Janulis boys drove the tractors. Thus it seemed that in spring, summer, and fall, our *sovkhoz* [abbreviation for *sovyetskoye khozeystvo*, "soviet farm"] was sustained by Lithuanian exiles alone. Russian folks grew accustomed to this status quo. But the farm work was not without sensational incidents. In spring a few years back, when a combine (a harvesting and threshing machine) was being hauled from the Center's farm to ours, the unwieldy machine tipped over on a turn of the road at the bend of the Ursul River: the combine tumbled into the river, bringing with it a segment of the road. A committee chosen by the Center's farm and the regional center proceeded with a long and thorough investigation of the accident. One of the Janulis boys had been at the wheel of the combine. However, the committee was compelled by the evidence to acknowledge that the incident was not a political diversion on the part of Lithuanian exiles.... Fortunately, Janulis' skin was saved while the pile of scrap metal that was the combine rusted in the cold waters of the Ursul.

The rhubarb season came and went. The end of the school year was in sight. Although I was not among the very best pupils in my class, I wasn't trailing behind the majority. After all, my circumstances were not particularly conducive to school work, and I was still struggling with the Russian language. So I was happy to receive the message that I would be promoted to second grade, and I quickly relayed the news to mother, who was sawing firewood by the smithy at the time.

Incidentally, even when the war ended, mother was not paid for her work but rather given those same "magical" food coupons. Rations of bread, groats, and other products increased somewhat, but we boys had grown in the meanwhile. So there was no relief from the shortage of food, and we constantly felt underfed. Vytukas had even come down with rickets (*rakhitis*), evidenced by his bloated tummy.

That spring, as in the past, Algis and I used to go to Jelo at least once a week for whey and buttermilk, and we did everything else mother asked us to do.

Summer of 1946

As in previous summers, our main job was harvesting. Whether we were paid for this work or reimbursed in another way, I do not know.

<…>

Once in a rare while we played outdoor games with local boys. The most popular ball game was then "Hit and run!" Our balls were made of cows' hair. We did not have any of better quality, nor had we seen any other kind of ball. Another game involved a right-angled stick, with ends sharpened in opposite directions. Whichever way it fell, you would have an end you could strike [with another stick] so that the stick would move in a chosen direction and, after a few more strikes, land in the goal.

We also liked playing "War." We used to draw a large circle on the ground, divide it into sections according to the number of players, and give each of these sections the name of some country. Then we declared war on one or another of these "countries." We had to aim and throw a knife into that country's territory so that it would pierce the ground; then we could claim and "cut" a piece of the territory indicated by the slant of the knife's blade.

The summer of 1946 was exceptional in the life of the village due to the arrival of movies. The apparatus was primitive, consisting of a motor turned manually by a handle. So turned, the little motor produced electricity, which lit the lamp of the camera. There was only a moving picture on the screen, with no sound. Since we had no money, we used to ingratiate ourselves with the movie operator and try to persuade him to entrust us with the turning of the motor; this way, we could also watch the movie.

Films made for a new stage of cultural life, one might say a revolution in the culture of the village. Why, that screen showed us images of life far from our home—not the hills surrounding us, which had grown tiresome long ago. How realistic it all was did not matter to us. We were interested in seeing people from a totally different world: seeing how they behaved and how they dressed; what houses, cars, and other things were like in their environment. That screen was a kind of window on the world. Even if the early films featured mainly wars and battles, we had a chance to see what we longed for: the world beyond our village and something of life in other places.

There was still no electricity, nor a power station in our village. We used portable kerosene lanterns or lamps with glass shades for lighting. There was a telephone line between the Center and our village. However, the soviet authorities communicated with Karakuba by dispatching a rider with a verbal message or a sealed letter. Occasionally, I was called on to serve as a rider. I did this with pleasure because a good steed and a saddle were always provided for the task. I used to gallop those several kilometers with the wind. I did not care whether I would be paid for the job. On those errands I would even forget the sores on my buttocks that had not healed since the harvest. The experience of riding a swift-footed steed was all that mattered to me; it boosted my spirit. I was also glad to be entrusted with a task for the Administrative Center.

Fall of 1946

Here was my third year of school. I attended second grade while Algis was in third.... Mother sawed and split wood, as usual. Exiles were now paid money for their work; food coupons were abolished. They used to pay five *chervonec* (one *chervonec* being equal to ten rubles) for one cubic meter of sawed, chopped, and piled firewood. This pay had to be divided between two workers because the work of preparing firewood was always done in pairs. As I recall, this currency didn't have much value. I didn't pay attention to the prices of products sold at the little store in our village because I had no money. But I remember clearly that a former soldier sharpened the saw mother used for five *chervonec*. He used to do this job in about an hour, working indoors. Evidently, there was discrimination against exiles. And could it have been otherwise? The rate of pay for various categories of work was determined by soviet officials and always to the disadvantage of exiles.

At school, we never heard mention of Lithuania. The denial of the Baltic countries was apparently regulated by the authorities. In our school there were about thirty students, including no more than ten Russian children; however, all subjects were continuously taught only in Russian. Of course, the teachers did not speak or write in Lithuanian, but a Lithuanian teacher might easily have been found among the exiles, had they wanted to accommodate Lithuanian-speaking children. Why, almost all the mothers had completed higher education in one field or another, and Bronius' father was a professional teacher. The soviet authorities obviously showed no political inclination to foster Lithuanian identity. Our mothers constantly reminded us to speak only Lithuanian at home.

...Once, while playing, we noticed that bread was being delivered from the Center to our village store. We waited until they finished unloading the loaves from the container in the cart and then rushed to collect the crumbs in that container. By luck (or rather ill-luck), I was the first one in the cart. Meanwhile, one of the fellows standing outside frightened the horse, and it let loose across the fields—dragging the cart with the container in which Fabius and I were stuck. The horse stopped only when it had recovered from its fright and grown weary. Fabius and I had more black and blue spots on our sides and bumps on our heads than we could count. Then we got additional black and blue spots from our mothers.

Winter of 1946-1947

<...>

Algis, who was a third-grader while I was a second-grader, was summarily superior to me, and I could not but defer to him. The more so because I was wearing his worn-out shoes and the shreds of his former clothing. I knew very well that there was no way out of my predicament, but I was especially jealous of my older brother that winter. When mother somehow obtained a pair of worn but firm felt boots, Algis, of course had priority in wearing them. The two of us made ice skates from sticks and some iron, and we used to tie them onto Algis' felt boots with some leather straps whenever we went skating on the frozen Ursul. My own boots were too threadbare to have anything tied on them, so I used to wait for my turn on the ice until Algis had skated to his heart's content. By the time we exchanged boots, it was usually getting dark. Thus I rarely had a chance to skate much unless Algis had to stay home due to illness or was not allowed outdoors for some other reason known only to mother. Vytukas was almost never allowed outdoors or on the ice. He still attended kindergarden and came straight home afterwards. He was a sickly child with fragile health, and so considerably smaller than Algis and me.

Algis and I tried to spend as little time as possible within the four walls of home. Sometimes we even went calling on people in the vicinity of the barracks, and we did so assiduously at Christmas time. We memorized a short prayer and whenever doors opened in front of us, we burst out with a recitation. Occasionally we received a slice of bread or a fried potato, and we always brought something home for Vytukas.

<...>

Every winter New Year's Day was a school holiday. We were unable to hold Christmas Eve celebrations because we had none of the food that was typically spread on the table on that occasion. And we couldn't celebrate Christmas because exiles were forbidden to organize get-togethers and sing hymns. It was said that such gatherings were banned because local soviet authorities did not understand the hymns or the talk associated with these events. Our mothers did not wish to conflict with the authorities. Moreover, there was no priest or other minister among us who would rally the Lithuanian exiles and bolster their morale. So we had to reconcile ourselves to celebrating Christmas on the New Year. We prepared for the New Year as if it were the most important religious holiday for us Lithuanians as well. We used to set up a fir tree in the barrack and decorate it with all kinds of ornaments and paper toys we made by cutting, folding, and pasting pages of old notebooks. We celebrated as we knew how and as best we could.

...During the second half of the school year I again ran out of ink and notebook paper. That winter my mother had given me a very special pen, with a nib inserted at the tip, but my delight in this instrument was short-lived. On the way home from school one day, we children got into a fight and started hitting each other with our school bags. I didn't even notice when my magical pen fell out of my bag.... How I searched for it! How I lamented its loss! I found it when the snow began melting, but it had been crushed by the wheels of some wagon.

That winter brought a conflict between my mother and my teacher—the first, to my knowledge—with a certain political flavor. It began with my teacher's complaint that I spoke very poorly *na rodnom yazyke* ("in my native language"), that is, Russian, and that I even spoke Lithuanian with my friends at school. She wrote a note to this effect. Upon reading the note, mother was very upset and rushed head-on to the school to explain to the teacher that her son's native language was not Russian but rather Lithuanian. The teacher showed her a Russian language textbook with the title *Rodnoy yazyk* ("Native language") on its cover. Her gesture was equivalent to saying, "From now on your son's native language is Russian." It was like a stab in the heart. Mother, perceiving the teacher's obstinacy and unwillingness to understand the essence of the matter, perhaps indicative of her political convictions, realized that any further argument or attempt to clarify the matter of her son's native language might tip the scales, and so she decided to withdraw from the "field of battle." Controlling herself, at great cost to her nerves, she bid the teacher good-bye and left the school, without even telling me about the conversation. Later, while the teacher insisted on my speaking Russian in school, she used to remark, "You can speak your native language at home." That showed a considerable political gain on mother's part. Tribute be given to the teacher as well, for she never took the incident out on me at school.

We exiles were not protected by any international organization. Why, no information was disseminated from the depths of this mountainous region to the rest of the world. Nor did we have the protection of any local alliance or party. In the Soviet Union as a whole there was one professional workers' union and one communist party. Both of these organizations were founded in the Kremlin, in Moscow, and they were subservient to Stalin and his henchmen. No legal institutions defended us. In fact, exiles had neither citizens' rights nor relevant documents. So how could they appeal to anyone about violations of their rights? Our very exile was approved by the founders of those same institutions, more precisely, the Kremlin....

For a long time after the war, while Stalin was in power, we didn't have the right to send or receive letters. We were fenced off from the world by high mountain ridges. Families certainly could not expect any help from fathers because they were in concentration camps or prisons—or long since tortured to death, shot, or otherwise murdered. Needless to say, we could not receive aid from our relatives around the world, who, as we learned much later, had emigrated to the United States of America, Canada, Australia, and Venezuela. At the time, we knew nothing about them, nor did they know about us. So we had to come to grips with the misfortune that had befallen us without anyone's help, relying only on ourselves, our intuition, reason, and intelligence. Mother insisted on our education, so that

The Zubinas brothers among schoolchildren at the Second farm school: first row, second from the left – Algimantas; third row, first on the left – Romualdas, and behind him, standing highest, Vytautas.

we would grow up self-reliant and self-confident. We studied to the extent allowed by our particular material and social circumstances. What a blessing it was to have a physically and spiritually strong personality like mother beside us then!

In honor of our women exiles, I must say, they kept their heads and fended for their children as best they could. Finding themselves unexpectedly in extreme conditions while still very young, with no previous physical or psychological training for such circumstances, they displayed remarkably exemplary behavior. They deserve not only their families' but also their country's highest respect. Why, some of them returned to Lithuania with all of their children and succeeded in bringing them up in the national Lithuanian spirit, providing them with higher education, and thus preparing them for life.

Elžbieta Zubinienė with her sons (left to right) Vytautas, Romualdas, Algimantas

Romualdas Zubinas. *Tremtinio Metraštis* ("An Exile's Chronicle"). Kaunas: Naujasis Lankas, 2010.

Romualdas Zubinas returned to Lithuania in 1956. From 1960 to 1963, he served in the Soviet army in Liepaja. Upon returning home, he married Genovaitė Puodžiūtė. A daughter, Diana, was born.

In 1959, Romualdas graduated from the Kaunas Polytechnical school; in 1976, he graduated from the evening program in Industrial and Civil Engineering at Polytechnical Institute. He held various positions in the field of construction until he retired in 1999. He resides in Kaunas.

Romualdas' mother, Elžbieta Zubinienė, died in 1997. His brother Algimantas Zubinas died in 2006.

Nijolė Ambrazaitytė in Igarka, ca. 1951

Nijolė Ambrazaitytė (first row, second from right) in her class at the Igarka school, ca. 1950

Nijolė Ambrazaitytė

In 1948, at age nine, Nijolė Ambrazaitytė was exiled with her grandparents and her aunt's family from Raseiniai to Igarka, by the Yenisei River in the Krasnoyarsk region of Russia, within the Arctic Circle. In 1956, they were relocated from Igarka to a settlement known as Maklakovo.

Nijolė Ambrazaitytė is a renowned singer, a former soloist of the Lithuanian National Opera and Ballet Theater, and one of the signers of Lithuania's Declaration of Independence in 1990. She was awarded the Cross of Commander of Lithuania's Grand Duke Gediminas' Order in 1998.

WORK BEGINS

As soon as I reached my tenth birthday, I had to report to the timber labor exchange in Igarka. I arrived at the office without any personal documents, no birth certificate or health records. The supervisor looked me over and said, "*khorosho*" ("good"). Apparently he was pleased to see my little purse with a crust of bread and an attached note dangling from the string that girded my quilted jacket. I gave him the note, which stated that I would soon be twelve years old, for that was the minimum age at which youngsters were accepted for heavy work. (The note had been signed by some well-wisher.) It was May. School was out only yesterday, and tomorrow I would be called to work at 6:00 a.m. by the sawmill's siren.

The colossal sawmill was constantly short of workers because its machinery ran day and night, necessitating alternate shifts. So starving children like me were also employable. The vicinity of the labor exchange resembled a deserted, uninhabitable frozen city. At closer range, the sawmill appeared to be a huge lumber enterprise, with enormous piles of logs, stacks of boards, firewood, and sawdust ever increasing in bulk and height. Igarka was the lumber capital, known for its quality wood products across the seas. Though this lumber capital looked like a fossilized specter of a city, it nevertheless held a distinctive title—that of a wood-drying labor exchange. It had its own governance and regulations, its wooden streets, alleys, and squares. Wherever you looked, boards were strewn by the wayside, wood bark creaked under your feet, sawdust whirled in the air, and sticks littered the ground, tripping workers and betraying the general disorder. Summer and winter, workers like ants kept moving those scrap piles from one corner of the mill to another in the course of a continuous work campaign, in which I would now participate. It didn't matter to me that all this was not a rubbish heap but rather a strategic resource for the Soviet Union, worth a mountain of gold in the world market, or that I would have to sort remnants—sticks (*gorbyl*), boards, and stumps—of cedars, larches, and other valuable trees and pile them onto enormous stacks; that I would have to cover roofs and dismantle them. All this I would learn a few years hence. What awaited me now in this disorder was an acquaintance with the procedures and internal regulations at the mill.

I walked between rows of wood piles, set on raised platforms and evidently held in esteem, for constantly scurrying about them were overseers or supervisors as well as accounting clerks with trim rectangular briefcases. Those piles were attended by sorters, inspectors, brigade leaders, perhaps even the office supervisors. It seemed to me that these people were in control of everything here. They sniffed and touched boards to check for dryness, and they didn't let the workers out of their sight. If a worker was drowsy on the job, he or she lost that workday. I understood that here, as in a battlefield, was an on-going struggle for work and pay.

That cold morning I hurried to my first day at work along with cheerless grown-ups. Together with everyone else, I waited at the labor exchange office for my assignment and soon joined a group of three workers. Our group followed the brigade leader to the rows of wood piles, referred to as "stacks" (R. *shtabel*). Pointing to the roof, which seemed to merge with the clouds, and then at me, the brigade leader said, "*Nu, rebyatnya, davayte*" ("So, young men, get to work"). That word *davayte* meant that I would have to get to the top of the very highest stack, lift boards from its roof and throw them down to other members of our brigade, who would have to pile them in order and align them on runners, until the entire cubic capacity of the stack would be hauled away by a straddle truck.

I stood there a while figuring out how I could reach that roof, for I had no ladder or rope, nothing to hold on to. The day's work norm was high—a few of those roofs per shift—so I had to storm that roof without further delay. I started climbing upward, board by board, because sluggishness on the part of one member of our brigade might cost everyone's pay or its decrease. I had to cast downward as many boards as I could, as quickly as possible. With this goal in mind, I thrust myself into internecine battle with the enemy, the massive stack of lumber. My hands and feet suddenly transformed into a centipede; they clutched at boards as I clambered up the vertical wall and before I knew it, surmounted the roof's sharp edge—escaping a fall backwards into the gorge between heaps of boards—and finally found myself on the roof. Great, the fortress surrendered to me.

I pry and lift the heavy wet boards, shouting "Ohohoii!" at each heave, warning those below to watch out. And so for several hours you hear only "Ohohoii!" and try to skirt the falling boards as they crash against the ground. From the top of the stack, as from a fortress tower or mountain peak, the town of Igarka is in full view, and I survey the grey scene.

Igarka stands shriveled, dotted with colorless, lopsided houses, mostly temporary barracks, and surrounded by grimy, boundless tundra. I despaired that my home was in such a monotonous

place, though behind one of those protruding chimneys were my grandparents, who awaited me today as always. I set to my task more deftly, anticipating my pay. I furiously pried those heavy boards, permeated by water and ice, and throwing them down, yelled energetically, “Ohohoii—here it comes!” warning those below to get out of the way.

After three hours of work came the well-earned lunch break. I climbed down from the stack, settled on some fallen boards, and pulled my lunch out of my jacket: two slices of bread with a fatty substance of unknown origin fortuitously inserted between them. Letting that wonderful food melt in my mouth, I savored it like a delicious pastry. Then I examined my bruised arms and legs, rubbed the black and blue spots, patted the aching sores, and pulled splinters out with my teeth. Following my grandmother’s instructions, I applied ice to my bruises and thus treated others’ wounds as well as my own. When my shift was over, I barely

dragged my feet homeward and had no desire to participate in a game of *lapta* (a ball game) with other children that day.

Next morning I was standing at the door of the lumber exchange again, waiting for my work assignment. This time a different brigade leader ordered us to follow him. As we approached an iron building, shrill sounds of creaking metal accosted us, growing louder. I was led to the screeching machinery, which was a huge lathe for splitting and shaping logs. Its iron blades turned so fast that in the blink of an eye the log caught in its clutches was transformed to sawdust and scraps of bark while an iron crane raised the thick, shapely boards above my head and lowered them mechanically on the other side. Could any girl conceive or dream of the kind of work that confronted me here? Chills ran down my spine as I looked at the jaws of those iron cutters. It was impossible to converse in the midst of the screeching noise; there was no way to express my fear and no one around to hear me.

The brigade leader shouted something straight into my ear, but I understood only from his gestures that I would have to deal with the plethora of sharp sticks, sawdust and chips flying in all directions on my own at these gates of hell. He handed me a large shovel and went on his way. To my astonishment, as I braced myself for very dangerous work, my fear left me as if it were lifted by an invisible hand. With one eye, I vigilantly watched the movement of the transporter; with the other, I attentively followed the iron chains that turned large and small gears with saws and clanked loudly from stretching and pulling.

The gigantic saws warned me of imminent danger as they rattled terribly, demonstrating the force of their iron teeth. There was no time for idling: I had to look out lest those gears do any harm. I concentrated on the task and in a while, I got used to the ear-shattering noise of crashing lumber and became a part of that hellish mill. The clattering gears ceased to frighten me, but I didn't know how my initial fear vanished. Perchance Medeinė, goddess of woods and forests, inspired me with courage, for she alone could have watched over the hubbub of that sawmill.

I moved about like a mechanical spinning top, pulling remnants of logs to the side, shoveling and piling wood chips and sawdust. This powdered my chestnut braids yellow. It got into my eyes and mouth, choking me. Toward the end of the shift, the brigade leader came in with a machinist, bringing grease for the machinery. They stopped and waved in my direction. From the movement of his lips, I understood the machinist saying, *"Gde tvoyi muzhiki, shto dityo stavish?"* ("Where are your men that you've assigned a child?"). The brigade leader merely parted his hands, and they walked out. At the end of the shift, a stocky man came in to replace me. I handed him my shovel and ceded my position without a word.

I left the sawmill very tired, with aching arms and back. Had I needed to proceed with that work for another hour, I simply could not have lifted the shovel—nor a spoon.

HOMEWARD ACROSS THE YENISEI WITH A SACK

Every day we dug potatoes and pulled up carrots and beets. The monotonous day work ended with singing by a campfire, baking potatoes, and sweet sleep in our beds. Washing at a stream one morning, we were surprised to see the edge of the forest sparkling with frost while mist bared our faces and hands. As everywhere in Siberia, winter came early.

I thought of my hungry grandparents ever more frequently and felt obligated to return home. Were they well? Did they have enough to eat? These questions kept turning in my mind. I approached the teacher and asked his permission to leave the field earlier. Those who dug vegetables could have some—as many as one could lift and carry. I made haste for home.

I filled a half sack and pulled on it. Oho! It was heavy, but I threw it over my shoulders. I turned in the direction of the Yenisei, toward the station of rowboats that served as ferries. From a distance, I could see a string of large and small boats rocking in the water along the shore. I looked about for a boatman, who should be nearby. I sat down and waited, waited long, but no boatman showed up. I decided to cross the river on my own. I chose a rowboat that looked quite new, bailed out some water, and loaded my sack with vegetables.

At first I merely dipped the oars and splashed water, letting the boat circle along the shore, but once I pulled away more forcefully, the current began to carry us. In the distance, I could clearly see the pier on the opposite side of the river. I felt confident and certain that I would soon reach the opposite shore. I worked the oars and was soon in the middle of the Yenisei. The river looked different from the boat than it did from the shore. I remembered that the local inhabitants called the river *Biy Khem*, meaning the Great Yenisei. It really was big as I looked, though narrower here and therefore swifter than it was in Igarka. It was truly *Biy Khem*. Suddenly I felt a strong current lifting and carrying my boat along like a piece of straw. Oaring became increasingly more difficult, and it seemed that the boat just stood in place without moving. The palms of my hands ached and I had blisters, but the flow of the current did not cease pulling. I grappled with the oars, but the boat did not cooperate, and the pier on the other side of the river was out of sight. All around, there was nothing but water, dark and deep. Whirlpools spinned the boat. This must be the locus of the most dangerous rapids and vortices children talked about, where someone was always drowning. Strangely, it was not fear that overtook me but a desire to wrestle with the current. I felt whirlpools pulling my little boat forward, but I kept raising my oars without a moment's respite, chopping deeper into the water at each turn. I hardly noticed when my boat lurched toward the shore, and I, helpless, with bloody hands and stars in my eyes, touched upon swampy, longed-for land. As I dragged my wet sack ashore, I felt as if I were landing after a great battle. Having conquered the water, I felt elated, as if I were entering a triumphal arch rather than a swampy strand guarded by hordes of mosquitoes. I stood up, took a deep breath, and shouted at the top of my lungs, "Yenisei, I crossed you! I crossed you, *Biy Khem!*" Then I turned around and saw in front of me a steep ragged bank, blocking my way home.

Such a high embankment was not visible from the other side; if it were, I would have seen it. While I was wrestling with the current, it must have carried me around the bend, maybe fifteen kilometers to the north. So the pier I had seen was now far away from me. Here, the Yenisei shore was badly washed by frequent floods. One could see ravines and holes in the ground, as if someone had been digging and burrowing in it. Perhaps gold seekers of sorts had wandered here from the Klondike or Magadan and, becoming frustrated in their search, expressed their anger by uprooting trees and devastating the shore. Here and there slender pines were still holding on by their roots, but evidently not for long.

My old sack lay on the ground like a rock while I tried to figure out how I could carry its weight up the nearly perpendicular, rugged embankment. If my grandfather were here, he would think of something, but I was alone and had to depend on my own wits. I looked in all directions. The steep ragged wall I saw in front of me extended to the right. If I walked forward, my path would be obstructed by a wide stream flowing into the Yenisei; going backward, I would come upon a swampy marsh, with the decrepit bank at my back. There was no way out but to climb that slippery slope. I hastened to investigate the most propitious route before nightfall. The moon shone above the embankment, but its light did not reach beyond a ridge of trees in the distance. I would have to climb in the dark. I'll climb a ways myself, I thought, and then pull the sack up. To see how secure the rocks were beneath my feet, I gently jogged a clod. It went rolling down and hit the side of the boat, crumbled and plopped into the water. As the noise subsided, I searched for firmer ground under my feet. As far as I could reach, I explored the terrain with my hands and fingers to see if it was sturdy and supportive. I clutched at some twisted roots, improvising a step, and climbed upward, pulling the sack after me. It worked. Thus step by step, gropingly, I rose upward. When I thought I had reached the top, I fumbled, and my sack tumbled down, plumb into its former spot by the rowboat below.

I had to start all over again. Now my fingers were feeble on my thin hands and I couldn't effectively grasp the sack, which seemed to grow heavier and stubbornly resist my clutching at its corners. I rumpled it and groped at the vegetables inside until I made out top and bottom. It was totally dark when I finally dragged that stupid bag up the bank, exhausted from pulling. I curled up in a ball, afraid to stir lest I roll down with my sack. Thus I nestled on the ground, waiting for dawn. I was frantically hungry. And why does a human being want to eat so frequently? It seems I had lunch just yesterday, and now hunger is tormenting me again as I dangle here above the Yenisei. I can't believe I've come to a place with no roads leading anywhere.

I thought I might listen to the night or versify some kind of story or pastoral about a shepherdess. Though I tried to listen to the sound of fish splashing in the river, my mind was occupied by those same thoughts of food, my cheerless home, and hungry grandparents. In this desolate spot, I remembered lines from my mother's letter. She wrote from a white stone house in Canada about my brothers and sisters. They didn't want to drink cocoa with cream in the morning. And what was "cream"? There in Montreal they didn't like hot "tostai" [toast] with butter, ham or cheese. The sentence was incomprehensible to me. What were those "tostai" and ham? I had heard of butter, but I had never tasted it, nor cheese or ham. There in the province of Quebec they spoke French and baked a cake called *Buche de Noel* for Christmas. I noted new words—*steak*, *shrimp*, *French*—but how could I guess what they meant? Yes, my parents lived in a big white house near the St. Lawrence River and they drove a white Rolls-Royce. They had a few stores called *Chemist* and a turkey farm in the country. The letter was full of unsolvable riddles.

I rummaged inside the sack and grasped a large coarse lump. I thought it was a carrot but found a beet as I bit into its sweetish, juicy pulp. No one ate raw beets, but they tasted good to me as I chewed on them. I felt very sleepy but could not fall asleep here; I had to watch my bag so that it wouldn't roll down to the Yenisei again. Thus curled up, I waited for morning.

The day broke. Morning above the Yenisei was awesome, but I couldn't delight in it; I had to climb up the bank, to the very top. I crawled in zigzags and was nearing the goal when my head hit against something hard. That was the last but most difficult obstacle. Above me hung a crumbling earthen ceiling, propped up by tree roots twisting crosswise and some rotten trunks. How could I get through such a tangle? One clumsy step and I could slide down. I decided to pick at that ceiling carefully and began to dismantle its clay and rock borders. Holding my sack in place with one hand, I scratched and clawed at the ceiling while it crumbled straight onto my head, inside my jacket and dress. Sand creaked between my teeth and got into my eyes as I burrowed like an animal, but I produced a small hole and squeezed myself through it. I widened the gap for my poor sack and dragged it onto the bank. Good thing I didn't let go of it when I had lost hope of success.

I looked down from the shore to the trail worn by my sack and to the channel of the Yenisei, marked and pressed in as if by a gigantic mold. I rejoiced at my night's work. I stood on the protruding bank amid sky, woods, and water, fearing neither the height nor big waters. It didn't matter that I was alone in this wilderness and didn't know if Maklakovo was far away.

With a triumphant gesture, I threw the vegetable sack on my shoulders and strode into dense woods. The sack helped me clear a path in front of me, flinging aside thorny branches and nettles as it propelled me forward. I marched over the taiga without any trace of a path or sign that anyone had set foot here before. Like a small ant carrying a pine needle, I elbowed my way through brushwood and tiptoed across puddles, bending snags and nettle thickets along my way. Cranberries shone red at my feet, blueberry bushes carpeted the ground green, and orange-caps by the side of white birch trees looked at me wondrously. When I happened upon some raspberry canes, I stopped for rest and breakfasted on ripe berries. My grandfather used to say, jokingly, that my blood was untasty and unsuitable for mosquitoes, for sometimes they just buzzed around and didn't bite me. But now, unfortunately, they would not leave me alone. Flying about in blackish hordes, they hit upon me and attacked me incessantly. They just buzzed and buzzed, searching for exposed skin to bite.

I had to wade from one swamp to another. The moment I reached drier ground, there was another quag in front of me. The swamps were covered with cranberries; in drier places, there were tussocks bulging with bilberries. Walking onward, I heard the drone of a car engine in the distance and turned in its direction. The noise of cars sounded like salvation to my ears. I soon wended my way to the highway and sat down on my sack with anticipation.

Passing cars were few and far between. I sat there, looking about, rubbing my bruises and stinging feet. Then a car pulled out of the mist and stopped. The driver stuck his head out the window, muttered, "*S gruzom nye beryom*" ("We don't take [passengers] with cargo"), and drove off. A few hours later, when I had lost hope of getting a ride, a dump truck drove up, rattling. When I heard "*Kuda*?" ("Where?"), I answered, "*Tuda*" ("There"). The driver got out, lifted my sack and me into the cabin, and shouted "*Derzhys*!" ("Hold on!"). The iron door of the cabin banged shut and we sped forth. I held onto the dashboard with both hands. The cabin shook so much that I was jerked straight up from my seat and flung down again. I rolled about and gasped at sudden turns, trying not to lose hold of my sack or fall out myself. It seemed as if I were riding on the back of a furious bull that wanted to be rid of me at any cost. And so I see-sawed with the truck from pot-hole to pot-hole all the way to Maklakovo. The taiga landscape, resembling a candy wrap and I. Shishkin's famous painting "Morning in the Woods," came to an end. I thought, if I ever get one of those candies, I must glue its picturesque wrapper into a scrapbook. I got off the truck with shaking feet and fog in my eyes, but I managed to drag the sack home. My grandmother, with tears in her eyes, was the first to judge my feat heroic, while my grandfather, jogging the sack, just shook his head and kept saying, "Oh, what a strong girl you are!"

Nijolė Ambrazaitytė. *Virš Mūsų Poliarinė Pašvaistė* ("Northern Lights Above Us"). Vilnius: Lithuanian Writers' Union Publishers, 2005.

Nijolė Ambrazaitytė returned to Lithuania in 1957. After graduating from high school, from 1959 to 1966, she studied voice at Lithuania's National Conservatory (now the National Academy of Music and Theater); from 1979, she taught at her alma mater. In 1966 she became a soloist at the Vilnius Opera and Ballet Theater.

From 1992 to 2000, Nijolė Ambrazaitytė was a member of Parliament of the Republic of Lithuania.

She resides in Vilnius.

Onutė in Siberia, 1950

Onutė, Leona, and Juozas Jakubauskas, 1950

Onutė Jakubauskaitė-Linkūnienė

On March 26, 1949, Silvestras Jakubauskas (1887–1968) and Magdalena Jakubauskienė (1896–1983), peasants from the rural district of Pajevonis in the county of Vilkaviškis, were exiled with their children Irena (b. 1933), Onutė (b. 1936), Juozas (1937–2001), and Leona (1940–2008), to the Krasnoyarsk region of Russia. Their daughter Teresė remained in Lithuania.

...Through the slits of windows beneath the ceiling of our wagon, we could see the Ural Mountains. They were so high that their summits were invisible. We saw miles of rock surface, sparsely overgrown with shriveled, stunted pine trees. Even the strongest among us were overwhelmed by this view. Mother was very strong, but looking at those mountains, she said, "This will be the end of us," and fainted. It seemed that if we were let off here, starvation was unavoidable. But we rode on. Whenever the train stopped at a larger station, Russian women ran up to us, vending pancakes and milk. They would pull a frog out of an earthenware jar and, dangling it by its leg, offer it to us: "It's fresh, chilled. Buy it." Those with small children had no choice but to buy such products. Then the frog disappeared into the jar and the train rolled on. At the next station, more of the same. We crossed the Urals. Beyond those mountains the landscape looked a little better.

We'd travelled three weeks when we approached the Sayan Mountains and the Siberian steppes. One morning our boxcar door was opened and we heard an order: "Get off with all your things." The assembly of people who got off with their bundles extended as far as the eye could see—a multitude of people waiting to hear where they would be placed. A few men, apparently overseers or supervisors, walked by us. They gestured to some people to step forward, then to others...but again they passed us by. After they had selected all those fit for work, our turn came. They indicated a dump-truck. We loaded our bundles, which they tied down with ropes, and we sat down on top of the bundles. We held onto the ropes tightly because the bundles were tied down while we were not. What if, driving beyond town, they raised the tailgate and we fell out while they rode on with our belongings? Thank God, that did not happen. Having been intimidated so much, we were prepared for anything.

It was mid-April, still very cold in Siberia. They drove us about a hundred kilometers. As we rode, it seemed the road was coming to an end and we would hit a mountain side, but somehow the road unwound and we came out to a plain on the other side of the mountain. Then again we were up against a mountain but came out on the other side. Throughout the entire route we passed no settlements; there was only desert and emptiness. Yet we began to smell a strange odor of smoke. Quite chilled by now, we looked around. In the distance we could see an inhabited area: strange houses made of rounded logs, their roofs covered with boards, and barns like sheepcots woven of willow and slathered with cowdung so wind wouldn't blow through the cracks. They were plastered thus on both sides. Very convenient: while the cowdung is warm, they spread it; then it freezes and holds. Wherever this "plaster" drops, it is collected into piles and used as fuel. That is the source of the strange smell wafting from chimneys.

We didn't know where they had brought us. We were taken like a cat in a bag so that we wouldn't know how to escape. It was a soviet sheep-herding farm (*ovcesovkhoz*) in the environs of Askiz, Khakassia, in the Krasnoyarsk region. There were 36,000 sheep, or thirty-six flocks, each with a thousand sheep, on that soviet farm. Our family was the last to get off the train because we were fit for nothing other than herding sheep. We were settled with local Khakas people. For about a week we sat and lay on our bundles, set down in a porch. The dwelling was infested with bedbugs. When these got the scent of new people, they fell straight down from the ceiling on us and bit painfully, especially at night.

While we lived with that family, we feared them and they feared us. Strange people, resembling Mongolians. The women wear dresses wide at the neck, with wide shoulders. They have long braids, and for holidays, they weave numerous little braids, which they adorn with sea shells, tied on by little holes drilled in them. That is their traditional dress. The Khakas have no beds; they all sleep on the ground. At night they spread a large woolen blanket in the middle of the room and lie down on it, with all heads in the middle: the husband, wife, three children, including a one-year-old, and a great-great-grandmother, over a hundred years old. She watches the little one and smokes a long, thin pipe with a tiny bowl. When the child starts crying, the old woman pulls out her withered breast to suck on, maybe a substitute for a pacifier. The old woman's son is ninety years old; his son is sixty, and the child's father is thirty-five.

As time wore on, we grew accustomed to these people, and we ceased to fear one another.

The local people did not know how to prepare meat. They slaughtered a pig and threw out its intestines for dogs and cats. Seeing this, my mother asked why they didn't make use of the intestines. "Let the dogs have them," they said. We were starving at the time, so mother asked if she could take those intestines. "Take them, grandma," they said. That meant a feast for us. We collected the fat, as much as there was, cleaned the intestines, and made some potato sausages. We invited the Khakas woman and served her some. She liked the sausages very much and asked how we made them, what ingredients we used. Neither did they know how to cure meat so that it would last longer. They butchered it, threw out the intestines, set it in a hole in the ground, and covered it with snow. The snow melted and they were out of meat. Later they learned many things from the exiles.

They kept two cows. They milk them, pour milk into jars made of birch bark called *tuyasok*. They collect the cream as needed and pour the milk into one big barrel. The milk sours until a crust rises to the top. Then they take out that crust with their hands, press it, and throw it on some cloth to dry. They eat those dried crusts. From the whey they produce a homebrew vodka called *ayran*. They also pour this vodka into birch-bark jars, *tuyasoks*, then treat themselves and entertain.

They do not have normal tables, only very low ones. They sit on the floor with their legs crossed beneath them. Before drinking-bouts, they bring an armful of hay into the room, scatter it around the table, then drink and spit into that hay. When the hay gets wet, they collect it, take it outside, and bring in more hay. Whenever they visit relatives or friends, they always make sure to bring along a few *tuyasoks* of *ayran*.

After our first week there, we were given a separate room, partitioned off by a wall of boards. On the other side of this wall was another family. There were bedbugs here as well. We had some trouble getting rid of them because they crawled through cracks from the other side of the partition, but eventually we succeeded and they ceased to suck our blood.

The Khakas appointed father to transport fuel to the tractors. Father harnessed a few ash-grey oxen without sidechecks or throatlatches, traces or reins, with only two sticks attached to their necks by the hame and a long whip in hand. The cart consisted of two levers set lengthwise and three barrels, each holding two hundred liters. There was no room for a tray or a seat, so father used to sit on the front barrel and drive with the whip. When the sun was hot and mosquitoes attacked them, it was impossible to control those animals. They went wherever they wanted to go, most often into water, and stood there as long as they liked, while the driver could just cry.

Thus father transported fuel for about a month. He became swollen and could not fasten his trousers by a hand's width. We had little to eat, and he did not have the strength to proceed with this work. Father sought a doctor, who informed him that his kidneys were failing and there was no help for his condition. Then mother went to another doctor, two tablecloths in hand, begging for help.

She had no money yet. Finally, father was hospitalized, nourished, and, thank God, restored to health. When he got well, he was assigned to sheep herding.

I was assigned to herd local inhabitants' cows. In the morning, at the break of dawn, everyone began to turn out their cows and calves to pasture. I didn't know those fields or pastures; I didn't know the people. Everything was strange and unfamiliar to me. I had no dog or horse. I went on foot, stick in hand, following fifty cows and as many of their brood, hardly keeping up with them. There were no pastures nearby; grazing land on the hills was about five kilometers away. At midday, when the sun was high, mosquitoes and *moshka*, those miniature flies, began to attack the animals. Oh, my God! How the cows ran about madly! They tossed their tails on the small of their backs and ran. They ran, and what was I to do on foot? I feared losing them because I would have to account for them at day's end. I ran as far as my legs carried me, but how could I catch up with the animals? It seemed my heart would come up my throat, my legs refused to go further, my mouth dried up, while the cows had run about half a kilometer ahead of me. I fell down on the ground and wept, wondering what to do—I was responsible for those animals. After some time, I calmed down, got up, and walked in the direction the cows had run. About a kilometer further on, I found them wading in a swift river, up to their sides in water, splashing with their tails, defending themselves from mosquitoes and flies. That day I became acquainted with the Sayan Mountains and the Khakas' cows. Later, when I grew accustomed to my herd of cows, the spacious hills and pastures, and came to understand the

animals, I did not worry so much because in the evening, the cows usually headed for home.

The greatest difficulty was hunger. I didn't have anything to take for lunch, so I didn't eat from morning 'til evening throughout those days at pasture. Mother used to make a groat soup and dispatch my little brother Juozukas and sister Leonėlė to bring me at least this groat soup, even if it had no protein or fat in it. Every time they tried to bring me lunch, they couldn't find me: it was too far for them and they were afraid of getting lost. So they used to return home with the pot full of soup, and I was left with an empty stomach. After a month of herding, I began to call on people for milk because I earned a half liter of milk and five rubles for each milking cow and five rubles for each calf. Then we had something to pour on the groats. Can you imagine that I had to work half-starved for a whole month? We were young and maybe hardier, so we didn't swell as father did.

The first month was the worst. Later, every evening after driving the cows home, I used to collect the milk due me from the local houses. There were Khakas women who used to take the milk just gotten from the cows and strain it through their hair. They all wore long braids, so they would undo the ends of a braid and, even though it was full of nits, strain the milk through it. Seeing this, I still had to drink that milk because there was no choice. I used to regurgitate that milk before I got used to it. Once boiled, even the lice-ridden milk served to improve soup or groats.

Every day, summer and winter, the cows were driven to pasture, and I herded them for two years. Later, a shepherd (*chaban*) invited me to be his assistant in sheep herding. It was a herd of pedigree brood ewes. In April, the sheep began to give birth to their young, so we had to transport them back from the fields. I had a horse and a wagon with a cabin, into which I lifted the sheep and then drove them to their pen (*koshara*), an enclosure for keeping sheep. I transported them in this way until all the sheep had lambed. The sheep had lots of wool. In summertime, they itched from the heat and we had to bathe them in an antiseptic substance (*creolin*) so they would not scratch themselves and scatter wool. The bathing place was far away, maybe eighteen to twenty kilometers, and there was only one for the whole soviet farm. Once, while driving the sheep, it grew dark. I met another shepherd with a flock of sheep along the way, and we spent the night there. I was treated to porridge cooked with sheep's milk; it wasn't bad though it smelled a little of sweat. The next morning we headed far over the hills again, to the bathing place. I herded sheep for a year.

We worked every day and we also had to report to the commander every week to prove that we had not run away. Every time he reminded us not to think of home. "You'll live here forever," he said. I never believed that we would live here forever, but I dared not shout back at him, "You'd better shove those words up your butt because that's not how it's going to be."

The west wind was tinged with Lithuania's fragrance for us, the more so because my eldest sister, Teresėlė, had remained in Lithuania. At the time we were deported, she was attending medical school in Kaunas. She also suffered hunger, and there was no one to help her out with food or money. In Stalin's lifetime, she was afraid to write letters or to receive any lest she be arrested and deported. She lived in a state of semi-starvation. She used to sell her blood for a few rubles and a food coupon for that day. Later, after Stalin's era, we used to send her as much tallow as we could muster and sometimes a goose roasted in fat.

There were eight hundred young lambs in the flock. The following year, each flock yielded an average of twelve kilograms of wool. The average weight of a lamb was eighty kilograms. For such results our brigade was awarded a prize of 40,000 rubles, an invitation to

the Soviet Union's nationwide agricultural exhibition in Moscow, and a medal.

In summertime we used to drive the sheep to the mountains, about ten kilometers away. We brought along a tent (*balagan*) for living and sleeping; wooden fences about three meters high with which to enclose the sheep pens or two wooden poles each to tie on wire fencing; a crow bar, an ax, and three dogs. We would find a location where there was a stream. During the day we let the sheep graze and before nightfall we drove them into the pens. As a senior herder, I had to guard the pens against wolves that might invade and kill the sheep. There were dogs at three corners of the pen, and I stood watch at the fourth corner. The pen was large, twenty-five by twenty-five meters, and every three or four weeks, we had to relocate it so that the sheep's wool would not get dirty. Wool was very valuable and it had to be clean.

Once in wintertime it was unusually windy, so we kept the sheep near bushes and brush. We herded them across a frozen river, and they were calm. In the evening, while driving them homeward, we saw a natural wonder: water flowing above the ice in a stream at least twenty centimeters wide. What were we to do now? Try as we might to drive them, the sheep would not proceed through the water; they turned in a circle. It was getting dark and we were tired. And how could we step into water wearing felt boots? Then, out of the blue, we saw a Willy (jeep) approaching on the opposite shore, stopping and beaming its headlights in our direction. It was the chief zootechnician coming to our aid, but the sheep would not move. We decided there was no way out but to wade into icy water and drag the sheep out by their horns, one by one. It worked. A few crossed the stream and then others followed, up to their stomachs in water. We herded them home. Apparently, it was not the first time water flowing down the mountains formed a stream over the frozen river in March. We each drank a hundred grams of whiskey, as per instructions, and did not even come down with colds.

In 1953, when Stalin died, the commander became a different person. We had more freedom. We bought a house with the money we earned, though a small one (three by six meters), and moved to the town of Askiz. Father went to work as a carpenter for a local enterprise; my sister found work in a sewing factory, and I at butter production in a dairy. My brother and other sister attended high school.

I haven't mentioned that my mother's eldest brother was an army doctor. In 1940, when the Russians occupied Lithuania, they arrested and deported all educated people in the army to Siberia (Norilsk). My uncle's wife, also a doctor, emigrated to the West with their three children during the war years. After Stalin's death, when prisoners were released, my uncle had nowhere to go, so he joined us in Siberia. When the commander heard that a new person had arrived, he asked for his documents. Handed my uncle's passport, the commander would not return it, saying, "You'll be an exile." From the sorrow and stress of his predicament my uncle had a stroke. He was paralyzed over half his body, and in another half year, he died. We buried him, erected a cross at his gravesite, and put up a fence around it. Many years later, when my sister Leonėlė travelled to this location, she could not even find the gravesite. Everything in the vicinity had fallen into decay and changed beyond recognition. And so my uncle's bones remained in the depth of Siberia.

When I began work at the dairy, there was no machinery; everything was done manually. Another girl and I were assigned to churn butter. They poured cream into the churn, a four hundred-kilogram barrel, and we had to stir it until the butter was churned. It was January and the premises were not heated. The cream cooled, so that sometimes we had to mix the butter into the night, until early morning hours. When I came home, even my padded jacket was wet from the work of stirring. Thus I worked until spring. The dairy's supervisors noticed that I worked conscientiously and sent me to a course in butter production. After completing this course, I worked in the dairy as a lab assistant. When I had left to attend the course, they could not find a replacement for me, a work mule who would churn butter in those conditions. They had no choice but to install a mechanical churn and so put an end to that slave's work.

The following year, they sent me to a course in cheese production. When I returned, I worked as the cheese forewoman. For the entire summer, I was assigned to the dairy's other production plant in the mountains, fifty kilometers away, with three other girls. The four of us were settled in a dormitory. We worked in two shifts: one shift produced cheese from the morning's milk; the other, from the evening milk. Incidentally, the cheese factory was built in the mountains so that it would be near the collective farm that delivered milk.

In summertime there were all kinds of berries in the woods. After the night shift, I used to go berry-picking and then made preserves. Once, while walking in the woods with my pail of berries, I fell asleep; stumbling into a hole, I woke up from my dream. I had been so tired.... But one can do anything in one's youth, with desire, of course. I dug up a garden bed by our dormitory and grew cabbage. I bought a few suckling pigs and raised them on whey by the following autumn. I brought home many goods that fall. By winter, there was not much to do there. The place was called Verkhniy Askiz. When the season of cheese production was over in the mountains, they took us home to Askiz. Then I proceeded to work as a lab assistant in butter production at the dairy, as usual. Of course by then we were no longer hungry, but homesickness did not cease to affect our health.

Here in Siberia, there was nothing good in the stores; there was alcohol. It was so cold inside the store that bottles of alcohol on the shelves were covered with frost. Bread was apt to be frozen if you didn't get it when it was delivered to the store. We could buy flour from the local people; we missed yeast most of all. Later, we learned how the locals produced their yeast: from a little flour, grated potatoes, and hops.

During my last year in Siberia before I was allowed to return to Lithuania, I had all kinds of dreams. For instance, I was flying so high that no one could reach me, waving my hands and rising, rising higher. It felt so good! I also dreamt of a floor that I washed very white and clean; then, donning a white dress, I stood up straight before a huge mirror on that floor. It was hardly a month after the latter dream when the director of the dairy told me to stop by his office. I went in afraid, thinking I'd done something wrong. He asked me to sit down, politely, and began to inquire how I was getting on at work; whether I missed my homeland. I told him that I missed Lithuania very much and that if I could, I would leave for Lithuania that very day. Fidgeting with a sheet of paper on the desk in front of him, he proceeded to inquire about my life. Finally, he raised the sheet of paper, saying, "Here, I am giving you this certificate (R. *spravka*); as of today, you are free and have the right to live where you like. You can stay here or you can go to Lithuania." The joy I felt brought me to tears. As I recall, I just had wits enough to thank the director and say good-bye. Returning to the dairy, I must have appeared a little crazed to the other workers. I dashed to embrace one of them, then circled the line, kissing another and a third one…. "Good-bye, girls, I am leaving. I am free, free!" And so I bade farewell to all of them while they, perhaps puzzled by my joy, remarked, "Onutė, you've lost your mind." The following day I did not go to work. I didn't even ask for my pay; my parents retrieved it. Within three days, I left for my precious homeland.

Mes sugrįžom ("We Returned": Reminiscences of Exiles and Political Prisoners from the Region of Vilkaviškis). Kaunas: Naujasis lankas, 2010.

Onutė Jakubauskaitė returned to Lithuania in 1958. That same year she married Petras Linkūnas. They raised three daughters and now have eight grandchildren. Upon returning to Lithuania, Onutė had no possibility to pursue her education. She worked on a collective farm for many years.

Currently Onutė and Petras Linkūnas are retired and reside in Vilkaviškis.

The Tenth Point: barracks inhabited by the Čėsna family and other Lithuaninan exiles.

The Tenth Point: the exiles' cemetery.

Teresė Čėsnaitė-Paulienė

On September 1, 1950, the Čėsna family (the mother with seven children) was exiled from the village of Džiaugėnai, near Šilalė in western Lithuania, to the Khabarovsk region in Russia.

The Čėsna family:

Ona Auškalnytė-Čėsnienė (1907–1981)
Ona Čėsnaitė-Venckienė, b. 1927
Jonas Čėsna, b. 1929
Teresė Čėsnaitė-Paulienė (1932–2009)
Marijona (Marytė) Čėsnaitė-Jašinskienė, b. 1934
Leonas (Levukas) Čėsna (1936–1953)
Antanas (Antanukas, Antanėlis) Čėsna (1939–1952)
Elena (Elenytė) Čėsnaitė-Juraškienė, b. 1943

Kazimieras Čėsna, the father, b. 1895. He was not exiled due to illness and died in 1951.

... We hadn't been in Siberia a full year when we received the sad message from our homeland that our beloved father had died.... We were left only with mother.

Shortly after this terrible blow, we met with another misfortune: mother became severely ill. We had to be clever, persevere, and support the patient.... We took her to a hospital thirty kilometers away by rowboat on the Khor River. No one believed that she would ever rise from her sick-bed....We did not have the means to improve her nutrition because we earned very little money. We used to go without food a day or two ourselves.

But to our delight, mother gradually regained her health. In a month's time, she returned from the hospital. I was then rafting timber with one of my sisters. My older brother was logging twelve kilometers away. My younger sister Marytė was at home with my little brothers and my sister Elenytė. Upon hearing that mother was returning from the hospital on foot, my brother Antanukas harnessed a horse to a sled and went off through mud and slush to meet her. He found her on the path, exhausted and weak. Worn out himself—pale, hungry, and ragged—he broke out in tears of pent-up longing and joy as he kissed mother's gaunt hand. When he calmed down, he quickly scouted around for some hay in order to seat mother comfortably. Sighting a little stack, he took the hay to the sled at breakneck speed, the sooner to reach the barrack and escape the irksome attacks of flies and other insects. The horse, taking fright of those insects, thrashed about, restless, and strayed from the path; it went galloping through slush, over tree trunks and stumps. All of a sudden, Antanukas realized that the sled was lying on its side. Aghast, he carefully helped mother up from the fall, for she, weakened by illness, couldn't get up on her own. He set the harness and sled right again, and they returned home without other mishap.

But what would they find at home when we had no bread or money? – Bare cupboards and bare shelves. My little brothers, Antanukas and Levukas, eagerly looked for work. They thought they'd earn some money and help the family survive hunger and hardship. But their wishes and good intentions took a totally different turn….

At the time, there was an abundant crop of cedar nuts. In the fall of that year, everyone made a living by nutting. Antanukas and Levukas, unable to find employment in our settlement, prepared to go to the work site at Khasamy, where our older brother, Jonas, was already working. My little brothers thought they'd gather nuts, sell them, and get plenty of bread for the family.

October 14, 1952, was a warm, sunny, beautiful autumn day when mother anxiously let her boys go off to work. They said their good-byes. When mother admonished them not to lose their way in the frightful depths of the taiga, Antanėlis told her not to worry: how could they get lost? With a rosary in Antanėlis' pocket and backpacks on their shoulders, my two young brothers departed on a muddy, puddled path for the work of nutting. Mother followed them with her eyes a long while, as far as she could see, until her little boys disappeared from view. The two of them trudged slowly, miserably, with loads on their backs, further and further into the taiga until they reached the work site at Khasamy. It was early evening. Tired, wet, and dirty, they entered a cold, dark barrack and, throwing off their backpacks, prepared to rest.

In the morning, they went nutting. For a few days, they gathered nuts successfully. But one day, October 17, the older brother, Levukas, stayed in the barrack to clean nuts while Antanukas went nutting in the woods with his friend Stasiukas, a Polish boy. They were accompanied by my brother Jonas' friend Petras. With confidence in their older companion, the youngsters trekked far into the taiga. However, they didn't find any nuts there. Petras told Antanukas and Stasiukas to return home to the barrack and without further word, walked out of the taiga, leaving his two young friends alone in the woods. The two youngsters then ran deeper into the taiga to look for nuts. Finding a cedar tree abundant with nuts, Stasiukas climbed it lithely while Antanukas ran onward to try his luck. All the while, they thought their older friend was still nearby. Taking a break, Stasiukas shouted from the top of the cedar:

—Antanas! Antanas!

By way of jesting, Antanukas did not respond immediately. When Stasiukas scurried to look for his friend, Antanukas poked his head through some branches and laughed aloud.

Evening approached and its shadows urged the boys to return home. They began to call for their friend Petras.... Alas, no one answered their call. Suddenly overtaken by fear, they still hoped to find their way home on their own. Evening shadows spread darkness over the woods. Not one golden sun's ray could be seen between the huge mountains and the thickets of trees. Now the youngsters were terror-stricken. They began running in one direction, then another,

unable to discern the right way homeward. The strange, unfamiliar location became more and more frightening and dreadful to them. The sun set beyond rows of gigantic cedars. As darkness, black and discomforting, descended on them, fear and anxiety overtook the unfortunate strays. It seemed that horrible nocturnal ghosts were threatening them, frightening them in shifting shadowy forms, as if warning them that a terrible misfortune will not let them out of its grip. So the two hapless boys wandered in dark woods, over desolate hills.

When night came, the boys lit a fire to warm up. Poor Antanėlis, wearing a light summer shirt and light trousers, thin socks, and summer shoes, felt a chill shiver. Stasiukas was more comfortable in his thick padded jacket and warmer footwear. The two wretched boys conferred as to what to do while they tried to warm up, but they felt the night growing colder. Shivering from both cold and fear, they grasped the rosary and prayed. Feeling hungry, they searched their pockets for a bite of food. They shared the piece of bread Antanėlis had brought from home. Hav-

ing soothed their hunger, they looked about with trepidation.... Alas, they saw neither a path nor a trail—only abysmal dark forest. Suddenly, Antanukas was shaken by chills. When Stasiukas asked him what he' d seen, Antanukas told him of his vision of a specter, a black human form, running through the dense forest. At first they both thought someone might be looking for them. But silence surrounded them, and every rustle and murmur in the trees was all the more frightening. Overwhelmed by fear, they left their campfire and began running they knew not where, as fast as their feet could carry them, thinking they'd find a way out or be rescued. To their distress, the hapless wanderers were caught in a heavy autumn rain as they elbowed their way through thickets of shrubbery, their clothing torn, their faces and hands bruised and bloody. Without rest or respite, the drenched and bruised boys kept on running, stumbling and falling, over the hills, as far as their meager, sapped strength allowed.

When dawn broke, they were still wandering, looking to save themselves. It grew very cold. Yet greater distress beset the boys when they were accosted by early autumn snow and sleet. The despondent youngsters cried bitterly from exhaustion, hunger, and cold. They moaned, shouted, and hallooed—perchance someone would respond to them. But in vain. No one answered their calls. They had no way to light a fire because their matches were thoroughly soaked. Nor did they have any defense against hunger. They had consumed the only piece of bread they had the previous night and scattered all their nuts while running.

On the second day of wandering, the boys were totally done in by snow. Seeing that his friend Stasiukas could walk no further, Antanukas sat down to rest by a stream. When the boys espied traces of old barracks, they supposed there had to be a road nearby. If not for exhaustion, hunger, and cold, the wretched boys might have averted further affliction. But once they sat down to rest, the two friends did not rise from the spot. They sat there, beneath a scraggy fir tree in a damp forest valley, hungry, wet, and shivering from cold, huddling close to one another for a touch of warmth and comfort....

The sun provided no warmth, and fierce autumn winds did not spare the youngsters. At night, the temperature dropped well below freezing. Morning frost covered the ground as well as the lost boys with its white shroud. Frozen stiff, their clothing glistened white each morning. Nestling close to one another, shivering, starving, and destitute of help, they prepared to die. Taking the rosary from his pocket, my brother Antanukas urged his friend to pray. "No one is likely to find us," he whispered; "Dying would be better than suffering like this....We may yet find ourselves among blissful martyrs."

They were tormented by thirst. Antanukas, unable to budge from the spot, asked Stasiukas to fetch water. But neither could Stasiukas make a move. They both merely longed to see their mothers for the last time. So they sat for five days, suffering starvation, cold, and exhaustion. Just before he passed away, Antanėlis said, "How I'd like to die, and how sweet it would be.... If only I could die more quickly...." A few minutes after voicing these words, and thrice agonizing, he gave up his soul to the Lord. It was October 22.

...For eight days we did not find the missing boys. One day less, and our Antanukas would have been found alive. The rescue effort was misled by a Russian man who spread the rumor that the boys had been seen at another work site. On the fifth day after the youngsters had been reported missing, the family, appeased somewhat by the rumors, set out on horseback to the designated work site to retrieve the boys. But they returned dejected, without them. The cruel supervisor of that work site strictly refused to assign more people to the rescue effort on the pretext that he knew nothing about the youngsters' misfortune. For seven days, only Antanukas' brother Jonas and Stasiukas' father searched for the boys.

The commandant was away at the time, so there was no one to demand assistance for the rescue team. When the commandant returned, he was immediately informed of the lost boys' plight. He then made haste to the work site at Khasamy, on Tuesday afternoon, and called together a search team the following morning. The commandant led the team to the forest and divided it into brigades, instructing each one as to the section of forest to cover and ordering them to search for the boys until they were found—not to return without them.

Having searched a broad belt of forest, the brigades proceeded deeper into the taiga. One brigade of Russians went straight in the direction of the lost boys' resting spot. It had passed this location when one member of the brigade—the same Russian who had spread word of the boys' return—retreated to get some water to drink, as if urged by some unseen power. Looking back and seeing that his teammates had left him behind a distance, he began shouting. Suddenly he heard someone's weak little voice responding. Surprised, he looked in the direction of the sound and, walking toward it, saw the taiga's victims. His brigade soon joined him and summoned the others. So they found the ill-fated boys, freezing in that swamp beneath a scraggy fir tree, on the afternoon of the very day Antanukas had expired, October 22.

Antanukas' cold body lay beside Stasiukas. Jonas and his friend carried my little brother's body to a pile of logs three kilometers from our barracks. They carried Stasiukas, still alive, to the barracks. The boy kept saying, "Whatever will become of me.... I will lose my legs anyway." His legs, turned coal-black from the freezing cold, hurt very badly. They took him, moaning, to the hospital right away.

In the morning, they lifted Antanukas' body from the log pile, set it on the sideboard of a cart, covered it with hay, and travelled seventeen kilometers on a swampy, muddy road to Khasamy. That same morning I set out on foot for the Tenth settlement (called *Desyataya Tochka*, "the Tenth Point") to relay the sad news to mother. All the way, I cried grievously. I saw mother standing behind the barrack, looking in the direction from which she expected her lost son to return. Not knowing how to phrase the terrible message, I uttered emotionally, "Mother, do not worry and do not be afraid. Our Antanėlis has given his soul to the Lord and is now resting in eternal peace.... His friend Stasiukas is still alive."

Mother was on the verge of fainting, and I could hardly walk her back into the barrack. She sat, stricken, as if unconscious, for a long while. Then we began to prepare for the funeral, which would be twelve kilometers away in Khasamy. In the meantime, my younger sister returned from potato harvesting in Kutuzovka. She had been away from home the entire month, so she hadn't heard about the tragic event. When she saw us grieving and heard about the circumstances of Antanukas' death, she cried bitterly.

Walking on the muddy, puddle-ridden path to Khasamy was a hardship for mother, weak as she was from illness and grief. As we approached Khasamy, we met the commandant, who informed us that the body of the deceased had not yet been transported to the work site; we would have to return to the Tenth Point and hold the funeral there. So we turned around. About half-way back, near the pass, we saw my brother Jonas with his friend, pulling the hay-covered body on a cart. They were very surprised to see us returning from Khasamy; they hadn't expected to run into us and, in fact, wanted to avoid this encounter. Perplexed as to how to prevent mother from seeing her son's lifeless, bruised body, they came to a stop; but we had already noticed them. Mother, crying, rushed forth to the hay-covered body on the cart, and when she brushed the hay off the bloody face, scratched up in the forest thickets, we heard her crying aloud and wailing. We pleaded with her to come away from the body and to calm down. Then slowly we all followed the cart back to Khasamy.

In the evening, all the Lithuanian youngsters came together to chant hymns and pray. Next morning, they adorned the casket with beautiful wreaths as we prepared for the funeral. Then, unexpectedly, came a telegram from the authorities in Bichevaya, with an order to bring the body to Bichevaya (thirty kilometers away) for an autopsy. We were all disappointed and worried about transporting the weary body of the deceased on that awfully bumpy, muddy road again, but we had to follow orders. We set the casket on the same sideboard and departed for Bichevaya.

The road was horrible. We came upon huge swamps, which we had to circumvent on a winding path through backwoods. The casket was knocked about on the sideboard, and the wreaths were torn off. When we reached the Tenth Point (our barracks), we received a telegram retracting the order to go to Bichevaya: we could hold the funeral here.

That evening we kept watch over the deceased in the tenth settlement. In late afternoon of the following day, October 25, we led a funeral procession to a hill on the taiga, not far from our barracks. That is where my thirteen-year-old brother Antanukas was buried. We erected an ash-wood cross with a memorial inscription, at his gravesite. My brother Levukas constructed a decorative fence around the cemetery, so that Antanukas' grave would not be trampled or neglected. Yet it pained us to leave him in strange woods on the taiga.

After a few months in the hospital, Antanukas' friend Stasiukas remained an invalid. They had to amputate both his legs, which had turned coal-black from the cold. To this day, the hapless boy cries, complaining of his fate.

At the exiles' cemetery.

In the spring of 1953, my older sister, my brother Jonas, and I were on assignment to raft timber on the Khor River. One early morning, our supervisor came to our tent with a telegram bearing the sad message that our fifteen-year-old brother, Levukas, died on May 20. The supervisor availed us of a rowboat, with oarsman, so that we could get home as soon as possible. We navigated along with the current, in a propitious direction, and reached home in late afternoon of the same day.

Levukas had fallen ill after Antanukas' passing, and his whole body swelled up. They conjectured that his kidneys were failing, and there was a lack of proper food for the patient. Though he used to eat very little even before his illness, during the week before his death, Levukas would swallow only a spoonful of tea intermittently. He could not speak. All the while mother took care of her young son. Wanting to know whether he was conscious, she would say, "Press my hand if you hear me," and Levukas answered by pressing her hand. He died of starvation, wasted by illness.

Erškėčių keliu ("On a Path of Thorns": Reminiscences, narratives, and articles about exile and the wounds of soviet occupation in the region of Šilalė and other locations in Western Lithuania), Part II. Kaunas: Naujasis lankas, 2009.

The Bakaitis family: (from left to right) Jonas, Anelė Bakaitienė, Onutė, Pranas Bakaitis, and Antanas. Kargala, ca. 1953.

Onutė Bakaitytė's class. Onutė is in the second row, second from left.

Ona Bakaitytė-Švilpienė

In 1951, four-year-old Onutė Bakaitytė, with her parents, Anelė and Pranas Bakaitis, and her brothers, Jonas (b. 1937) and Antanas (b. 1943), were exiled from Jokeliškiai, a village in the rural district of Kiduliai, county of Šakiai, to the Krasnoyarsk region in Russia.

Unfried Pancakes

Chug chug chug… rumble the wagon wheels laboriously…. The train, long as a giant snake, with boarded windows, begins its journey on October 2, 1951, at the railroad station in Vilkaviškis, packed with families of farmers from Suvalkija [southwestern Lithuania], henceforth called exiles. Ten years have passed since the first deportations, June 14-18, 1941. The Lithuanian educated class and landowners are semi-starved or already exterminated by the Laptev Sea, in the Siberian steppes, in prisons and hard labor camps…. But the boundless latitudes of Siberia are apparently insatiable; they await new faces.

In one cattle car, huddled together on their scanty belongings, are the Andriulaitis, Aleksa, Bučius, Žemaitaitis, Sriuoginis families, and many others. Among these are Anelė and Pranas Bakaitis, their fourteen-year-old son, Jonas, eight-year-old Antanukas, and the four-year-old baby of the family, Onutė, looking sadly through a crack in the boarded window.

Chug chug chug…churn the wagon wheels, rattling a tune without end. Further and further eastward they go, to Si-be-ri-a, Si-be-ri-a, Si-be-ri-a…. Little Onutė, perched on the family's bundles, cuddles close to her parents and remembers yesterday.

… The golden-hued autumnal orchard at home is blanketed with fragrant, tart winter apples. They thump against the ground as they fall. My parents, waking early, chat about making apple pancakes for breakfast.

Suddenly, there is knocking at the door: "Get ready! You are being deported for life…." Frightened, mother loses her bearings and with trembling, stiff hands gathers her children into her arms. The luminous windows of our homestead grow dark.

Onutė wonders why her father slaughters such a small, immature suckling pig in a hurry. Yet she hops around, eagerly anticipating the repast: "Antanukas finds the snout very tasty!"

We didn't have a chance to taste apple pancakes that morning—nor for seven subsequent long, hard, and hungry years.

Onutė's parents' farm, nestled close to the picturesque Kregždantė stream in the village of Jokeliškiai, district of Kiduliai, is left behind with its carefully tended orchards and gardens, mother's bee hives, thirty-eight hectares [about eighty acres] of land, spacious barns and sheds, and father's pride—the manor, a section of which houses an elementary school. Here the good teacher Irena Gulbinaitė gave lessons in Lithuanian reading and writing, exemplary conduct, and love for our country. Once she even admitted little Onutė to a drawing lesson.

The children who attended school that memorable morning of October 2 were given a live history lesson. "They are deporting the Bakaitis, Pranaitis, and Totoraitis families…," people whispered, cowering; "The neighboring Šilingas and Dimaitis families have long since been deported…."

Four-year-old Onutė does not understand why mummy didn't boil the snout for Antanukas and why she didn't broil the butchered meat. Why was the family riding on a truck, on their hastily packed belongings? Even more perplexing: Why was mother crying bitter-

ly while father was singing a song through his tears? Why were we surrounded by armed men? Why did our neighbors want to throw feather-beds into the passing truck, and why did armed guards prevent them from doing so?

The truck soon turns into the homestead of my father's sister, Marijona Pranaitienė, whom we lovingly called our "Fat Aunt." My aunt Marijona and cousins Pranas and Teresiukė are hoisted onto the tailgate. My cousin Jonas is no longer here; he is sitting in prison, they say. "Why is he sitting? Can't he walk or sleep?" – The little one doesn't understand grown-up talk.

When the truck stops at the homestead with a splendid windmill, the deportees have to crowd together more tightly. Onutė remembers riding to the beautiful windmill with her father to grind flour. But now the windmill was not waving its magnificent wings; it was standing still, rigid and dark.

The miller Pranas Totoraitis, his wife, Agota Totoraitienė, and their daughters, Birutė and Agutė, also climb into the truck. Then the truck turns in the direction of Vilkaviškis. … Thereafter, images flicker in the girl's mind as in a backlit negative: a train of cattle cars, bundles, people, a toilet pail, hunger, thirst….

The train stops for a short break, and the boxcar door is opened. Onutė gets out with her dad and they take a breath of fresh air. People relieve themselves under the train while armed guards walk about.

Onutė fearfully pulls her dad toward the boxcar door lest the train move on without them. An armed soldier takes her gently by the armpits and lifts her into the wagon. "Maybe he has a little girl like me, so he treats me kindly," Onutė reflects and again presses herself to the crack in the boarded window.

Chug chug chug…rumble the train wheels again. We reach the Ural Mountains. Beyond the Urals is the end of the earth…. Chug chug chug… "I'm thirsty. I'm hungry. I want to go home," cries the little exile, guilty though guiltless.

The first winter in Kargala

The wheels of the train slacken their pace and come to the end of the long, tiring, and painful rumble we endured for half a month.

We arrive at the Krasnaya Sopka station in the region of Krasnoyarsk. When they tear open the door, we see stretches of dazzling white snow. There is a harnessed sled waiting for us, and beside it, a figure in fur. Was it a human or beast? From head to toe it was dressed in fur, girded with a chain and holding in its hands a twined leather whip with a short hilt. Onutė would find out later that the fur garment, called a *docha*, was made of dogs' hide with the hairy side out, and the whip, *bichik*, was used to urge horses forward.

People are seated in the sled. About twelve kilometers away, we come to the village of Kargala in the vicinity of Beryozovka. All the exiles are led inside a clubhouse. They sit down on their belongings.

The windows of the club house are low and seemingly large, translucent like Xrays. Local people peer through them; some come in, quietly look around at us exiles, and go out again. In their glances, Onutė feels naughty, but she cannot understand why.

— *Fashistov privezli…* ("They've brought fascists"), we hear them saying in an incomprehensible language.

Onutė, her brothers, and parents, are settled with a Russian widow, whose husband perished at the front. She has three children. The eldest daughter usually lies on her untidy bed with her baby, covered by a down jacket. Her brother, Shura, and her sister, Zoya, attend school. On the anniversary of the October Revolution, Zoya and Shura, children of a fallen soldier, were given presents: one pair of laced canvas boots.

"How will they be able to share that pair of boots?," Onutė wonders. "There are more feet than boots!"

In the widow's room, in the most conspicuous spot on the wall, hangs a *balalayka*, tied with a red ribbon. That is the family's pride. In one corner of the room is a large stove, with a few hens cackling beneath it. On the stove is the bedroom.

Onutė's family huddles together in another little room, with a small furnace (*burzhuyka*) fueled by coal. There is evidently nothing to eat. Ahead of them is a long, cold, and hungry first winter in Siberia and a small, frosty, snow-covered window on the world outside.

— Mummy, why didn't they bring us here in spring, when there is plenty of sunshine? We could plant potatoes then, observed the little one.

The strange odor of coal fumes, a hand scorched by the furnace, constant pain in the tummy, hunger, fear when left at home alone (when her parents and brother Jonas worked and Antanukas was in school)—such were Onutė's sensations during the first year of exile.

Many years later, her mother would say, "I didn't think that we would ever bring you back to Lithuania, my little one."

In the barrack

In spring, the family moves into a barrack. That is a building with walls made of wattles and cracks filled with clay. The roof is laid with boards, and the small porch roof is covered with sod. On both the outside and inside, the barrack is whitewashed with lime. There are two windows in this building, through which hungry eyes will gaze.

– We'll be staying in the middle room, which might be warmer than the others, Onutė's father remarks.

He constructs beds and hammers together a table. However, there is not much joy in this abode. At night, bedbugs attack both grown-ups and children. Mother gets up, though tired after the day's hard work, to burn bugs hiding in the cracks and cries after losing the battle with them.

To weed gardens, they have to walk quite far, about three kilometers beyond the pig pens, and they have to take Onutė along. The girl walks and walks, but only half the way:

– I'm tired, she says; my side hurts.... In her tummy, slosh, slosh goes the soup she had for lunch.

When she grows a little taller, Onutė accompanies other children to the shrubs that contain some wild black currants and bitter bird-cherries. They pick a few handfuls of those meager vitamins--substitutes, of necessity, for the apples, pears, plums, and cherries in the carefully tended orchard back home.

They tried to plant crab apple trees across the river, but the trees did not yield any fruit. As much as he tried, even cross-pollinating fruit trees, Michyurin, a botanist of the time, could not subdue nature in Siberia. His words, written on a billboard in the collective farm clubhouse, "We cannot expect favors from nature. Our task is to simply take them," were not justified, after all.

The winter of 1953

The girl is six years old already. With a stick in hand, she pokes snowdrifts and skates. Winter is very cold but dry. The climate is continental, so there is little humidity. Her brother Jonas comes down with pleurisy, and the doctor says to mother, "In Lithuania, your son would not survive; it's too humid there. But here, in Siberia, he will get well." The doctor is right. My brother pulls through the severe illness, though he would never regain all of his health.

As she wades through snowdrifts, Onutė dreams of making skis. But the village of Kargala is far from the taiga; it is surrounded by steppes, and there is no wood here. What joy it is to see them bringing at least an evergreen to the clubhouse for New Year's!

My brother Antanas manages to get two boards somewhere. He steams the board ends over mother's boiling potatoes, bends

them, and lets them set overnight. Then he hammers some straps on them – and forth from a springboard onto the snow!

"Maybe we could make a sled like the Russian children's," the girl muses. They form a hollow in a pattie of cow dung, fasten a rope to its side, and pour water on it. When this boat-like chunk freezes, it's as good as a sled! But Onutė's parents have only a goat, Zoyka, which constantly nudges her legs with its horns, though it also provides her with delicious milk. That milk is such a life-saver! Therefore, in wintertime, when they transport hay from stacks in the fields and pass by the barracks, Onutė always plucks an armful for the little goat. The hay is so fragrant, so-o fragrant!

When father worked in the fields, he often brought home some awfully beautiful flowers from the meadows. "They're prettier than flowers in Lithuania's gardens," he'd say. Siberia's scenic meadows hasten to blossom in spring, for summer is short and seeds must ripen. In those meadows, one can also find a wonderful, vitamin-rich Siberian herb called *cheremsha*, which is known to have saved people's teeth, maybe even their lives. Indeed, *cheremsha* is one of the three most important and ubiquitous things in Siberia, the others being *moshka*, miniature flies, which bug one's eyes, nose, and mouth in summertime, and *fufayka*, the padded jacket that is suitable for work, for holiday wear, and for cover, summer and winter.

… So we can't make a sled, for we have neither a cow, nor cow dung….

The girl's day dreams are interrupted by a kindly Russian woman, who approaches her and says, "*Umer Stalin. Vi smozhete vernutsya na rodinu!*" ("Stalin has died. You will be able to return to your homeland.") It would be some time before the woman's prediction is realized. They would endure more than one severe winter with its blizzards and freezing temperatures that sear the cheeks.

Of the terrible cold, father says, "When I spit, the spittle turns to ice and tinkles when it hits the ground." Onutė wants to see if father's account is true. She spits, but there is no bare ground around her—

only snow—so nothing tinkles. She is still confused as to whether father was telling the truth or not.

It is really very cold. She wears a long, wide scarf that is wrapped over her head, crossed on her chest, pulled beneath the armpits, and tied on the back. Over this, even a thin coat seems warmer. Russian women carefully protect their heads from the cold. First they tie a little scarf on their foreheads and then cover this with a large down scarf. The latter is a source of pride for the women. No less important are their felt boots. They pad the soles of their boots with some leather or tarpaulin so they will last longer. No one needs galoshes because there are no thaws in winter. How glad Onutė is to have her first pair of felt boots! She couldn't go anywhere without them!

Onutė in School

Onutė approaches age seven: time to get ready for school. But now, suddenly, her mother falls ill, and she hovers between life and death for an entire month. Consequently, Onutė begins school a month later, when her mother's health improves.

For this rite of passage, the good neighbor Sriuoginienė fashions a black bag with two hand straps for Onutė's books. She decorates one side of it with a letter "A", sewn from multicolored scraps of fabric.

The teacher, Mariya Ivanovna Malchikova, asks for Onutė's name.

– Ona, says the new first grader.

– With a double "n"? the teacher inquires.

– Yes, answers Onutė assuredly, though she does not understand what a double "n" means. And so Onutė Bakaitytė becomes Onna Bakaites, with an erroneous spelling of the surname as well.

The teacher calls on her to read, but Onutė, the late pupil, is silent. The teacher reads a syllable, then Onutė repeats it, and so, syllable by syllable, to the bottom of the page. The teacher does not scold her.

One day, while retelling a narrative about vegetables, Onutė can't think of the Russian word for potato stalks. When the teacher asks her to say the word in Lithuanian, the class bursts out in laughter. That hurts her feelings....

Nevertheless, Onutė completes the second grade with excellent marks (5's). A window onto the world of knowledge opens for her. At the school's year-end assembly, the honor student receives a certificate of commendation. Onutė is obliged to give a speech for the first time in her life. Prepped by the teacher, she says,

— *Ya poluchayu pokhvalnuyu gramotu i zhelayu yeshchyo luchshe uchitsya!* ("I am receiving a certificate of commendation, and I want to do even better in school").

Not only does Onutė study diligently, but she also tries to help her parents. They work very hard, as do all Lithuanian exiles in Kargala. At sowing time and harvest time, they work day and night, without respite, because summer is short, and wheat must be cultivated. They usually work until the stacks of golden wheat piled up in the fields are covered by snow.

The soil is black, rich, and fertile. It does not have to be fertilized. Dung is used to build fences: it dries and hardens, making for sturdy, high fences. One can sit down on them or step up, the more easily to mount a horse.

Father transports water on horseback, so he lets me ride along sometimes. Earlier, father worked in a saw mill. He used to split and saw logs. Once Onutė and Antanas brought him lunch to the saw mill. The soup smelled so good! Onutė tasted a spoonful, then Antanas took one, and so the children supped the soup.

– Daddy, don't you want any?

– No, I get lunch here, he responded, telling a white lie.

This was not the only serving of soup father denied himself. Mother and father forego numerous spoonfuls and morsels for the sake of their children.

When he grows some, Antanas herds animals and rides horses very well. He has a real whip (*bichik*) and knows how to crack it loudly and briskly so that capricious animals instantly turn in the direction they are supposed to go. Onutė's brothers don't have the option to attend school; however, they would grow up to be good, honest people.

After our return to Lithuania, on the occasion of a neighbor's funeral, four youths rode as guards of honor. Onutė heard women whispering, "And who is that young man, riding so beautifully, sitting astride the horse as if cast for an equestrian statue?" She was proud that this rider was her brother, Antanas, who had graduated from "riding college" in Siberia.

While repairing a pig pen roof on the collective farm, father suffers a fall as the roof caves in and injures his back. His kidneys give him pain that becomes unbearable. They have to take him to a hospital in Krasnoyarsk, 300 kilometers away. He undergoes surgery to remove a kidney. Mother keeps watch over the patient and stays with some wonderfully kind nurses, also Lithuanian exiles. One of them gives mother a photo with the name Staselė. Where are you now, good sisters?

While mother is away, taking care of father for a few weeks, Onutė's stockings tear, and she doesn't have any others to wear. She finds a scrap of black material and attempts to sew stockings so that she might cover her legs between her dress and her boots. She sews them together and tries them on, but they keep slipping down her legs. Again she sews and tries putting them on, but she cannot get her feet into them. Then she takes them apart and, in her third attempt at sewing, succeeds. She attends school with her handiwork on her feet. Yet how glad she is when mother returns from Krasnoyarsk and brings her some real stockings!

When father recuperates, mother brings him home. But he would never fully regain his health after that injury and operation. He had just enough strength to return to Lithuania and enjoy his homeland for another year… to pick the last of the winter apples….

The exiles in Kargala

This village is extremely poor. Not only the Lithuanian exiles but the local Russians suffer wretched living conditions. In the collective farm established here by the name Chkalov, there are few Russian men left—many died at the front. Consequently, the women try to spare the remaining men and do heavy work on their behalf. When they hear bad political news on the radio, they walk around wailing, "Let's hope there won't be another war!"

There is a change in the Russians' attitude toward Lithuanians. They see that these exiles are not the criminals they were said to be when they arrived, but rather an industrious and responsible group of people: Lithuanians performed every task diligently, and they could be trusted.

There are two streets in Kargala. One is long, maybe a kilometer and a half in length. The other stretches parallel to the first and is called German Street. Volga German exiles and most of the Lithuanians live on this street.

We still live in the barrack that looms over the end of German Street. The barrack recently acquired a radio cable, so my parents often listen to the radio, hoping to hear news about Lithuania. Once they heard a Lithuanian song on the radio!

Beyond our barrack are the collective farm's fields. One year they planted hemp nearby. Onutė would sneak into the hemp field and rub her palms with hemp leaves—how yummy! Father would pour a spoonful of hemp oil or sunflower oil into a bowl. Then we dunk some bread in it and delight in the taste of those fragrant morsels. Oh, for more of those!...

Our closest neighbors are the Andriulaitis family. Their Teresiukė has a lovely blue dress with a flower design. When she adorns herself with that dress and dances with Stasys Aleksa, they look beautiful together! Stasys is a photographer. With his old camera, he has made a record of the Lithuanian exiles' tired faces.

My brother Jonas and Juozas Andriulaitis are best friends. Both of them are obsessed with technology, and they are always talking about tractors. Juozas drives a tractor while Jonas is a coupler. They buzz around the tractor and turn various knobs until, after much effort, they finally get the tractor started. It is more cheerful when the two become interested in music and begin to play the harmonica.

Jonas Andriulaitis is a born veterinarian. He tends to every sick or injured animal. He has invented names for all the goats on our street.

Old Mr. Andriulaitis is a veteran of World War II; he marched as far as Berlin while serving in the army. However, his family did not escape Stalin's regime. The men in the settlement—Onutė's father, Aleksa, Žemaitis, and others—gather for conversations with Andriulaitis. Onutė hears talk about politics and "forest brothers" [partisans]. She doesn't understand why those brothers had to go into the forest, why they couldn't stay in their little houses. Many things are not discussed in public. Even when the former exile Juozas Gustas, mother's relative and priest (who had studied theology in Rome), visited from Krasnoyarsk and Onutė received her first Holy Communion, she was not allowed to share her joyful experience with anyone. She was admonished by her parents not to peep a word to anyone about this event.

Later, my parents received the sad message that Rev. Juozas Gustas was found dead in his apartment in Krasnoyarsk under questionable circumstances….

The Lithuanians in Kargala organize dances. Aldotas and Justinas Stanaitis play the bandoneón (a kind of concertina). Youths from other villages in the vicinity, Shepilovka and others, also come to these dances.

Onutė's cousin, Teresė Pranaitytė, visits from Krasnaya Sopka, and Onutė goes to the market in Krasnaya Sopka to sell father's woven baskets. It is so much fun to visit with her cousin and her dear "Fat Aunt"! The miller Totoraitis' family, exiled the same day as Onutė's family, lives in another village.

* * *

What could be more important in Siberia than a package received from Lithuania or a letter from one's loved ones? Packages sustained our bodies while letters lifted our spirits. Thanks to our dear relatives, the Gustas, Simokaitis, and Stravinskas families, for every strip of bacon, for tallow, and dried apples; for lovely knitted gloves, stockings, and scarves, which mother used to exchange for food products. Thanks to mother's uncle Kazimieras Gustas for the packages he sent from the U.S.A. What joy it was for the family to open a package together! How cheerfully our hearts beat then! How delicious the fragrance of dried apples! Dear relatives, you helped us survive.

Life goes on

There are numerous baptisms among the growing Lithuanian families. The Andriulaitis family had little Petriukas; the Žemaitis family – Gintas, and the Grinius family – Stasiukas. Three daughters were born to the Stanaitis family: Zita, Leta, and Teresėlė.

Juozukas Žemaitis is Onutė's classmate. They both enjoy exemption from wearing the Pioneer tie, which is an obligatory part of other school children's uniforms. Juozukas' younger sister Laimutė has grown taller since her arrival in Kargala at six months. When the Lithuanian exiles were assembled in the clubhouse, Laimutė lay in a little metal tub, propped up on a pillow and all tucked in, only her eyes peeking through the covers and attesting to her vitality.

The blue-eyed Aleksaitė sisters, blond Elytė and darkhaired Matilda, could not complete their schooling in Lithuania, though they were capable and intelligent girls. They had to give up their pretty dresses and smart shoes, muffle themselves up in standard Siberian apparel, the *fufayka*, pull heavy canvas boots over their graceful teenage feet… and work, work, work, without rest, without holidays or leisure days….

Little Jonukas Aleksa is a very good pupil in school and the brave Antanas Aleksa knows how to scare the Russian boys so they go running for their lives.

Their dad, Mr. Aleksa, knows Russian very well and is reading Leo Tolstoy's *War and Peace*, thus earning Onutė's respect and inspiring awe. "When could he read such a big book?" she wonders.

The soul of the Aleksa family is the mother, a woman who can dance or pray, as suits the occasion. Thanks to her initiative, the Lithuanians in Kargala gather to pray and sing, practice their customs, cherish their national identity, and foster reverence for their homeland.

Onutė's best friend is Genutė Sriuoginytė. Her mother is an excellent seamstress and her father, a good-hearted, curly-haired person, reminiscent of the painter Repin, whose portrait is featured in her textbook and whose painting "Loggers by the Volga" reminds Onutė of the exiles' hard life in Kargala. Genutė has an older sister, Elytė, who is studying in the city, Barnaul.

Onutė is acquainted with the pious P. Bučys, whose extended family includes two priests, one of them a Russian orthodox bishop. P. Bučys herds the collective farm's sheep, constantly turning the pages of a prayer book, now thoroughly worn and faded from use. When Bučelis, of slender and ascetic frame, stands with his head raised, in front of his sheep, he looks like Jesus with his flock.

There is the Grinius family with two daughters, whom the parents always call lovingly by their diminutive names, Aldutė and Mildukė. Perhaps they are related to the former President of Lithuania Kazys Grinius? The Jančius family, with long-braided Birutė; the Venius family with three men, sturdy as oaks, and their sister, Salomėja, and other Lithuanians also settled in Kargala. Since 1951, fourteen Lithuanian families have eked out a living, grieved, celebrated, and prayed in Kargala.

…One day in 1956, Andriulaitienė comes to bid Onutė good-bye. She is going back to Lithuania, where the sun shines more brightly and the land, with its luxuriant apple orchards, awaits returning exiles. Being treated like a grown-up, Onutė is so deeply moved and saddened that words catch in her throat. She says to herself, "When I return, I will eat a treeful of apples." This would later happen: by the time the apples ripened, not many would be left on the tree.

The brief summers in Siberia keep turning into cold winters…. Finally, it is December, 1958, and Onutė bids good-bye to Kargala! She is going home, home to Li-thu-a-ni-a, to celebrate the sacred holiday of Christmas!

When they return to Lithuania, family friends marvel, "How tall Onutė has grown!" and mother answers bitterly, "Siberian bread was very tasty…."

We shared Christmas Eve wafers with our loved ones that year.

Onutė's mother, Anelė Bakaitienė, in Lithuania the first spring after her return,1959.

Mus skaičiavo vagonais ("They Counted Us by Cattle Cars": Reminiscences of Political Prisoners and Exiles from the Region of Šakiai). Kaunas: Naujasis lankas, 2007.

When she returned to Lithuania, Onutė Bakaitytė attended Kiduliai High School in the region of Šakiai; later, the pedagogical school in Mariampolė and the Klaipėda branch of the Pedagogical Institute of Šiauliai. Since 1969 she has lived in the town of Gelgaudiškis near Šakiai. For seventeen years she worked as a preschool teacher, and for twenty-three, as a High school teacher in Gelgaudiškis.

She raised two daughters and now has five grandchildren.

Her parents and her brother Jonas have passed on.

Onutė says, "My little pupils could not comprehend the theme of exile—nor could I, their teacher."

Arimantas with his mother in Kaunas.

Back from Altai, Arimantas with his uncle Juozas Mažuolis and his wife, Bronė, 1948.

Arimantas with his godparents, Marytė Sinkevičiūtė and Vytautas Činikas, several months before exile.

The „zemlyanka" inhabited by the Dumčius family: initially a covered dugout, it was later enlarged with walls and roof.

Arimantas Dumčius

With his mother, Konstancija Mažuolytė-Dumčiuvienė, and nanny, Marija Liutkutė, one-year-old Arimantas Dumčius was exiled to the Altai region of Russia in 1941. Marija Liutkutė died in exile in 1944. Arimantas and his mother returned to Lithuania illegally in 1947.

Arimantas' father, Stasys Dumčius, Chief Firefighter in the city of Kaunas, was separated from his family. He died in 1942 in the course of cruel interrogation procedures at the Puksozero concentration camp in the region of Arkhangelsk.

Arimantas Dumčius is a professor, a renowned heart surgeon, and trailblazer in the field of cardiosurgery in Lithuania. He participated in the independence movement prior to 1990 and is currently a member of Parliament in the Republic of Lithuania.

My life's odyssey

The most educated and well-to-do Lithuanians—teachers, farmers, government, military, and service personnel—were the first to suffer from "the great Bolshevik experiment" of June 1941.

My father, Stasys Dumčius, Fire Chief of the city of Kaunas (from the village of Eiciūnai in the district of Šakiai), my mother, Konstancija Mažuolytė (from Pandėlis in the district of Rokiškis), my nanny and relative, Marija Liutkutė (also from Eiciūnai), and I, just past my first birthday, were arrested and exiled. We were separated from my father at the outset. I was informed about my father's fate only in the late 1980's by the accounts of Alfredas Savickas (d. 1989) and Stasys Jameikis (author of the memoir *The Train Rolls to Eternity*, 1991; d. 1991), who fortunately survived the same hard labor camp to which my father had been deported. Jameikis' memoir was the basis for A. Maciulevičius' touching film *Eyes Look Above the Cross.*

From about fifteen hundred of father's fellow prisoners at the hard labor camp in Puksozero, only five survived and returned to Lithuania. From the twenty-four fellow countrymen in father's group who had been accused of plotting an insurrection together with Latvian and Estonian prisoners, thirteen men were condemned to execution by gunfire (J. Linartas, L. Maziliauskas, J. Reklaitis, J. Masiliūnas, J. Vinča, J. Jurgelevičius, A. Dailydė, B. Stasiūnas, A. Vilimas, K. Mickevičius, B. Merkelis, M. Naudžiūnas, J. Blochas). Eleven men died as a result of torture in prison interrogation chambers. Among these was my father, who perished on May 16, 1942, and was buried in a common grave in the tenth zone of the Puksozero prison camp in the district of Plesetsk, region of Arkhangelsk. Now a gas main from Tyumen stretches across this site.

Like other families, we were shoved into cattle cars at the Kaunas railroad station. (Later, we ascertained that my future wife, Ona Elona Kleizaitė, and her mother, Sofija, were on the same train from Kaunas.) Eventually we found ourselves in the Altai steppes, the fifth section of the Martovka soviet farm in the Khabarsky district. En route, when I was severely ill from prolonged diarrhea and unable to stand on my feet, I was cured by mother's pancakes fried in pork fat. Later, when I almost died from pneumonia, I was saved by good-hearted local Russians and Kazakh and Ukrainian exiles, who healed me with various herbs from the steppe.

Four-year-old Ona Elona Kleizaitė in Barnaul.

We lived in a dugout in which water accumulated after rain, especially in spring. The women labored hard on the farm or did agricultural work in the steppes. My mother, who had a degree in economics from Vytautas Magnus University in Kaunas, milked cows, herded sheep, and worked as a logger. The daily food ration for working adults was 600 grams of bread; for children, it was 200 grams. Exiles were divested of their personal documents and allowed to go no further than ten kilometers from the settlement. Lithuanians were constantly inspected by local security officers. Men from 180 households were called to the front. Most of them died or returned invalids—except for three communist supervisors, who managed to evade the war. These three continually oppressed both the local inhabitants and the exiles in any way they could. We often heard wailing and laments for the deceased in our settlement.

Some of the stronger exiles were relocated to the shores of the Laptev Sea. In our settlement, there were eleven Lithuanian families, with no men, for they were incarcerated in hard labor camps. Most children were five to eight years older than I (Algimantas Gudavičius, Romas Savickas, and others); Dutis Vaitaitis was two years older. Relations among the families were very friendly. However, exiles were totally at the mercy of the administrators of the collective farm and local security personnel. For taking some wheat or potatoes from the fields at harvest, one was threatened with a three-year prison sentence.

We suffered the worst hunger in wintertime. Women used to secretly dig holes in the ground and store some wheat for winter; I used to discover grain hidden in ground squirrel burrows. These caches helped us avoid starvation. Finding models with local inhabitants, mother made a simple grain grinder: two grates inserted into one another, with one mounted on a wooden base and the other turned by a metal handle. As the device turned, it ground the wheat strewn between the graters, sifted the flour, and ground again. Then we baked wheat or oat scones, adding even sawdust in winter. We nibbled on sunflower cake (sunflowers divested of oil), which was usually fed to animals. Another source of salvation for me was the rubber thermos in which mother used to bring me a liter of milk, which she procured secretly while milking cows on the farm.

Of course we also suffered from extreme cold in winter. The women addressed this problem by extracting wool from dung in the sheep barns, shredding it, and knitting stockings, socks, trousers, and other clothing. Their example was followed by the local people.

When I grew a little older, I became the chief ground squirrel catcher in the steppe. The ground squirrels, called *susliks* by the locals, fed on grain and were the only meat available to exiles. In exchange for their beautiful furs, we used to get pencils, paper, ink, and other items. In summer, I used to gather birds' eggs and wild strawberries in the steppe.

At that time, our mothers did not know that their husbands, their children's fathers, had perished in the concentration camps. R. Gudavičienė's husband, former Supervisor of the District of Kaunas and member of Parliament, had died. J. Martinkėnienė's, B. Misiukonienė's, V. Karpuvienė's husbands, my father, Stasys Dumčius, and others had also passed on. My mother found out about my father's death when a package she had sent to him was returned. In response to her inquiry, it was briefly noted that S. Dumčius "departed on May 16, 1942" ("*ubyl 16 maya 1942 goda*").

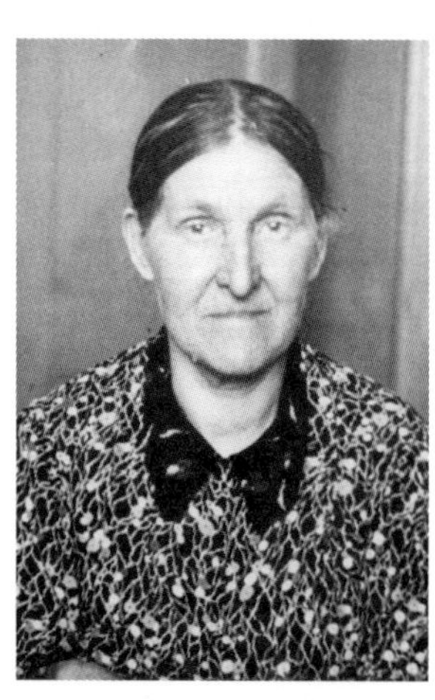

Nanny Marytė Liutkutė

Arimantas with Saša, a childhood friend, by Marija Liutkutė's grave in Martovka, the Khabarsky district of Altai, 2011.

Toward the end of 1944, I woke up one morning in our cold, wet dugout to find the stiff, lifeless body of my nanny, Marija Liutkutė, beside me. I had been very close to her and used to call her "Tulytė." She died from typhoid fever. The whole settlement accompanied Marija to her resting place; the local people were impressed by the ceremonious Catholic funeral rites. In 1945, G. Vaitaitienė's twelve-year-old daughter Vidutė, who had been the soul of the settlement and a lovely singer, died of pneumonia.

In 1984, my mother secretly wrote her reminiscences of exile, which I submitted to the "Toward Freedom" Archives in Chicago at the onset of the independence movement in the late 1980's. I cite a passage from her memoirs: "The local people became open and sincere with us exiles. They used to tell us about their experiences, their hatred for the Soviet government and its lackeys. They sympathized with us but could not help us in any way because they had nothing themselves. Wrapped in rags, wretched, they were driven to work half-naked and instilled with fear of imprisonment as well as separation from their children. And that's what happened. Every month a throng of people from the vicinity of our settlement was sent to prison.... The soviet farm was gradually emptied of both people and animals. At the end of the war, in spring, two thirds of the animals died of starvation and were buried in the ground."

After the war, when the animals had expired from starvation as well as pervasive disorder and ruin on the collective farm, we felt that our lives were also in jeopardy. In a state of hopelessness, my mother and G. Vaitaitienė began planning an escape to Lithuania. They sold off the last of the garments they had and the cows which they had acquired the previous year in exchange for their deceased husbands' clothing. My mother received 400 rubles for her cow. They paid some local Russians to drive us to Novosibirsk on their heavy (1.5 ton) truck.

In the spring of 1947, mother and I, G. Vaitaitienė and her son, Dutis, seated on the tailgate of the truck, took off on the Barnaul

highway toward Novosibirsk. Along the steppe, we were chased by starving wolves that attempted to jump into the tailgate. I thrashed their paws with a switch to fend off their attack. At Novosibirsk, we could not obtain train tickets to Moscow. For three days we hid in the woods in the outskirts of the city (about forty kilometers away), so we were not caught and arrested. My mother and Vaitaitienė had no choice but to bribe a train conductor at the railroad station in Novosibirsk for travel to Moscow. The conductor would lock our compartment, and I would hide in a huge suitcase on the upper shelf during inspections. So we made our way to Moscow, and from there to Vilnius and Kaunas. Later, we heard that G. Vaitaitienė, M. Bertienė, and B. Misiukonienė were arrested, returned to exile, and imprisoned for their attempt to escape. We lost touch with our friend in misfortune G. Vaitaitienė and her son, and never learned of their later fate.

In Lithuania, mother and I were confronted with the unexpected: fear, mistrust, deportations, and executions. In Kaunas, my uncle Vaclovas begged us to leave his family as soon as possible. We were briefly sheltered by the academician Vladas Kuzma's family, then the firefighter's Jonas Lapelis' home on Paneriai Street. In my father's birthplace, Eiciūnai (now Gerdžiūnai) in the region of Šakiai, my grandfather's, the renowned teacher's Petras Dumčius', house with its school had been collectivized. We were afraid to be seen there. My uncle Liucijonas, who had been a farmer in Eiciūnai, was exiled with his wife and daughters, Liucija and Elena, to the Krasnoyarsk region in Russia. Their Petriukas, born on the train, died two years later from exhaustion and pneumonia. Then my grandfather Povilas Mažuolis and his brother Juozas' wife, Bronė, were exiled from the village of Liepeniai, my mother's birthplace near Pandėlis. My grandfather died in the Krasnoyarsk region; my uncle Juozas knocked about in neighboring Latvia until his death.

For lack of other options, I was taken from Kaunas by my loyal godmother, Marytė Sinkevičiūtė (from Eiciūnai) to my aunt Valė Gervienė in northeastern Lithuania and unofficially adopted by her family. I entered the elementary school in Vilkoliai, district of Pandėlis. The teacher, a courier for the partisans (freedom fighters), knew of my identity and escape from exile. In the meantime, my mother obtained a passport in her maiden name, thus legal status, with the help of relatives and friends in Kaunas. It seems that we survived by the protection of God's blessing.

My aunt in Vilkoliai was exiled with her three children to Buryat Mongolia for her connections with the partisans. I avoided a second tour of exile by mere chance: when my aunt's family was being deported, I was pushed out of a window and took shelter with the neighbors, the Dovydėnas family. My mother, with the help of her cousin B. Mažuolis, obtained temporary work as an accountant on a soviet farm in Viešintai and soon came to retrieve me from Vilkoliai. As we entered the town of Viešintai, we saw bodies of partisans—three men and three women (former teachers)—left desecrated on the ground by soviet security agents ("*stribai*"). The freedom fighters had defended themselves in the swamp to the very last bullet and then taken their own lives.

Aunt Valė Gervienė with her children Irena, Vidmantas, and Birutė in exile in Buryat-Mongolia, 1948.

In Viešintai, we settled with Mrs. Petrylienė, whose loved ones were serving sentences in Soviet concentration camps. In 1949, we moved to Kupiškis, where mother worked for the Department of Agriculture, and I attended school. We were destined to witness more of the horror of partisan warfare as well as the process of collectivization of private land and farms. I used to see the profaned bodies of freedom fighters lying in the town square and caravans of trucks on their way to the railroad station with deportees to Siberia.

The townspeople were very much opposed to collectivization. We children were divided into opposed groups: Lithuanians and little "*stribai*" (soviet agents), whose parents were mostly Russians, revengeful people, or petty criminals. We held official "battles" by the shooting range or the Kupa River, fighting with sticks, slings, tin cans filled with live coals, and other weapons. Our (Lithuanian) leader was Valdas Ožalas, the mathematics teacher's son; Vincas Rubliauskas and I comprised his staff. We had dug a bunker in the yard of the Stukas family's abandoned house and drawn a town plan. Once, after we beat up the son of a leading soviet agent, the boy complained to his father, and they tracked down our bunker. Valdas and Vincas did not betray me, but my mother was scared, and we soon moved from Kupiškis to Juodpėnai, on the edge of the forest of Šimoniai.

In Juodpėnai, mother obtained work as a Russian language teacher in a primary school. The language skills and practice she acquired in exile proved to be useful.... After Stalin's death, we breathed more freely; however, we were beset by fear throughout those years. Although teachers and village folk supported and protected us, the soviet administrators defamed my mother as a "bandit." People thought that my father, supposedly an army officer, had emigrated to the United States, confusing him with Captain Antanas Dumčius, who had served in Kupiškis and emigrated during the Soviet occupation.

Liucijonas Dumčius' children (marked by dots) in the isolation ward for infectious diseases in Goriovka, Ingash district of Krasnoyarsk, 1950.

One of my schoolmates, Antanukas, was the son of the legendary partisan leader Antanas Starkus-Montė, of the Algimantas command. A. Starkus had single-handedly vanquished a gang of soviet agents from Šimoniai. He died with his mates, fighting rather than surrendering, in a partisan dugout in the forest of Šimoniai. At about the same time, my mother's cousin, the partisan leader Jonas Baltušis, was killed in northeastern Lithuania, and her cousin Vanda's husband, Bronius Vaivada, formerly Director of the Hydrometeorology Bureau for Lithuania's Civil Aviation, was killed in Tuskulėnai.

In 1959, I graduated from Kupiškis High School with a silver medal. I still remember the words of my botany teacher, K. Pajarskas: "You must strive and get ahead in order to fill all the official positions in the country; otherwise they will fall into the hands of foreigners. And woe to Lithuania in the event of decisive historical moments." I passed the entrance examination for the Kaunas Medical Institute with high marks. In my autobiography (curriculum vitae), I omitted mention of formerly being exiled. The Pro-rector, who chaired the admissions committee, and the Secretary of the city's communist youth committee demanded certification as to whether my father had died among freedom fighters in 1942. In despair, my mother requested a certificate at the Civil Registry Office and, to her astonishment, they issued a certificate of my father's death… in Kaunas! (Later, in conversations with colleagues whose experiences were similar to mine, I learned that Security officials, foregoing legal procedures, used to register the names of deceased prisoners by their former addresses.) So I entered the Kaunas Medical Institute and ventured into the second half of my life's odyssey.

Mus skaičiavo vagonais ("They Counted Us by Cattle Cars": Reminiscences of Political Prisoners and Exiles from the Region of Šakiai). Kaunas: Naujasis lankas, 2007.

CHILDREN ON ICE

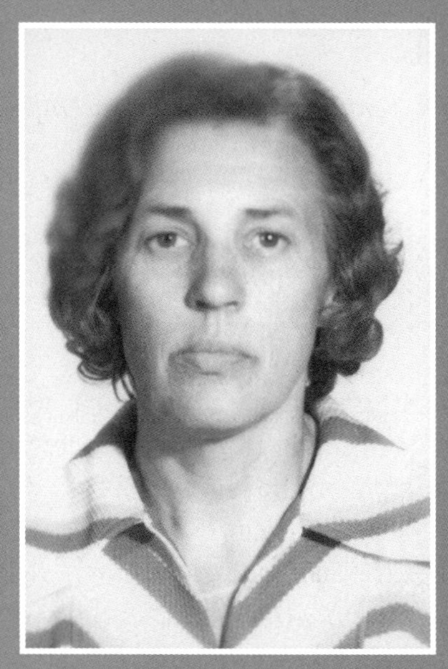

Irena Milaknytė in Lithuania, ca. 1979.

First-year students at the Yakutsk Pedagogical Institute, Natural Science Department. Irena Milaknytė is in the second row, first on the right. Yakutsk, 1952.

IRENA MILAKNYTĖ

On June 14, 1941, eleven-year-old Irena Milaknytė, her parents, Veronika and Juozas Milaknis, her grandmother, and two sisters were exiled from the village of Mitragalis in the district of Rokiškis to the Altai region of Russia. In 1942, the family was deported from Altai to the Bykov Mys promontory in the Lena delta, within the Arctic Circle by the Laptev Sea.

The drivers were angry, unsympathetic men. They didn't allow us to pack food, clothing, or other belongings for the journey. But fortunately, father was not separated from the family in Naujoji Vilnia, so he was deported with us to the Altai region. We rode in a cattle car crammed with people and things. For several days we were submerged in total darkness, for not only the boxcar door was locked but the windows were tightly sealed. Later we sailed on the Ob River, until we were let off in the town of Kamen by the Ob.

From the very beginning, we met with awful hardship. We lacked food and warm clothing. We kindled fire with dry cow dung because there were no woods in the vicinity. Our cooking utensils had been stolen on the train, so we had no way to heat water and prepare food. We could not find a decent pot to purchase in the town of Kamen. There were only badly fired clay pots, which cracked easily. Often, just before our soup was cooked, we'd find it spilling on the embers. We'd be left hungry, and there was so little food.

Our grandmother died there in Altai on Christmas day, 1941. She was buried in the town of Kamen. The grave sites have been destroyed, with only some hillocks marking the area of the cemetery.

As we were beginning to settle in Altai, in the summer of 1942, we were deported for the second time, somewhere further. At first we rode by train and then sailed by boat on the Angara River. We were driven by truck from Zayarsk to Ust-Kut, and then we travelled by steamboat on the Lena River as far as Yakutsk. Here, in Yakutsk, we were loaded onto barges. The hold [cargo space in the hull] of our vessel, lined with three-tiered bunks, was crowded with people and packed with bags of salt and building materials.

I recall a telling incident on the steamboat back on the Angara River. Some actresses from Irkutsk—young, beautiful women—were also sailing on the boat. Among the exiles was a woman with her little girl. The actresses tried to persuade this woman to give them her young daughter. The exile was clearly disturbed and puzzled by the proposal: why should she give her daughter away to strangers? She did not understand, nor did she surrender her daughter. The actresses knew, but how could the exile have known that they were taking her and her child far north, beyond the Arctic Circle, to fish in the Arctic Ocean by the Laptev Sea?

The exiles did not know where they were being taken. The Soviet propaganda system was efficiently deceitful in spreading misinformation that exiles were being taken to…America. Therefore, people did not try to hide or escape en route. They suffered all the discomforts along the way and travelled willingly…to so-called America.

The journey lasted almost all summer. At its source, the Lena River is scenic, with mountainous shores; beyond Yakutsk, it is increasingly wider, reaching two to three kilometers across. Further north, the river shores are low and overgrown with barely visible scraggy brush. Toward the delta [mouth], the river widens up to twenty kilometers and branches out in numerous channels. So it abounds in islands, islets, and promontories. The Lena delta is far beyond the northern Arctic Circle. That is where exiles began to disembark. Some people were left on the barely inhabitable island of Tit-Ary; others on Trofimovsk…while we, remaining on the barge, were still sailing happily to America…. But suddenly, the icy promontory Bykov Mys reared its head, and our journey to America came to an end. Those who had died on the barge were thrown overboard. When the vessel tied up at shore, another group of exiles, including our family, disembarked.

We found ourselves in a settlement called Bykov, on a high icy promontory surrounded by tundra. However, the tundra there was different: instead of earthen ground, there was ice beneath our feet. A layer of soil, barely thirty to fifty centimeters thick, was superimposed on the permafrost. During the brief polar summer, this layer is covered with soft moss and small trees, osiers [willows], protruding here and there from the moss. Warmed somewhat by sunlight, the soil spurts puddles and small ponds. The tundra even adorns itself with flowers and birds coming to hatch. But summer, with its polar days of non-stop sunlight, is short. Frosty winter creeps in, bringing three months of polar night. The thin layer of soil freezes over with a cover of ice and snow. Terrible blizzards set in, often raging for weeks, whipping huge masses of snow into maelstroms that appear to merge earth and sky. It is impossible to hold one's ground in such wind. Caught in this kind of blizzard, one loses all sense of direction, and with prolonged struggle against the elements, is likely to perish. True, the northern lights in the Arctic are awesome, but they neither warmed nor cheered the exiles. Sometimes not only the sky but also the snow turned a rich crimson, as if seeped in blood.

A huge, dilapidated barge loomed over the shore of the Bykov Mys promontory. That is where we were initially sheltered. At night, a storm rose and rain fell. It was only mid-August, and snowflakes fluttered in the air. The shoreline sparkled with an icy crust. Cold Arctic water splashed over the sides of the barge. It was dark, cold, wet…and frightening.

From the very first days of our arrival, adults and teenagers were forced to work. Some fished; others built yurts. I began to prepare food. There were a few outdoor stoves on shore. Luckily, while sailing, we had purchased a few pots from Yakut passengers, and one of them was a good cast iron pot.

After constructing the first eight yurts, the exiles moved into them. It seemed that our life improved. But living conditions in the yurts were hardly normal. There were about seventy-five exiles in each of the yurts. It was cold and damp. We used a metal barrel [half of a metal drum] for a furnace, which we had to heat constantly. Yet our clothing and footwear did not dry overnight. The locus of all our activity and rest were two-tiered bunks, infested with lice. People came down with dysentery, scurvy, and respiratory ailments. My sister Aldutė became ill with scurvy (R. *cinga*). People began to die from illnesses and starvation. The dead could not always be buried immediately; corpses would often be lying in the entrance ways, and we children used to be afraid of passing by them. The cemetery at the end of the promontory began to disappear. Washed by waves and driving rain, coffins jutted out from the ice.

During our first winter in Bykov, when I was going on thirteen, I also went fishing. We pulled fish from beneath the ice. The fishing brigade consisted of about thirty people, divided into teams of three or four. Before the ice thickened, we had to ax out ice holes in which to set nets. Every day throughout winter we had to chop through the ice holes (which froze overnight), scoop out ice, pull out the nets, collect fish, and shove the net back through the ice hole. We worked in freezing cold, reaching down to – 45° C, quite far from the settlement, where the fish were. We didn't have any gloves, so we pulled the wet, icy nets and untangled fish with unprotected, bare hands. We used to go to the ice holes even during blizzards, in light clothing that did not shield us from the wind. If we didn't chop through the ice holes every day, they would freeze over with a thick layer of ice, making it extremely difficult to pull out nets. During winter the ice was apt to be one and a half to two meters thick.

Our team of four was comprised of one adult man, two teenage boys, and me. We were assigned thirty nets. However, our work proved futile because we were all too weak to pull out a large soaking wet net with fish from an ice hole. Working without gloves, we developed blisters and sores on our hands from the icy water, wet nets, and fish. The icy cuffs of our jackets rubbed the sores open. Besides, being inadequately dressed, wet, and frozen, we could not endure staying on the Arctic ice for long.

In 1943 my older sister Aldutė nearly perished in a blizzard. She was working in Mostakh, sixty kilometers from Bykov. When she finished work, she had to return home. There was no sleigh by which to ride back that day; moreover, the superviser said he was out of bread cards. So my sister had no choice but to walk home, and she left on foot. This incident was described by Aldutė's companion on the trek, Ona Sirutienė, in the chapter titled "The Wounds of June 14, 1941" of her book *Let Us to Our Homeland (Leiskit į Tėvynę)*, as follows:[1]

"We asked the superviser how many kilometers Bykov was from Mostakh. He replied, 'About sixty; try walking. Tomorrow morning, 6:00 or 7:00 a.m., I'll bring you a slice of bread each, some sugar, and walking sticks.' The journey would be rather long. We had neither food nor money, and Aldutė's felt boots were heavy with their sewn-on soles. When Karpov, the superviser, came by next morning with the supplies he had promised, the woman with whom we were staying asked in astonishment, 'What if they happen upon a blizzard? How will they walk home? –It's a long way.' With a glance at Aldutė's felt boots, Karpov shook his head.... I asked Aldutė in Lithuanian, 'Ką darom?' ('What are we going to do?'). She answered briefly, 'He wants to be rid of us, so let's go.' We thanked our hostess, said good-bye, and left. The superviser escorted us up to the straight road, gave each of us some spare rope, and advised us to walk at a normal pace and to eat the bread and sugar in parts. He added, 'Midway, you will see a small cabin, but don't go inside to rest; if you sit down to rest, you will fall asleep. Good luck on your way. You'll reach Bykov about noon.' Then, turning 'round to us again, he shouted, 'Stay on the left shore of the river and do not lose your walking sticks.'

So the two of us set out on our journey. Of course, first of all we crossed ourselves because we were both believers. I was about thir-

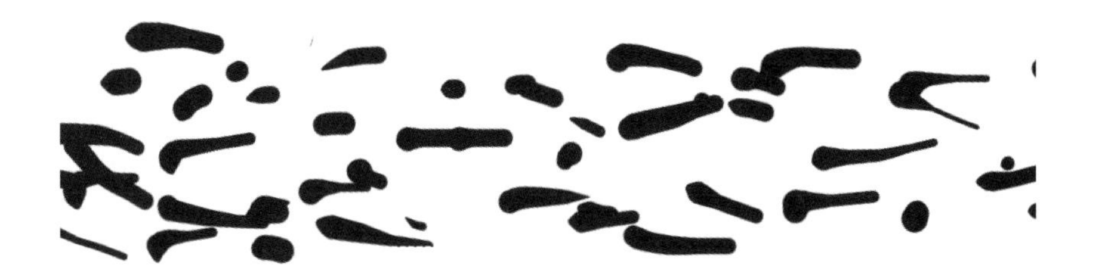

ty-one years old and Aldutė was eighteen [sixteen—I. Milaknytė's note]. I walked ahead and Aldutė followed, conversing very little. We were both dressed in wadded clothing; mine was borrowed. On my feet I had deer hide boots. On my head was a hood I had sewn from a doubled bag; I had tied my mother's scarf around Aldutė. She said she'd already eaten half of her bread whereas I was not even thinking of food. I kept reminding her to hold on to the walking stick. We walked on and on but came to no cabin. Aldona began to complain that her knees were shaking and she was ready to drop. Then, unexpectedly, we felt gusts of stormy wind. When I turned around to look at Aldona, I saw that she was covered with snow and heard her muttering that she could hardly walk. I advised her to take a few pieces of sugar. She said she'd already finished the sugar; she was very tired and wanted to rest. I wondered what would become of us further on. A blizzard was howling and the two of us were alone on the tundra—in bad weather. When we saw a sleigh approaching, we raised our hands and begged the driver to give us a ride to Bykov. The Yakut answered curtly, 'No! I'm hurrying home. There's a blizzard.' So we continued trudging along, leaning on our walking sticks. Turning about, I inserted a piece of bread with sugar into Aldona's mouth; I took her rope, girded her, and tied her to myself. Asking her if this made walking easier, I was glad to hear that it did. 'Are you really going to pull me like a billy-goat?,' she queried. The wind subsided. I noticed a grey shape on my left, so we'd reached midway. Lest Aldona notice the cabin, I pulled her scarf lower on her face and gave her another small piece of bread with sugar. Later I remarked that we'd passed the resting place and she must now think of home because her parents and sisters were waiting for her; moreover, she was the main worker in her family. Aldona teared up, asking why I hadn't let her know when we'd come to the cabin. She didn't have the strength to go on. I had grievously suffered the death of my young son, so my only wish was to bring Aldutė home alive to her parents. Again, the wind diminished somewhat, and I decided to pull Aldutė like a sled. I asked her to sit down, tied her rope around her chest and pulled it under the arms to harness myself with it. We began to move forward, and this was easier for both of us. Then Aldutė began to complain that her trousers would tear. As I could not think of another solution, I kept pulling the live 'sled' silently. I remembered Christ's words from the Holy Gospel: 'If you love me, take your cross and follow me.' Though it might be difficult, I must sacrifice myself for my loved ones. I was so glad when I espied a rosy hue in the horizon! I shouted that Bykov was near, and I wasn't mistaken, for the sky grew lighter and lighter. Nevertheless, it was very difficult to lead Aldutė all the way home. When we entered the yurt, her entire family woke up. They helped Aldutė out of her heavy clothing, and she, collapsing on the bunk, uttered, 'If not for Ona, I wouldn't have returned home.' It was 2:00 a.m., so we had walked a long time. Slowly, I crept to my yurt. The door was unlocked. I entered quietly and undressed by myself, for I didn't have a family. When I attempted to climb up to my bunk, I found that I didn't have the strength."

In 1943 Aldutė was sent to Arangastakh for summer work, and our whole family went along this time. Arangastakh is a hardly inhabitable island to the north of Bykov. It is flat, with low shores, thus totally open to the wind. During the summer, the island sprouts moss. On the shoreline, one might see a discarded log, frozen in winter.

In Arangastakh, the exiles dug a pit in the ice, making for an ice cellar. During winter, fishermen loaded it with the fish they caught. During summer, the fish had to be processed and sent to the front lines. So in winter, men, women, and strong teenagers fished on Arangastakh; in summer, women and children were brought there to trim and salt the fish. It might seem like easy work, but the frozen fish, ice-cold water, and salt were peculiarly harmful. Cold water and salt irritated our hands, inducing sores, for which we had no medication or bandages. A platform of boards was laid out on the ground to thaw fish; beside the platform was a pile of salt. We didn't have all the tools we needed for the work, nor gloves. Some workers lifted frozen fish out of the ice cellar with their bare hands; others brought it to the platform, and still others slit and gutted the fish, scraping out the intestines. They loaded the fish in tubs and carried these to the water, to clean the fish, which they then salted. After a few days, the salted fish was again rinsed in sea water and packed in barrels. Later, stronger men pressed down the fish and secured the barrels.

We processed fish until late autumn. Work days for both grownups and children were twelve hours long. The work continued even with the onset of snow. Frequently, the cutter arriving to transport people and tools could not reach the shore because it was ice-bound.

During our first year in Arangastakh, we lived in a cattle-shed, and in a tent during our second year. Exiles sewed tents from the bags in which American flour was packaged. In winter, they covered the tents with layers of snow. As there was no firewood on the island, we often lacked kindling and wood needed to light the stove and cook food. Inside, the tent was cold and damp. We'd take off our padded jackets and shiver with cold, but the jackets would not dry overnight.

Food was scarce. Officially, a worker was allotted only two to three kilograms of fish per month.

I remember walking along the shore one day after work, in cold, damp weather. My clothing was soaked and my hands ached from sores chafed by salt. The shrill cries of seagulls accosted me. I had the urge to drown myself, but I kept walking, walking and crying…. I thought I heard my echo in the distance, but it was not an echo—someone else was also wailing out there. As I walked further, the wailing grew louder... and before long I could see my Jewish friend Leah's silhouette.

I worked on Arangastakh for two summers. My dad worked in construction; my mother collected moss for use in construction. During winter, after returning to Bykov, I split firewood. Later, we two teenage girls and two other women, harnessing ourselves to sleds, transported firewood for the officials in Bykov. In our settlement there was only one horse, employed to transport water from the bay. The water in this bay was not as salty as sea water, so we could use it to prepare food.

In 1947, when the war was over and father's health deteriorated, we obtained permission to move to Yakutsk. We sailed just before the sea froze over, in the last steamboat. However, we lacked some kind of documentation, or so they said, and we were directly thrown out on the ice in Kyusyur. We lived in Kyusyur for four years. I attended school and worked there. My father, Juozas Milaknis (1900–1950), died there. He was buried in the cemetery at Kyusyur. But when the shore was washed out by flooding and masses of moving ice, the graves drifted out to sea. The Kyusyur cemetery has now been relocated, and Lithuanian exiles erected a cross there.

In 1951 my sister Aldona Milaknytė died in Yakutsk and was buried there. Her grave has also disappeared: a fire burned out the section of the Yakutsk cemetery where she had been laid to rest.

After the war, in 1946, exiles' children were allowed to attend school. Danutė Milaknytė (1937-2010) graduated from the agricultural secondary school in Yakutsk. She returned to Lithuania in 1956. She died in Vilnius in 2010. Her son, Remigijus, died in 2009, leaving her daughter-in-law, Danutė, and grandsons, Rimvydas and Eimantas.

I, Irena Milaknytė (b. 1929), graduated from the Yakutsk Pedagogical Institute in 1955. In 1957, my mother, Veronika Milaknienė (1897–1967), my sister Aldutė's daughter, Marytė, and I returned to Lithuania. My mother died and was buried in Vilnius. Marytė Baronienė now lives in Rokiškis; her two children, Giedrius and Jūratė, live in Kaunas.

Bykov Mys is now a part of Russia's border zone and is closed to travelers.

Recorded by Irena Kurtinaitytė Aras
Vilnius, 2010

[1] *Leiskit į Tėvynę* ("Let Us to Our Homeland"). Reminiscences of Exiles. Compiled by Kęstutis Pukelis. Kaunas: Šviesa, 1989.

From right to left, Jonas Markevičius, Adelė Markevičienė with Remigijus in her arms, Danutė Adelė, and a few of her classmates, ca. 1940.

Adelė and Jonas Markevičius (sitting); Danutė, Remigijus, Audrius, and Elytė Markevičienė (standing, left to right) in Kaunas, July 26, 1971.

Danutė Adelė Markevičiūtė-Bakevičienė

With her mother, Adelė Markevičienė, and four-year-old brother, Remigijus, fifteen-year-old Danutė Adelė Markevičiūtė was exiled from Kėdainiai to the Altai region in Russia on June 14, 1941. A year later, they were deported to the uninhabitable Tit-Ary island in the Lena River delta within the Arctic Circle.

Danutė's father, Jonas Markevičius, a civil servant, was separated from the family at the Naujoji Vilnia station and deported to the Reshoty concentration camp in the Krasnoyarsk region. After eight years of imprisonment, he was exiled to Denisovo, a village in the Dzerzhinsky district of Krasnoyarsk.

We disembarked on Tit-Ary August 21, 1942, after a long journey on the Lena River, past the center of the Bulun district. The island shore was steep and sandy. We got off the barge with our bundles and via a little foot-bridge, touched ground on the island. Stopping at a tarpaulin-covered pile of logs, we sheltered ourselves from the north wind and, huddling awkwardly on our belongings, we fell asleep. When we woke up next morning, we looked around to see where we could settle. The Lena River flowed northward, with hills lining its right shore, above which on the east side, there was gloomy sunlight. Finnish and German exiles, brought from Leningrad, had already built a shelter and settled on the island.

We had dozed only a few hours when we heard the call for work. Mother got up and joined the others. When she returned, she said she was assigned to construction; they would be working fourteen hours per day. Children and teenagers were not driven to work yet, so Remigijus and I remained perched on our bundles. My brother was four years old, twelve years younger than I.

We had to figure out how to bring water from the river and how to heat it. I told Remigijus to stay where he was, for the wind was cold. Luckily, we had a pail and a pot. I drew some water from

the Lena; it was *so-o* cold.... Now I had to look for firewood and somehow kindle a fire. Remigijus, shivering as he sat there on our belongings, was asking for food and drink. It was snowing already, snowflakes whirling around my feet. I found an old brick, some stones, and twigs on the river shore. The twigs were damp and kindled very slowly; then the flame was put out by a gust of wind. I saw a fire burning by the Finns' barrack and went to ask for some coal. But how would I carry the red-hot coals? After a few trials, I brought some smoldering twigs back in my pot and unloaded them on the campfire I had stacked up. The damp wood hissed and wheezed while Remigijus kept asking for something to drink. I was afraid to give him cold water. I knelt down and blew on the smoldering wood... and so labored a few hours before I succeeded in heating the water. I poured in some salt, which I had found in a pile on the ground. We still had a piece of bread, so I managed to feed my little brother. Mother returned from work with some flour. We poured flour into turbid water and ate our first meal on the island. Sustained by this slop, mother left for work again while I went looking for more fuel. I asked Remigijus to tend the fire by adding twigs

before the flames died out. So the two of us kept the fire going day and night and provided hot water.

Mother worked pulling logs ashore. She used to return exhausted and wet, and there was no place to dry out. She received food cards: 500 grams of flour for a worker and 300 grams for a non-worker or a child. In sum, she got one kilogram and a hundred grams. She was also given an advance of one hundred rubles (*chervonci*). Every day we had to pay 3.3 rubles for bread (or ninety-nine rubles per month). Mother said we had to save that money because it was difficult to achieve the day's work norm, and she could not anticipate how much she would be paid at the end of each month. We decided to buy a half kilogram of sugar and 300 grams of butter with the food card. Nevertheless, we began to suffer hunger because mother could not attain the work norm every day and received only sixty rubles at month's end. There was insufficient money to buy butter before the next advance payment.

After several days, they let us move into the Finns' barrack, where there were bunks secured to the walls and a few iron barrels with apertures for loading fuel. We could heat water in pots atop those barrels. Around them, we warmed pieces of brick to take to bed and warm our feet, as it got ever colder at night. We tended the fire in turn with Bartkienė's children. I used to bring water for everyone and gather fuel; the children kept the fire going day and night.

Finally, they set to building a barrack for us Lithuanian exiles. First they chopped (axed out) holes in the frozen ground and set logs in them; then they covered the logs with sod and poured water over the sod to secure the logs. After setting logs for the walls in this way, they proceeded to construct walls with boards, leaving apertures for doors and windows. The boards, split and sawed from logs, were narrower at one end than the other, so ill-fitted with one another, making for cracks. Sod was forced into the cracks, but it was frozen and did not fill the cracks properly. Consequently, the walls were open to drafts of wind. The windows were covered with paper because there was no glass. They laid the roof with boards and covered them with moss—while there was moss to be found beneath the snow—and more frozen sod.

<…>

In a few days, they nailed two-story bunks to the walls. Our bunk was in the middle of the barrack. Bartkienė was younger than my mother (who was forty-six), so she volunteered to occupy the upper bunk with her children. One day, they finally set up an iron furnace (*burzhuyka*) by our bunks. The temperatures dived lower below freezing, the wind tore the paper off our "windows," and cold air penetrated the crack-filled walls. Several women, including my mother, were assigned the task of mending walls to warm the barrack. They dislodged the window frames, took them to the river, and stuck them through ice holes into the freezing water to soak. Overnight, they froze and were then brought back to the barrack and reinstated in the window jambs. Six women transported a cask of water on a sled: some, harnessing themselves to ropes, would pull the sled while

others kept the cask from sliding off the sled. The water swished and splashed the women walking alongside the sled; they were drenched as they worked and could barely drag their feet.

The women who mended walls were not much better off. They poured water on snow and spattered the wet slush onto the walls. While they applied it at arm's length, it wasn't bad, but when they hurled it upward, some of the slush fell back on the "plasterers." Mother used to return from work with a coat of ice all over her. Since there was nowhere to dry out, she had to go to work wet next morning. She used to say that while her clothes were in the process of freezing, she felt miserably chilled; when they were frozen, the cold was bearable. Before long, however, she was down with a bad cold. She forfeited her worker's card when she was sick, and we then received barely over a kilogram of bread each. Fortunately, I was already working in the children's brigade.

Mother had taken an advance loan of 600 rubles, to be paid back in installments over two years. Each month, twenty-five rubles were deducted from her pay, in addition to the income tax (*podokhodniy nalog*), so she used to receive only 100–120 rubles. I used to earn eighty to ninety rubles, working ten to twelve hours per day.

When the children's brigade built a school house, children were registered for school. I also signed up. There were seven of us enrolled for the seventh grade: two Finnish and two Lithuanian girls, two Lithuanian boys and one Russian boy. After the first few days of school, the boys did not show up; a Lithuanian girl also quit. Four of us remained. They had promised to pay us 180-ruble scholarships, but only the Russian boy, a Finnish girl, and I received scholarships. Russian was very difficult for me at first. I received an unsatisfactory grade for language and lost my scholarship. When mother fell ill, I went to the Director, the Yakut Aliokhin, and said I could not attend school any longer because we would not have enough money for the daily bread ration. The Director then promised to pay me and the other Finnish girl a scholarship of ninety rubles each. I added that if

I didn't go to work on mother's behalf, mother would be deprived of her work card. He advised me to work half of mother's shift and stay in school. I agreed because I wanted to study very much.

To be sure, it was not only the desire for education that drew me to school—where I would be warm and more at ease than at work—but also my aching legs. Earlier, near Cheremkhovo, I had been attacked by those miniature flies (*moshka*) and developed open sores on my arms and legs, which would not heal. When the weather turned cold, my feet and toes were frostbitten and did not heal. My toe nails came off and the toes festered. We had no shoes. We used to wrap our feet with rags, secure the soles of old shoes on our feet with bags (which we could buy), and tie them on the outside around our ankles and calves with scraps of netting. Our feet looked like frozen blocks, and we could hardly drag them.

With neither footwear nor winter clothing, we covered ourselves with whatever we could find. We wrapped ourselves with bags that we sewed together. Our faces used to freeze, so we hid them behind "masks." When we breathed, those masks soaked up steam and froze forthwith; sometimes they had to be torn off along with our skin. People suffered so much while adapting to new conditions.... Many exiles could not endure the Arctic conditions and died of hunger or cold. Memories of those years still haunt me....

While working in the children's brigade, we carried boards, window frames, and doors from the river shore. We had to achieve a day's norm. Once, trying to do the work faster so we could have some leisure time, we stacked more boards on a door and began pulling it uphill. Four of us carried a door, one at each corner. As we climbed with such a heavy load, I suddenly felt pain in my abdomen and fell, weighed down by the door. I can't remember how they pulled me out from underneath that door. Some women dragged me to the barrack, where I lay without getting up for a few days. The brigade leader came around every day, cursed, and threatened to take away my food card. And that's what he did.

Consequently, I had to get up and go to work though I could hardly walk; my legs and stomach ached. But I was glad they assigned me to fuel and tend the stoves at school. I had to work fifteen-hour shifts, splitting wood and kindling fires in newly set stoves so they would dry out. At first, I heated only four stoves, but every day they would set up another one, giving me additional work. It was very difficult, and I could hardly split enough wood for all those stoves. The firewood was wet and kindled very slowly. I began to fall behind, and when I didn't attain the day's norm, my pay decreased.

Fortunately, mother and I were not sick at the same time. While one of us was ill, the other was well; so we suffered through that first winter of 1942–1943. At one time, however, we were short of money for bread and lived on water and salt for three days. Mother was sicked and stayed in bed. I returned from work with some wood chips I had gathered and started a fire in the furnace. Remigijus asked if I had brought home some bread. I replied that we had no money to buy bread. He started whimpering, saying through his tears that he was not asking for much. With his little forefinger and thumb set together, he showed that he was asking only for a wee little crumb....

We drank some water, lay down, and huddled together for warmth. Remigijus used to lie between us, but that evening he would not lie down, complaining, "Mummy, Danutė, I feel dizzy and have a stomach ache. I want a little crumb of bread to suck on so very much," again setting his forefinger and thumb together to indicate a wee bit of bread. We tried to pacify him in many ways and consoled him that in another day or two we would have money and buy bread, but the child sobbed and would not be appeased. It was getting late; we couldn't fall asleep and were keeping others awake. From a corner of the barrack came the voice of a former Minister's wife: "What sort of mother can't control her child? If she'd give him a good whack, he'd be quiet." Whereupon mother, losing her restraint, spanked Remigijus, and he cried the more bitterly. Then he kissed mother, saying, "Mummy dearest, what are you spanking me for? I'm a good boy. I sit on the bunk day in and day out though my feet are frozen; I only get off to pee. I sit alone in the dark all day though my legs hurt. I listen to you. When there are some wood chips for kindling, I heat the furnace. Why are you spanking me if I just want a crumb of bread so very much?" That pitiful complaint rings in my ears even now, fifty-seven years later, and tears at my heart….

When I got up next morning, I tried to waken mother and offer her hot water to drink, but she was silent and didn't move. By the light of a wick lamp, I saw that her eyes were shut, her mouth open, and face distorted. I tried to prop her up, but she was so heavy…. Then Remigijus and I began to scream. Women came running, looked at mother, and said she was paralyzed. They told me to hurry to the medical assistants' station and ask them to hospitalize mother. When I explained what happened to a doctor's assistant, she said curtly that there was no room in the hospital. A nurse who overheard our conversation remarked that someone died that day, so there would be a vacant bed. Then the doctor's assistant told me to bring the patient. I returned to the barrack. We wrapped mother in a blanket and with the help of a few good women, dragged her through the snow to the hospital; we did not have the strength to carry her.

Remigijus and I were on our own. All the chores fell on my shoulders: finding fuel, bringing ice and snow from the river for water, and then queuing for bread. I consoled myself with the thought that at least mother was warm and received soup at the hospital. They did not admit visitors at first, but a week later, I found mother looking brighter and beginning to eat by herself. In a month, she was released. But she was so weak that she could hardly get off the bunk to fuel the fire in the furnace. Remigijus helped her.

In the morning, I worked a half shift for mother: I transported wood from the island hillock with Finnish women. The trees were northern larches that grew almost horizontally on the ground, only their tips rising upward about a half meter. We had to find those larches beneath a thick layer of snow, shovel the snow, fell them, pull them out, and load them onto a sled. Six to eight of us pulled the sled, harnessing ourselves to ropes. Going downhill, two of us held on to the sled, so that it wouldn't slide too fast. In six to seven hours, from 6:00 a.m. to lunch time, we used to make two round trips to the hillock. The lunch break was a half hour. After the morning shift, I ran to buy bread, brought it to the barrack, and ate lunch—if there was something to eat besides bread.

In the afternoon, from 2:00 p.m., I attended school. When I was late, the Russian teachers would tell me to sit down quietly on the bench and proceed with the lesson. If the Lithuanian teacher, Miss M., was teaching the first lesson, she would order me to stand by the blackboard and recite, "*Prishol olyen, pust stoyit, yesli narushayet poryadok*" ("In came a deer. Let her stand if she can't keep to the schedule.") I used to stand there while ice melted from my frozen leg wrappings, forming a puddle around me, and children joked that I was peeing in my pants. It hurt me so much to be humiliated by a fellow Lithuanian, but I stood there and listened to what she was saying. If we didn't hear a lesson, we would fall behind and get bad grades; there was no one else to explain it. We had no books, and we wrote on the edges of newspaper sheets. After six or seven lessons, we were given some supper: a glass of hot water, fifty grams of bread, ten grams of butter, and twenty grams of sugar. I used to drink the water and bring the bread home to share in equal parts with mother and Remigijus. Mother would break off a bite of her piece for Remigijus.

I received a scholarship of ninety rubles and earned sixty rubles, sometimes less, on mother's behalf, so we could afford to buy bread. If the bread was dark, it cost three rubles and thirty kopeks per day, about a hundred rubles per month. With 150 rubles per month, we could also buy some butter or sugar. If the bakery produced white bread, it cost five rubles and fifty kopeks per day, or

170.5 rubles per month. In winter, fishermen were not allowed to bring any fish home for themselves. We used to be very glad to find some fish heads discarded in the trash, for we could boil them and thus supplement our diet.

It was so hard, but days passed. In the island of Tit-Ary the sun set far on the tundra. The Yakuts said that on November 18th the sun would set, to rise again only at the end of January. When the weather was clear, we used to see the sun's orb in the west before it set for the winter. But each day it decreased in size.... On November 18th we saw a slight streak of sunlight disappear and from that day, the sun was gone. It grew dark, and darker during the day than at night because the moon often shone at night. But the moonlight was eerie, seemingly lifeless, and did not console us. Blizzards raged frequently. It snowed and wind blew so fiercely that it seemed to surround us in a maelstrom. In such weather, going to the Lena River to cut ice was frightful—we might not find our way back. While protecting ourselves from the wind, we'd lose our sense of direction and stray from the path homeward.

One day, mother and I ventured to the other shore of the Lena, where Kazakhs fished. We set out in the evening before the moon rose, thinking that we'd return in moonlight. We brought a pillow to barter for fish. We entered one of the yurts and proffered our pillow, but no one was interested. Nor did anyone offer us hot water to drink. In another yurt, they gave us three pike-perch heads, some fish tails, and bones, for which we were thankful. But we turned around disappointed and tired. As we walked, a blizzard rose, mingling earth and sky, obscuring the path ahead. We soon lost track of our previous footprints, which at first we tried to re-trace. Covering up our faces, we could hardly see each other. Chilled, our feet freezing, we proceeded at a snail's pace, stopped and started, then stopped, not knowing which way to go. Mother pointed in one direction while I insisted on another. Angered by my opposition and stubbornness, mother walked away while I stood there and cried, muttering that she was going the wrong way. Though frightened, I wouldn't budge, for I was sure she had taken the wrong direction. I started shouting, "Mummy, if we die, let's die together!" Soon I could see her approaching me, silent. I pulled her in my chosen direction. When I felt uneven ground under my feet, I knew we were close to the shore, where ice chunks clash against each other, pile up, and freeze unevenly. Beyond the irregular ground, we found ourselves climbing uphill. So this was the shore of the island, we thought. In turn rising and sliding down, we slowly reached the top. Suddenly we saw a light flickering ahead of us. Someone must have opened the barrack door.... We were safe! Thanking God, we proceeded toward that light. It was a Kazakh barrack that we entered in tears, asking for water and respite.

The Kazakhs seated us and gave us tea, but offered no food. An old Kazakh man held a wick lamp to our faces, pausing by mine for a while. Then he went to a two-story bunk, chatted with someone sitting above, and returned. Mother offered our pillow in exchange for some flour, but he said they needed no pillows. Then he pulled me by the hand toward the young man on the bunk, saying, "Look, isn't he handsome?" What was I supposed to say? I thought, if I were agreeable, maybe they would offer us some food. Back by mother's side, he told us to wait: they'll have a little discussion. Then we saw a few more Kazakhs getting down from their bunks to talk. (Incidentally, these Kazakhs were brought from the Caspian Sea to teach local people how to fish.) Mother and I waited, wondering what would come of all this talk. The old Kazakh returned and started questioning mother as to how many children she had and how much money she earned.... When he had his fill of information, he chatted again with the men. Then he sat down on a bunk in front of us and said, in awkward Russian, "We've decided to wed your girl to that young man. She'll stay with us, and we'll pay you a good bride-price (*kalim*) to help you live. Mother glanced at me, shriveling by her side, and began to explain that I was only fifteen years old, too young to marry. They responded, "She'll live with us for a few years, grow up, and be a good wife. Why, she'll be his first wife, and that is a great honor! When he takes a second wife, she'll be the primary housekeeper, respected and obeyed by all. We'll give you an even larger bride-price because we like her." Mother rose, grabbed me by the hand, and tried to leave, but the old Kazakh stood in the way. Mother and I started screaming that they had no right to detain us; if they wouldn't let us go, we'd complain to the local government official (R. *partorg*, "communist party secretary"). Finally, we escaped and made our way back to our barrack. We went to work sleepless and tired that day.

So I was almost married to a Kazakh. Sometimes mother jested that I might have been "the Kazakh's most honored wife"—"Just think, the first one!" I was angered when she told other women about the chance she had to sell her daughter and forego the struggle for survival.

Once, returning to the barrack, I overheard mother conversing with the bearded man who had vied for the central spot in the barrack when we first moved in. He was saying,

"Just think, Adelė, after so many years, we've met up with each other here.

Do you remember how, during the early years of independence [Lithuania's independence 1918–1940], we used to organize gatherings of young people, teach reading and writing, and stage plays? And the plays! I remember 'Birutė' and your performance of Birutė. You had such lovely hair and you looked so beautiful that all of Vilkaviškis called you a star. Everyone wanted to be by your side, hoping for a chance to dance with you. What has become of you now? – a wreck, a sack of bare bones."

Mummy laughed, rejoining, "Dear Juozas, you are younger than I, but you sit here bent-up and bearded, a veritable stump!" Then he retorted, "I'll let you know that you've brought up your daughter badly. She is so stubborn that she challenged me when we were choosing bunks in the barrack."

– “And you, Juozas, used to be such a gentleman. What has become of you now, that you dared push my children around? I’m proud of my daughter. If not for her efforts, we would be settled further from the furnace, by the windows. Moreover, if not for her alertness and obstinacy, we would have been lost while crossing the Lena and would now be lying frozen, covered by snow, until someone found our bodies in spring. Or, carried away on the Lena’s ice, we’d be lying somewhere in the depths of the Arctic Ocean.”

The days began to grow longer. Sometime after February 4th, a streak of sunlight once appeared in the west. We all stood and watched it like some miracle. We looked at one another, appalled at our appearance: shriveled, exhausted, with soot-covered, dirty faces, we looked like ghosts surfacing from under the ground…. The sun rose higher every day. How joyful it was to get up with the sun! When it appeared above the hill crests in the east, we knew where the sun was rising. From the end of April, the sun would journey through the sky without setting for several months. Even if it didn’t yield much warmth, it would cheer us with its bright rays. Summer was coming….

<…>

Those who survived the winter of 1942–43 straightened up, mended, and adapted to the severe Arctic conditions. People began to fish. Though furtively, fishermen brought some fish home; we also tasted some that summer. Remigijus used to go watch the fishermen sometimes. Given a fish, he would hide it under his shirt and bring it home, proud to be helping us out.

In spring, before the school examinations, I came down with scurvy (*cinga*). My legs were cramped and full of sores; moreover, the sores were infested with lice—a horror to remember. When I was alone, I used to shield myself so no one would see, take a twig, and brush off lice along with the pus, then re-wrap my feet and legs with unwashed rags. I couldn’t bend my legs; besides, I was too weak to get up, so I had to stay home from school. Now Remigijus stood in line for bread, gathered firewood, and brought ice from the river. Mother worked salting fish. While she stood in a huge barrel (*chyan*), the skin on her hands and feet peeled off from the brine—it just came off like a glove. But she kept on working.

The Director came to our barrack, looking for me, because examination time was approaching. He began to scold me for staying home from school. No one had seen my sore legs, for I was ashamed of them, but now I uncovered them by way of response to his scolding. With a glance at those swelling sores—rosy, infected flesh with lice crawling about, surrounded by black and blue—the Director, turning pale, told me to cover them and go to a doctor's assistant as soon as possible. I snapped that I could not bend my legs and stand up. He asked whether I had already sought medical advice. I said I had, but the doctor's assistant had neither peroxide nor bandages. The Director wrote an order for buying bags with which to cover my legs, inquiring, "So you worked all winter with your legs in that condition?" I said, "Yes, and I attended school. But now my joints are contracted and I can't get up." He cursed, adding, "That's scurvy. Didn't you ever take any vitamins?" I replied that I had never heard of vitamins. – "We take them by the handful," the Director said, and with a wave of his hand, ran out of the barrack.

Soon he returned and gave me fifty-nine tablets, the size of peas, telling me to take two per day. I divided them into three parts, nineteen each, and swallowed the remaining tablets right away. When mother returned from work, I told her about the Director's visit and gave her two thirds of the vitamins. She kept eighteen for herself, an equal part for Remigijus, and gave me the extra two, saying, "These might help you get up and take your exams."

After the Director's visit, my teachers came by a few times to explain the lessons. My girlfriends came to see me and bring me homework. And what a miracle! After taking the vitamins for a while, I began to bend my legs. With some crutches they made for me, I returned to school. I passed the exams very well and received a certificate of graduation from seventh grade. The Director recommended further study for three of us girls at a pedagogical school in Kyusuyr.

The Director also arranged for mother's release from the fish processing factory (*ribzavod*). Mother was all swollen and had begun to retain water in her abdomen. Nonetheless, we set out for the *ribzavod* one day to collect mother's salary. On the way, she fainted. I tried to pull her up, but I didn't have enough strength. Passing us on the road just then, Vacys Ivaškevičius took mother by the armpits while I lifted her by the feet, and we carried her to the hospital nearby. Then I ran around looking for a doctor's assistant. Mother stayed in the hospital for eighteen months.

I did not leave for the pedagogical school. Remigijus and I were ousted from the barrack, and we lived in a tent for a while. I soon arranged for Remigijus' admittance to the newly opened kindergarden. I moved into a small barrack where I settled in a corner by the door and a stove; on the other side of a partition-wall was a Polish woman with two children. I tried to keep out of the school Director's sight because he had threatened that if I didn't leave for the school, I wouldn't be able to obtain work on Tit-Ary. I was working, transporting firewood. I joined the Yakut brigade because I had an ax. I was the strongest among them although my legs were still full of sores. The Yakuts procured high fur boots for me, with soles of soft leather and no lining inside them. I cut soles from an old briefcase, sewed lining from bags, and attached some netting to the lining so it would not wear out easily. I made good money working for the Yakuts: 500 rubles per month.

At that time, the fishermen received more coupons for flour than they could use and gave me some. I bought a forty-five-kilogram bag of American wheat flour, fifty kilograms of oats, and a seventy-kilogram bag of oat flour. I also had enough money to buy butter and a kilogram of sugar. We were now well armed against hunger. After work, I used to prepare a pot of oatmeal and bring it to the hospital for mother. There was a Lithuanian attendant who would ladle the oatmeal into a bowl and return the pot to me. When I got back, I prepared a larger portion of oatmeal and took half of it to Remigijus in the kindergarden. Then I ate some myself. I used to wear myself out because I had to gather firewood, stand in a queue for bread, and bring ice from the river, in addition to working twelve hours per day. It was easier in summer when the ice floated down the river, and we didn't have to chop ice in order to draw water. Thus I subsisted on my own until mother returned from the hospital and found work in the kindergarden.

1945 came around and the war ended. We rejoiced, thinking that we may be allowed to go home. One day, on my way to the barrack, I met up with the school Director, the Yakut Aliokhin. He was surprised to see me and asked where I was working. I said I was transporting firewood and water. Indignant, he asked whether my legs had healed. "No," I replied. –"Why didn't you call on me? I would have placed you in an easier job." I said that I was afraid to see him because he had warned me that I wouldn't be able to work on Tit-Ary if I didn't leave for school in Kyusyur. He laughed, exclaiming, "What a fool! Let's go to the *ribzavod* office." I did as I was told. I waited by the personnel supervisor's door and heard him speaking to the supervisor: "You must find work for her; she's the only one left of the first graduating class of seventh graders. She has completed school." Finally he came out and said, "You'll work as an accountant in the office. You'll be warm there; maybe your legs will heal faster." Thus I obtained easier work.

When I arrived for my first day at the office, I didn't think I could do the work. Holding a pen in my hand, I sat there, oblivious and blocked, unable even to remember how to write a single letter or figure. I stayed until next morning, practicing letters and numbers. The next day, I barely managed to fulfill my tasks, sitting in the office from 8:00 a.m. until midnight, snacking only on a piece of bread and a cup of hot water. Thus exhausting myself for a few days, I got used to the work. However, I didn't work there very long. The post office was increasing staff and needed postal workers. They were anticipating the first mail delivery by airplane, so a landing place on the Lena River's ice had to be leveled. I was charged with supervising the workers in this task.

The workers labored for ten hours and went home, leaving me alone on the river. The ice field had been leveled and smoothed down, but a blizzard brought more snowdrifts. Afraid to leave, I spent the whole night shoving snow and maintaining the landing field. In the morning, before 8:00 a.m., the Post Master Sinicin came to inspect the landing area. When he found me clearing snow alone, he began shouting, "Where are the workers? Why isn't anyone working?" I said, they have not yet arrived for work. – "And who are you, that you're working?" I said I was an accountant. – "And you are in charge of this task?" – "Yes. Yesterday the workers leveled the ice field and went home. I stayed and cleared snow alone all night." He told me to go home and get some sleep. I could hardly climb the steep island shore.

That is how I became a post office employee. I worked there until 1949. During that time, our lives improved. The Post Master departed and I was assigned to take his place. When a commission from the Health Department came to Tit-Ary to see patients, I was designated as disabled, group one. I then resumed my studies with correspondence courses and raised my rank. I applied for admission at a technical school for communications. In 1949, I left for Yakutsk on my own, but I was late for the beginning of the academic year at the technical school. I found work at a primary school. Soon mother and Remigijus joined me in Yakutsk.

We obtained permission to move to Denisovo, a village in the Dzerzhinsky district of Krasnoyarsk, where my father was exiled after serving an eight-year sentence in concentration camp. This was nearer our longed-for homeland, Lithuania. But again, we met with hardship and disappointments. The yearning for our homeland was ineffable… a Lithuanian song on the radio would tear at our hearts. We longed and dreamed of returning without thinking where we would settle or how we would earn a livelihood. Only to get back, the sooner the better....

Finally, in 1955, we returned….

I rejoiced at Lithuania's independence in 1990, which neither mother, father, or Remigijus lived to see. But that is human fate.

I often remember the North, its terrible cold, and slave labor, wondering how I survived it. Hardship and work temper and toughen a person; one can endure anything. But it's a pity that I spent my youth in exile.

Danutė Bakevičienė, Kaunas, December 2009

In 1955, Danutė Adelė Markevičiūtė returned to Lithuania with her mother and brother. Her father, Jonas Markevičius, was not released from exile at the same time; he returned later. The re-patriated family stayed in Kaunas, where they had a difficult time getting settled. At first, they had to live separately from one another.

Thanks to Dr. Čepinskas, Danutė enrolled in a two-year course offered by the Red Cross and obtained work as a medical assistant in the health office of a factory.

Her mother died in 1974; her brother, in 1976, and her father, in 1990.

In 1987, Danutė married Stasys Bakevičius, also a former exile, He died in 1997. Danutė Adelė Bakevičienė is now retired and resides in Kaunas.

Linutė and Antanukas Abromaitis before exile.

Malvina and Jonas Abromaitis with their children, Lina and Antanas, in Yakutsk, 1947.

Antanas Abromaitis

On June 14, 1941, nine-year-old Antanas Abromaitis and his three-year-old sister, Lina, their mother, Malvina Abromaitienė, and father, Jonas Abromaitis, a teacher, were exiled from the village of Radžiūnai in the district of Alytus to the Altai region of Russia. In 1942, the Abromaitis family was deported from Altai to the island of Trofimovsk in the Lena River delta, within the Arctic Circle.

CHRISTMAS OF 1942

I woke up and tried to sit up, but I couldn't—my head was spinning. The barrack was dark, for the polar night had set in. None of us had a watch, so we didn't know the time and whether it was day or night. Someone was groaning on the upper bunk. From the other end of the barrack came the moans of death agony. On the bunk next to ours lay a stocky man, Adolfas Zabukas, shackled by scurvy and other diseases. We could hear his heavy breathing, interspersed now and then by his plaintive utterance, "I'm dying, dying...."

The make-shift stove, a metal barrel standing in the middle of the huge barrack, was not lit because there was no firewood. Rarely did anyone dare steal a board and light the so-called stove, for fear of imprisonment. Whenever someone took the risk and kindled a fire, people who could still walk came round the barrel to warm their stiff hands. Others brushed their clothing on the sides of the hot barrel to burn off lice.

The barrack door opened and I could sense mother returning. (My parents belonged to the work brigade which had to take the cold bodies of the dead out of the barracks.) Coming to the bunk where my little sister and I were lying, covered by rags, mother held her hand against my forehead. I understood that she wanted to make sure I was still alive. She helped me sit up, made the sign of a cross, and said, “Antanėlis, today is the first day of Christmas. I stole two board ends and bought some flour with the food cards.”

In the dark, mother tore a few splinters from a board, lit one, and handed it to me. The light of the burning splinter illumined the frosty ceiling and icy walls of the barrack. While I held the shining splinter, mother chopped the boards and started a fire in the metal barrel. Then she went outside to fill the only cast iron pot we had with snow and set it on the barrel to heat.

Soon father returned, all covered with ice. His fingers and hands were frostbitten through the wrists. The sores were not healing because we had no medication for them…. Unwrapping some rags from his hands, he dried them by the furnace. Mother poured flour into the pot, boiled the liquid, and brought it to our bunk—our table, chair, and bed in one. We had only two spoons. We crossed ourselves, then taking turns with the spoons, we supped on the watery broth. Thus we celebrated the first day of Christmas, 1942, on the island of Trofimovsk in polar Yakut country near the Laptev Sea.

A blizzard rose, with terrible winds howling and whistling. Their mighty gusts whirled away masses of snow several meters high, seeming to merge earth and sky in the maelstrom. I waited, expecting the vortices to flatten our barrack at any moment and so bring an end to our misery. Such blizzards often raged for weeks.

On the second day of Christmas, an old Lithuanian woman and two Finnish men died. Ona Baltrukonienė, formerly a teacher, left the barrack during the blizzard and did not return. Her little son, Jaunutis, about three years old, was crying on their bunk. He was an orphan now, for his father had been deported to a concentration camp and died there. A good-hearted woman, Stalauskienė, who had no children of her own, adopted the boy into her family and took care of him from that day on. O. Baltrukonienė’s corpse was found in the spring by Yakut hunters, five kilometers from the barrack.

On the third day of Christmas, Adolfas Zabukas passed away. And so day after day…. By spring, from over a hundred exiles, fewer than fifty remained in barrack Number 8.

FISHING

We woke early. Mummy, having lit a wick lamp (*koptilka*, a rag soaked in fish oil), was kindling a fire in the metal barrel. Father was tying ropes onto nets.

We didn't know what time it was because we didn't have a clock. We told time by the stars. Last night's strong wind had covered the door of the yurt with snow. I pushed the door open just a bit and went outside. The Pleiades constellation was above the right corner of the yurt, which meant that it was about 7:00 a.m.

When polar night approached, the sun did not appear; only a border of sky shone dimly for about three hours a day. In that short stretch of time we had to check the nets which we had set the previous day. Covering ourselves with whatever we had, then harnessing ourselves to a sled with all our fishing gear, we ventured out to check the nets. We left my six-year-old sister sleeping in the yurt. I was twelve years old.

A moderate wind was blowing, gently whirling snow above the ground. We walked along a series of landmarks, which formed a trail up to the shore of the island. Those were good guideposts, especially during a blizzard. Then we walked on ice. It was still dark, and we took a while looking for the nets we had set. When we finally located them, we hammered through the frozen ice-holes with a picket and scooped out chunks of ice. The wind grew stronger, spinning snow fiercely. It was still dark.

We began to check the nets in the absence of any light. In one ice-hole, we tied a rope, called *progon*, to the end of the net. From another ice-hole, we pulled out the net with our bare hands and began to untangle fish. Our hands stiffened forthwith from the cold—

about 30 degrees [C] below freezing—and our fingers grew numb. Strange, but the cold also pained the heart. One of us untangled fish from the net while the other tried to warm his hands, sticking them into ragged gloves. Mummy also took turns in the task.

As a streak of sky grew light, we hastened to make our round of the nets; there were two more to check. Mummy told me to run home, for my little sister was alone in the yurt. Sticking two *omul* [fish belonging to the salmon species], already frozen, under my armpit and approximating the direction toward the island shore, I ran. It was getting dark already. The wind whistled and snow glued my eyelids shut. I was impelled by one thought: to find the island; otherwise, death. My eyes brightened when I struck against the shore. Walking onward, I came to the first landmark. Thank God, I was home!

As I pushed the door of the yurt open, I heard my sister crying. The wick lamp had faded out and the yurt felt cold. I found some

matches, which we kept in a safe dry spot, lit the wick lamp, and kindled a fire in the metal barrel. Then I filled a pail with ice outside and heated some water. All the while I prayed that my parents would not lose their way back. In the morning, we had left without eating. So, when the ice melted, I mixed some water and flour for

flat-bread and fried the fish I had brought with me on a bent tin plate Daddy had made. Our diet consisted of fish and flour, which were often in short supply. There were times when we ate only fish. We forgot the taste of bread, not to mention vegetables. We tried to protect ourselves from scurvy by eating raw fish.

In about an hour, my chilled, hungry parents returned. With a pleasant warmth spreading from the stove and the wick lamp burning, our yurt felt cozy. We were glad we hadn't lost our way today, or frozen. Pushing aside the rags on our bunk, we sat down and ate our meal—breakfast, dinner, and supper in one. After eating, we prepared nets to set beneath the ice next day. I carved floats, burned holes in them with a heated twig, and tied them onto fishing line.

Thus we existed day after day. And there were very many of those same monotonous days in the five years we spent in the Arctic region.

Jonas Abromaitis. *Tremtis Užpoliarėje* ("Exile in the Arctic"). Kaunas: Naujasis lankas, 2010.

In 1946 the Abromaitis family obtained permission to leave Trofimovsk. They settled in Yakutsk and vicinity. Antanas worked, attended middle school and later an electro-technical school in Yakutsk. In 1956 he married Nijolė Vaičiūnaitė.

In 1961 Nijolė and Antanas Abromaitis returned to Lithuania with their two children, Marytė and Stasiukas.

Now Antanas and Nijolė are retired and live in Kaunas.

Pranė Grinkevičienė with her children, Dalia ir Juozas.

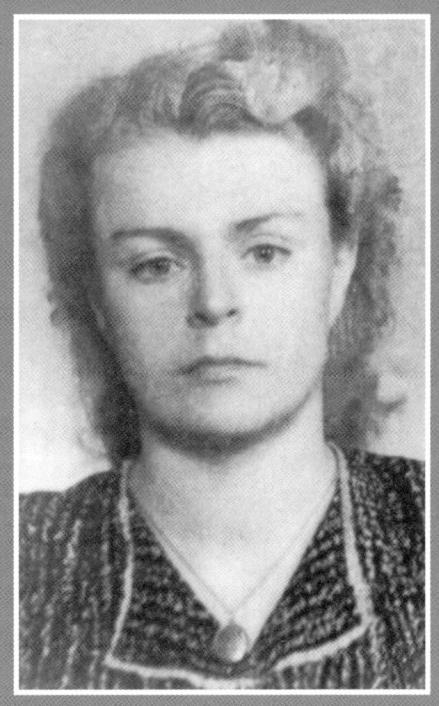

Dalia Grinkevičiūtė in Yakutia (on her neck, a medallion with a strand of her mother's hair).

The Grinkevičius family in Kaunas, 1937.

Dalia Grinkevičiūtė

Dalia Grinkevičiūtė (1927–1987) was exiled from Kaunas in 1941 (at age fourteen) with her mother, Pranė Grinkevičienė, and seventeen-year-old brother, Juozas. At first they were deported to the Altai region; a year later, to the island of Trofimovsk in the Lena River delta.

Her father, Juozas Grinkevičius, was separated from the family at Naujoji Vilnia and taken to a concentration camp in the Sverdlovsk district, where he died of starvation in 1943.

In 1949, Dalia and her mother returned to Lithuania illegally. In 1950, her mother died; Dalia was arrested and sentenced to three years at a concentration camp in the Gorki district. Later she was again exiled, in stages, to Yakutia in the Arctic Circle.

Our first really terrible and cruel polar winter, at the mouth of the Lena, began. Between the years 1942 and 1943 there were four hundred and fifty Lithuanians there.

In November the last rays of sun disappeared, a dark polar night set in, and terrible storms began their horrid dance of death. In our brick barracks it felt as if we were outdoors. With the storm howling, the last sacks filled with soil and sand were torn from the roof; the planks started creaking, and it looked as if the boards were also about to be torn off. Being wet, the mattresses, filled with wood shavings, froze to the floor. I had covered myself with all the rags I could find. I pressed myself against my mother and started breathing under the rags. It even felt warm. The snow did not melt from the top of the coverings, and that way it gave us some warmth. The wind had broken the door and had blown a mountain of snow into the center of the hut. The walls were covered with ice. Everybody kept silent, though nobody was sleeping. It looked like morning.

"Mummy, has Zagursky opened his shop yet? Can we get some bread?"

I heard Noreikienė's voice answering, "Be quiet, you animal. Yesterday we got a two days' ration, and we ate it all."

"Mummy, won't anybody give us a gram of bread?"

"Go and ask, and you'll see."

I got very frustrated. With a hurricane howling outside, we did not have to go to work. But I felt I could not go on lying there any longer. I crawled out from under the rags, shook the snow from my feet, and quickly pushed them into a pair of torn felt boots without soles. I had those boots since our time in the Altai region. On my legs I rolled some stinking wet sacking and bound it with string. I put on my thin wadded trousers and Juozas' jacket, which he had outgrown. On top of that I put on a wadded coat, made from a dressing gown, and breathed a sigh of relief. I sensed jealousy on the part of all those lying in that stronghold of ice and afraid to crawl out from beneath their rags, insulated merely by their breath. Finally Krikštanis crept out and started pulling on his trousers in a hurry.

In an attempt to form an exit through the door, both of us started tearing off the snow with our hands. In an hour we had made a hole at the very top of the door. I went on, lying on my stomach and working further. Suddenly my feet touched the upper frame of the door, and still I proceeded, gasping for fresh air. We were covered in snow because we had not built any kind of porch. The snow was getting softer, even trembling from the raging storm. With my hand I dismantled the last layer of snow that buried us. I wanted to shout to Krikštanis: That's it! But snow suddenly hit me in the face, glued my eyes together, went down my throat, hid inside my collar, and crept into my sleeves and mittens. My eyelashes were frozen and glued together with ice and, gasping for air, I started crawling back in. I fell to the floor with my face down, breathing very deeply. My heart was pounding heavily. The storm covered up my narrow tunnel again, but finally Krikštanis and I managed to crawl out. Everything around us was in the grip of the hurricane. A step and a half in front of us nothing was visible, and the whirling of snow was wild. We were immediately hurled down and fell on top of each other. Both of us started crawling on our knees and our bellies, fighting against the elements. We kept our heads down so the wind would blow over them and not obstruct our breathing. My heart was pounding for lack of air.

We clutched at every log, at every piece of ice, and continued crawling. I enjoyed the struggle, clenched my teeth, and, centimeter

by centimeter, fought the mad elements. I felt my hands going numb inside my mittens and my knees becoming wooden in my wadded trousers. Never mind, they would thaw out again. My trousers were filled with snow, which spread like a cold lotion over my body. Several hours must have passed. Finally, we found that we had reached a storehouse full of planks. We took five long planks each and began to run. The wind thrashed our backs and lifted us off the ground, together with the planks. I could not stay on my feet, I kept slipping, falling down onto my booty, getting up and running again. I was overwhelmed by a desire to laugh. Finally, the brick barrack came into view or, to be more precise, only the flat roof with the short pipes which were supposed to be its chimneys. We counted the chimneys and, finding our own dwelling, started digging our way towards the entrance. Though the hole had been covered up with snow already, we soon discovered a softer layer of snow and started pushing in the planks one after the other. Then we followed the planks. Krikštanis was the first to try to push himself through the opening, but with his wide shoulders, he kept catching on the door frame. Now his front half was in the barrack, but his bottom was still in the snow. Finally, his lower half disappeared as well, and in a few seconds we were both inside.

A couple of minutes later the thick planks were crackling away in the iron barrel, turning its thick sides and its pipe red. Everyone's mood lifted. We unpeeled the sacking and cloth from our feet and attempted to dry out. I heated some water in a tin and took it to my mother and my brother to drink. But hot water only irritated our stomachs and aggravated the hunger. When would it be twelve? We still had to spend the whole day in the cold, dark barrack, which would not warm up even if the whole store of planks were burned. Dirty, soot-covered faces with hungry, sunken eyes, glinted in the light of the yellow fire. All the faces said one thing only: Give us bread!

Every morning we crawled out of our barrack and started creeping through the grounds of the factory. We moved very slowly, hampered by the sacking on our feet and lacking strength. We went downhill to the shore of the river. There we saw huge piles of logs, stretching as far as Konstantinovka; another stack of logs was frozen in the ice. Our group consisted of Daniliauskas, Totoraitis, Totoraitytė, Štarienė, Nausėdienė and myself. Krikštanienė was our group leader.

We found the pile of logs covered with snow, and there was no sign of the hole from which we had taken our logs. We started looking for sledges, shovels and sticks. We found our sledges buried deep under the snow. We cleaned an area, uncovered a pile, and started tearing logs from it with levers. On one side of the hole medium-size logs were laid aslant, making it easier for us to lift them. Having dragged one out, we put one end of it on a small wooden sledge and, harnessing four of us to each sledge, tried to move one after the other. If the logs were not very thick, only about twenty centimeters in diameter, we put two on a sledge, but if they were very thick, forty or fifty centimeters in diameter, we found it very difficult to cope with even one.

"Ready, steady, go!" We heard the order from Krikštanienė, and with all our strength we tried to move. The ropes, strained to breaking point, hurt our shoulders, but the log would not even stir. We repeated the procedure. Once again we summoned all our strength and, biting our lips, we tried to break forward, but the log refused to move. Antanas Daniliauskas' rope snapped in two, and he fell flat on his face on the ice, blood smearing his nose. Eventually we managed to shift the log and started dragging it up the hill. An ice-covered track for sleds, about a meter in width, facilitated the upward trek. When dragging the log up, we had to support it on both sides with ropes lest it slide down the hill. The rope cut like a knife into my shoulders, and I heard blood throbbing in my temples and the arteries of my neck. We dragged a log halfway up the hill, all of us nearly fainting with weakness. Our bodies doubled over, our hands touching the ground. Somehow we took one more step, followed by another. The rope pressed my left shoulder, and it seemed pliers were squeezing my heart. Everything started reeling around me, snow and hill merging in the motion. God, help us drag this log up, just this one! One more step, just one more. Finally we reached the top. We allowed ourselves a rest there. Gradually shapes became clear, and the pain in my chest subsided. I wondered what other people felt. Did they experience the same things I did? Did they feel as if every step were tearing out their bellies and squeezing their hearts? Probably not, because they were much stronger than I was, mature. When I was sent to join her team, Krikštanienė told me that I would have to work the same as everybody else did; they did not have work for children. I could not work less, drag less, or lift less, for the pay was divided equally among all the members of her team.

We pulled the log up to a pile. We lifted it from the sledge and, all together, tried to heave it up to the third layer of the pile. Again I felt something like a knife piercing my bowels. It lasted only a minute. With our sledge empty, we went down the hill again. If only this part could last a bit longer! It was so good not to pull any ropes!

We managed to move two more logs. We lifted them out of the hole and, with some difficulty, laid them on the sledge. Again the rope started pressing against my back and my chest. Again and again and again, only this time it had to be faster and faster and faster. My blood throbbed, my legs slipped, and something stabbed my bowels. I wished I could grow up more quickly, so the work would not be such torture.

Days passed very slowly, every one of them unbearably difficult and oppressive.... But at one o'clock we threw down our tools and dragged our feet to lunch. That was the happiest moment of my existence. I used to look forward to it all the time and dream about it when sleeping! Lunch consisted of a cup of hot water and a piece of fragrant bread with a nice crunchy crust. I crept into the barrack and by the light of a burning splinter, I saw my mother lying on our bed. I saw two pieces of bread there, for me and my brother.

My head was dizzy with happiness and weakness, my mouth full of saliva, but I still tried to control myself. I managed to untie the strings and unpeel the ice-covered sacking from my feet. I turned the piece of bread over in my hands, the whole day's ration, and I tried to prolong the pleasure. My hands shook and my feet shivered. Another minute and my teeth would bite into this delicious bread. I tried to chew it slowly, to savor it, and to prolong the pleasure by drinking water in the process.

"Mother, was any cake ever as tasty as this bread? Could it be tastier than bread?"

A burning splinter flashed in the darkness, and twenty-five people, with their eyes fixed on one point, were eating. A light flashed in my mother's hands, and I saw her eyes, filled with very deep pain.

"Mother, Mummy, dearest, we shall live. We have to live. We shall return. Do you hear me, Mummy ??!!"

VI

On the first of December they started a primary school. I became a seventh-grade pupil. To earn my bread, I had to drag logs four hours a day until lunch time. At noon I felt as if I were reborn. When everybody went home to have lunch, I too threw off my rope, dragged my huge sack-covered feet to the barrack, and ate my ration. Then I grabbed the old briefcase, Krikštanis' inkstand, and ran to school.

Our school consisted of two small houses, drowning in snow. When I entered the classroom, I was greeted by my friendly classmates. They suggested that I sit closer to the iron stove. I unwrapped the ropes and sacking from my feet and pushed them under a bench. Then I tore the frozen headscarf from my face and brushed the ice off my eyebrows. The classroom was very small, with just enough space for four benches and a small table for a teacher. The bell rang and we took our seats. There were six of us. I usually sat on the front bench, together with Tautvilas Stasiūnas. A Finn, Kekonen, and a Yakut, Semyonov, took their places behind us, followed by two Yakut girls, Ptitseva and Trokhova.

While the teacher was speaking to us, I felt the odor of fresh trees, combined with the fragrance of a forest, something very agreeable. An infinitely pleasant warmth penetrated my body. God, let this lesson last longer, so that I do not have to return to that dark cave that is our barrack! I felt cocooned in sleep, but logs kept appearing in front of my eyes and the open blister smarted in my shoulder. Forty-five minutes passed like five minutes. Why had lessons seemed so long in Lithuania? Here I did not have the slightest clue about Russian grammar. Algebra was very difficult too. I knew that I should have been placed in sixth grade instead of seventh.

"You must have forgotten the basics of algebra. You do not seem to practice enough. Try and remember the rules," said the sympathetic Anna Mikhailovna.

In my torn felt boots and dirty wadded trousers, holding a piece of chalk in my hands, I stood at the blackboard. I wondered how I had got there. It must have all been a dream. I was warm, surrounded by burning candles, and I was being addressed as a human being: "You must have forgotten the basics of algebra." Alongside that, another voice kept ringing in my ears: "Go on, lift the log, and if you can't, you will leave our team." I kept lifting the end of the log, but everything started mingling and shimmering in my eyes, and it dropped. Curses ensued ... Then the school re-emerged. "Dalia, pay attention, you are dreaming again. Wake up from that stupor, please." Slowly, I recovered my senses, and my situation did not seem so strange any more. During the break, the six of us would sit around the stove, and each of us would impart something from our life stories. My classmates were as sorry for me as I was for them. They were devilishly hungry, just as I was, and lice, gaining strength from the warmth of the stove, started crawling across our backs. My classmates kept scratching themselves and shifting around. Like me, they would return to their cold, dark barracks, and all through the night, shivering under their lice-filled rags, just as I did, they would wait for one o'clock the following day, when they would be able to return to the warm school.

Finally, lessons ended. Lazily, trying to prolong the minutes in that paradise, we dried our foot-cloths by the stove and wrapped them slowly around our feet. We muzzled our faces with rags or scarves, leaving only the eyes uncovered. In the doorway, a raging blizzard grabbed Ptitseva's notebooks and, tearing them out of her hands, carried them skyward with a howl. Stumbling, finding it very hard to keep steady on our feet, we set out running across the snow-drifts.

Pressing my school bag, my father's old briefcase, to my chest, I crawled homeward. The wind thrashed my head and whipped my face, gluing my eyelashes together, fastening them so tight that I was unable to open my eyes. I had to pull my hand out of my mittens to wipe the ice off my eyes. The storm raged on. I crawled further, and still further, till I managed to locate the hole. I dug an opening into the barrack, lay down on my stomach, and crawled downwards. My head banged against the door. Finally, I was home. The school, like a beautiful dream, faded away. In the darkness I knocked over some-body's night pot with my unwieldy, ice-covered feet. The stench was sickening. On the way to my bed, I stumbled over someone, received a blow to my chest, and fell over. Krikštanis, Ašmantas Ad-olis, Kazlauskas and Žukienė were still sitting by the dying embers of the stove. There was no room there for anybody else. Krikštanis lifted a burning splinter to light a cigarette, and I saw his unshaven, soot-covered face, with its deeply sunken cheeks and eyes. His eyes glinted like a dog's from hunger.

"Kaunas prison, my friends, was a health resort by comparison. Every day they gave us a kilogram of bread and hot soup. They used to give us each a bowl of thick, meat soup, so fat that the steam could not be seen rising off it. Then they served the second course, which was also usually meat. The portion was huge. One did not suffer hunger there."

Silence. Everyone felt the torment of conversations, which evoked all sorts of associations. In an unhealthy imagination, hunger called forth various images of food. At night everybody dreamt about bread: this was the law of hunger. When you were about to start eating it, the bread disappeared. You would wake up with your head burning and your mouth filled with saliva.

"I dreamt last night that I was eating real country bread, and can you imagine how much I ate?"

The rascal was lying. He may have seen bread in his dream, but he could not have eaten it because it would have disappeared. Though nobody believed him, we allowed him to speak; it was tantalizing to hear somebody talk about bread.

Kazlauskas used to conjure the most fantastic pictures of food. He was psychologically unsound. Having been deported by mistake and subject to constant hunger, he had gone mad while serving his sentence in a political prisoners' camp. On being released, he joined his wife in the Altai region, and then they were both deported further to the north. On the way there he would eat all day long. He exchanged all his things for food so that he would be able to continue eating. Without recovering properly, he found himself plunged into a new kind of hunger. Interestingly, he even expressed regret at having joined his wife. "It was much easier in the camp than it is here," he used to say.

In the daytime, having harnessed up a cart, he gathered firewood for the bosses. On receiving his bread ration, he consumed it straightaway in the shop, unable even to leave the counter. When he was given his monthly ration of butter, he shoved it all into his mouth right away. The same happened with sugar. I once saw him sitting next to Krikštanis, holding a frozen piece of raw fish in his hands. He held the fish close to the stove, but without waiting for it to thaw, began to consume it. With fish intestines hanging from his lips and blood streaming over his hands, he went on eating, chomping loudly and trembling with excitement. His horrifying eyes glared occasionally in the dark. Five minutes later there was no trace of the scales or the tail, or the bloody intestines filled with excrement. You could never have expected him to boil the fish. I noticed Krikštanis smiling as he followed Kazlauskas' every movement. That was the end of the fish.

Kazlauskas also tried to take the dogs' food, when they were being unharnessed from the sledges and given their rations. It is not an easy task to take food from a ravenously hungry dog which has been dragging a sledge all day long. His face was very often bitten by dogs and covered with blood.

"Even in Lithuania I could never eat enough. How can you really satisfy your hunger? However much you ate, you would still be hungry. Ha, ha, ha ..."

He seemed to have gone completely mad. He was having hallucinations about being hungry in Lithuania. His small, thin body trembled, and he rubbed his hands, laughing silently. His clothes reeked of urine and excrement.

"I cannot understand, Mr. Krikštanis, how you, such an intelligent person, can speak like a rough yokel. Excuse my saying so," Žukienė prattled on.

"What a lady!" The democrat mocked her. "Why shouldn't I say things Remarque himself used to write?"

"Your Remarque must have been quite a cynic, Mr. Krikštanis."

"You call Remarque, the great realist, a cynic? If Remarque is a cynic, then you, madam, are an ass and do not understand anything about either politics or literature."

"Karl Kautsky once said, 'The famine is about to end because we have found some noodle soup here ...' Conversations we have reflect the kind of life we lead," Žukienė observed conclusively.

The barrack was completely dark. Everybody was lying on their bed, keeping their bruised legs bent. I would have been very happy to be able to bend my knees and not have to move them, but I knew that I would find it very difficult to unbend them in the morning. I would have to use force and suffer excruciating pain straightening out my stiff knees and lifting them up, just to put my feet on the floor. I took my place on my bunk and, seated between Prapuolenienė and my mother, I lit a candle, which I had stolen from the school. I was trying to do my homework for the next day. Ice started melting from the ceiling, and a piece of snow fell down my neck. My hands were freezing, and I was shivering with cold. I was trying to do sums. Friends and teachers kept flashing through my mind like mirages. The candle was flickering, and my head was dropping to my knees. The icy barrack, with its lice, hunger, and the stench of excrement, was drowning in darkness. As I squeezed myself into the narrow space between two bodies, images of my childhood flitted by, as if in a film. With my eyes wide open, I gazed into the darkness. I wanted the chance to speak to somebody, to press myself closer to them. I wanted moral support: to have somebody very strong standing behind me, helping me not to feel absolutely alone. I wanted somebody to console me. I pressed myself closer to my mother, wanting to kiss her, but I felt tears on her face.

"Mummy, Mummy, I shall graduate from school in the spring, and they will let me go to the technical school in Yakutsk. I shall get you out of here, Mother; we will make it and get on, I promise you."

My mother's hand was stroking my hair.

"Broniukas," I heard Krikštanis' voice. "We are sure to survive it all. We are young and strong, we shall live on. Grinkevičienė and Atkočaitienė are old and sick; they may not last very long. But we shall survive, and we have to go on."

Somebody peed into a tin, and then crept back to his place. Nausėdienė's cigarette glittered in the dark.

VII

Death, accompanied by typhus, lice, scurvy, and cold, settled into our horrible barracks. The hospital, in a neighboring building, was packed to capacity. It was more like a mortuary than a hospital. The sick and the dying lay on bare, snow-covered planks. The majority of them were delirious.

Vidokleriene, whose son died yesterday and was lying naked in the porch of the hospital, shouted, "Akaša, why are you playing a burial march for me?"

A storm had long ago covered the door with snow, the fire in the stove had died out, and the wind was blowing snow down through the chimney. The stove kept shaking and whistling with the storm. All around was darkness. The sick did not feel the cold. Some of them were even hot, others were unconscious, and still others had passed beyond the walls of the mortuary.

For three days nobody could enter the hospital, for the door was covered by a mountain of snow. On the fourth day, the hospital did not have any food or medicine, not a drop of water and no firewood. Corpses lay alongside the living, and the nurse, Onutė Polek, was unable to deal with them by herself. She moved from one patient to the next, to see whether they were still alive. Balčiuvienė, choking and wheezing, kept calling out for her husband. The little daughter, Zita, was lying next to her and shaking her mother's head: "Mummy, Mummy, don't die, Mummy."

"My God, Almighty, have mercy upon these people, have mercy upon the sick; stop this storm, please," Onutė pleaded, weeping hysterically, as she knelt in the center of the mortuary. "God, my God ...," she went on screaming, and in the dark you could feel her body shivering. Her crying merged with the noise of the wind, and with the wheezing and coughing of the sick.

Our barrack seemed to be illumined. Candles were burning on both sides of Atkočaitienė's corpse: a candle for each side, which meant that somebody must have stolen them from the office and saved them. Her nose was sticking out and seemed to be unnaturally long; lice were scurrying across her yellow, emaciated, and smoke-blackened face. I had never seen such a plethora of lice—

black masses of them crawling across the nose, eyelids, and lips, disappearing in her ragged clothing. I was taking advantage of the candle light, reading a history of the Middle Ages as I stood there.

Yesterday I had sat in front of the door of the stove, studying. Nobody bothered to drive me away because I had procured the boards which were burning in the stove; everybody had to keep a respectful silence. By the light of the fire, I noticed that Atkočaitienė, while making soup from her bread ration, was also ladling some pieces of bread out of Kazlauskienė's cup, where two hundred grams of bread were boiling in two liters of water.

I touched her hand and asked, "Are you, an ardent Catholic, not ashamed to steal?"

She grabbed her cup and, crawling back to her bunk, started to devour the food greedily. Only noisy gulping sounds could be heard in the dark.

Just the day before, that pious woman had been singing hymns and, rosary in hand, praying in the silence of the barrack.

On hearing her pray, even Aris had asked, "Daddy, where is God?"

"There is no God, Aris," thundered the "emperor's" voice in the icy darkness.

"My God, have pity on him, he does not know what he is saying," Atkočaitienė could be heard whispering.

Jasinskienė noticed that some of the grain which she had stolen from the collective farm in Altai had been pinched from her. After lighting a splinter, she saw that there was grain strewn around Atkočaitienė's bunk. She grabbed a stick and with all her strength, started beating the suspected woman on the face and hands. Atkočaitienė fell to her knees and started thumping her chest, swearing that she had never taken any grain, but pitiless whistling lashes kept falling on the old woman's shoulders. We pulled the stick out of Jasinskienė's hands. Atkočaitienė confessed to the deed, and Jasinskiene forgave her. She even kissed the woman's lice-covered face.

Led by Abromaitis, the team for taking away corpses arrived, and Atkočaitienė was now carried feet first out of our barrack. Žukienė appropriated the candles and advised me to occupy the vacated place. I considered myself very lucky.

I was sitting with Krikštanis by the stove. "Well, Dalia, you are very actively, even furiously, fighting with life," Krikštanis said. Blood rushed to my brain from pleasure at the compliment. Totoraitytė descended from her bunk and, turning her bottom towards us, settled herself on the bucket. She had diarrhea and ten times a day she took up this position, showing us all her bare backside. The bucket was full, the stench was unbearable, and her mother, unable to carry it out through the blocked door, would pour the stinking lot onto the heap of snow in the middle of the barrack. We could not bring any water in either, so we would take snow from the very same heap and, after melting it in tins, drink it.

The number of planks in the storehouse dwindled by half. As there was no firewood to be seen anywhere around, everybody stole; we did not have the strength to drag wood ten kilometers from the forest. Barrels and boards crackled in all the barracks. Sitting in front of the fire, we would roll up our trousers, pick lice, and clean the pus from wounds in our legs. Lice liked wounds, but they also made us itch. We all had open wounds, which did not heal for many months, and every evening we had to tear off our trousers, which were stuck to the wounds. It was painful, and we could barely endure it.

It was light in our barrack. Almost everyone had either a splinter or a candle, and we were all busy hunting for lice. This gave us a certain satisfaction: "Well, you rascal, you can bite me, but I can crack you between my fingernails, and that's the end of you." Hunting in our shirts was an easy job; it was much more difficult to search for them in wool, but that gave us an even greater satisfaction. Slowly, we perfected our skills: at night we managed to hunt in the dark and throw the lice into a glass, and in the morning pour them out through the crack in the door. Jasinskienė did it in a much more straightforward way. She chewed every louse and spat it out. Grockis, who was sick, and had to lie next to her day and night, complained that he could hear her grinding her teeth all the time. The sound began to get on his nerves. Because of scurvy, Jasinskienė had cramp in her legs. She could not stretch them properly, and a lying person would simply be devoured by lice. In Altai, she had been the strongest woman, able to carry sacks weighing up to a hundred kilograms. In Trofimovsk, she sold her two-year-old daughter's bread card. With the money gained she bought more bread on her own card, on which the two of them lived. The grain for which she had thrashed Atkočaitienė came to an end, and finally the two of them lived on six hundred grams of bread a day. Her daughter, Dalia, was constantly wetting her knickers. When Jasinskienė asked me, I hung out Dalia's sweater and knickers, but they were stolen by somebody. The woman cried despairingly. She could not climb down from her bunk. She relieved herself up there. Lying on the wet, stinking rags, she shivered all the time, and to get warm she pressed herself against Dalia's small body. Grockis also had diarrhea, but he still had the strength to climb down and use the pot. Juozas and Oldas lay with their feet frozen. Only a few people in our barrack were able to use their legs. I was one of them.

My mother fell ill. Her face and head swelled up, her weight dropped to thirty kilograms. She became as thin as a little girl. Her ribs stuck out and her legs became very spindly; they were like bones covered with skin. She looked as if you could just pick her up and carry her outside. She was burning with fever. She couldn't see because her eyes were so swollen. Juozas and I, transfixed by terrible fear, just stared at her. We hugged each other and cried.

"Dalia, if our mother dies, I shall stab myself with this knife," said my brother, lying on his stomach. I felt his weak, long, thin body trembling.

My mother lost consciousness. For the first time in all those nightmarish months I started praying.

"God, let my mother stay with me. Let Mother live," I implored, hugging her numb body, her ribs, and her red, swollen, formless face.

Somebody was trying to dig a passage into our barrack. He crawled in and shouted that the trial had already started, and they were waiting for me. I crawled out together with Žukienė, who was coming with me as a witness.

"Goodbye, Mother; goodbye, my dear Mother." I started kissing her unfeeling body, face, hands and feet.

Juozas and I understood what had happened. She had sentenced herself to death by starvation. She had been dividing up her ration and quietly giving her share to us. We, hungry beasts, frozen and tormented, would snatch the bread without even asking if she had eaten herself. Juozas, we killed our mother; we were beasts, you and I. Mother, all heroes paled in my imagination, unable to stand the comparison with your strength, love and heroism. Matrosov, who stopped a tank with his body, was a pygmy in comparison with you, who sentenced yourself to a slow and painful death. That is the essence of a mother's heart! Goodbye, my Mother, because when I return after the trial, you will be cold already. You will be happy because you will not see your daughter being sent to jail. Goodbye, Mother. Žukienė pulled me away from the body of my mother, who was still warm.

VIII

I was sitting in the dock along with the other five accused. We were all being tried for stealing planks from the storehouse. In front of us, a judge was sitting at a table covered with a red cloth and lit with five candles. The judge was an eighteen-year-old Yakut, who was an auditor by profession. The Party had ordered him to act as judge because it would have been unfair to have the local judge perform the task. A secretary was sitting on each side of him. They were busy taking down every word. One of the women was a drawing teacher, Novikova, a Komsomol member from Leningrad; the other was a tough "Oberkomsomol," Mironova. She used to do anything to make her bosses happy.

An empty barrack, which usually served as a sweatshop in daytime, had been turned into a court. The two iron stoves were red hot and exuded warmth. My head was in turmoil; I saw unconnected images and faces shimmering in front of my eyes. I felt very sleepy. My eyes seemed to have been glued together.

As if in a dream, I heard Riekus' voice speak out: "No, that is not true, Comrade Judge. I did not steal. That day I was making a coffin and brought home only remnants of the wood."

Why defend yourself? What an idiot! What difference would it make where one died--in prison, or in that majestic death factory of Trofimovsk? My head dropped to my chest, and sleep overwhelmed me completely. The barrack was filled with spectators, all of them buzzing and humming for no conceivable reason.

"That is not true, Judge. I did not take any logs; that is, I did take some, but when I met Sventicki and he shouted, I dropped them and did not take home even a splinter."

I opened my eyes. I saw a seventy-year-old Finn standing in front of me. He had terribly sunken eyes, like a tortured dog. His face could have served as a model for a painter to portray starvation. Having endured the siege of Leningrad, where he had lived on a hundred and twenty-five grams of bread a day made of chaff and clay, he was brought to the death camp at Trofimovsk, and a ration of six hundred grams of bread, cold, scurvy, typhus, lice and polar winters. He was deemed a criminal. He had wronged the state because he had taken back to his awful barrack some wood for the stove, to thaw the ice off his face and eyes, and to dry his clothes, which were frozen into an icy armour.

In front of me I saw the Pole Sventicki take up his place in the witness box. He could have been called Judas and Golovkov combined, a Columbus of Trofimovsk. He would look out everywhere for stolen planks. He noticed the property of the state disappearing, but he would not even see the heaps of naked corpses lying like logs in a pile outside each barrack, courtesy of the very same state. He did not see that we stole in order to stay alive. No, beast that he was, he did see all of that, but he wanted to be a faithful dog and build a career over our dead bodies. I felt an urge to jump at him and sink my nails into his revolting neck.

"I deny all the charges. I did not take anything. I found the plank covered with ice on the river, when our team was hauling wood. It was only then that we took it home. The whole team can vouch for me."

All, including Markevičienė, were lying. The whole team was lying. All of the Soviet Union lied and would go on lying for ever; all of them had stolen, and would continue to steal. All four pleaded not guilty. Behind me, I heard the supportive buzzing of the crowd. My turn was soon to come.

A week ago, returning from school, I had found my mother, very weak by that time, in the barrack. She kept asking everybody to give her some water, but there wasn't a drop to be had. Groping around in the dark, I found a bucket. At the bottom of the bucket there were a few slivers of ice, left over from the snow that had been thawed in it the day before. The majority of the people in the barrack were unable to get up.

Žukienė lit a torch, and said, "Dalia, fetch some planks and light the stove. We will melt some ice for your mother, you will warm up, and I will be able to heat some soup. Nobody has lit a fire today; the sick people want water. Only you can do it. Krikštanienė has been standing in the bread queue for the last few hours."

I crawled out of the barrack. Silence, a deep silence, reigned all around me. It even seemed strange: there was no storm, no wind, only the frost, locking everything around me in ice. The mouth of the river, the tundra, and all of us in our barracks seemed to be chained down. The northern lights shone in the sky. As it was so light, my task was going to be difficult. I crawled up to the storehouse, squeezed in through the fence, and grabbed three thick and impressive-looking planks. I was stopped by the sound of crunching snow. Having heard my footsteps, a guard, wrapped in dog fur, was approaching. I threw the planks aside and dropped down, pressing my body against the tundra and pushing my face into the snow. After some time, I raised my head. The long furs were departing. I crossed my fingers and pushed the boards through the hole in the fence. I was on the other side in a jiffy. Clutching the ends of the boards under my arm, I crawled and dragged them homewards. I had to move faster. Finally, I reached the king of the barracks, the red brick building. I had no strength left, my head was reeling, and I was unbearably hungry. I was chewing and biting my lips, and pushing snow into my mouth, but the hunger would not go away.

The sky, meanwhile, was sparkling with real beauty! The majestic aurora borealis was shining in all its splendor. The views around me were magnificent: the endless tundra, cruel and vast like the sea, the mouth of the Lena, full of majestic pieces of ice, the rocks at Stolb, many meters high. Against that background only we lacked majesty: we hungry dogs, infested with lice and ready to give up the ghost in our icy, stinking barracks.

There was a creature moving in front of me. It didn't seem to belong to our world; it was just a symbol of death. It was searching for something edible in the rubbish heap of the fifth barrack. Idiot, what could he find? What would people throw out into the manure? Soon the people, crazed with hunger, would eat their own fingers.

Finally I reached our barrack. As fast as lightning, I threw the planks inside. I cut them up, and soon the stove was hot. I melted some ice and gave it to the sick. They added some salt and started to drink it. I started spooning hot tea into my mother's mouth. She was too weak to speak. It was very difficult to see whether a person was a man or a woman. All around me were bones, nothing but bones.

Suddenly, Sventicki and Antonov appeared, and lit a candle. Building materials were crackling away in the stove, and another pile of cut planks was lying in the middle of the hut.

"Who stole those boards?"

The answer was silence.

"Who cut up those planks?" the sly Pole asked politely, as genteel as always.

Silence.

I covered my mother up and crawled down from the bunk.

"I did."

"You?"

"Yes, I did."

Several heads looked up from their rags. The others did not react, for they were totally indifferent to everything. I was afraid for my mother, but she seemed unable to understand the affairs of our world any more. They wrote out a charge. Žukienė and I signed it.

"The defendant, will you stand up, please."

I stood up. Slowly the judge inspected my terrible feet, wrapped in sacks, my torn wadded trousers, my jacket made out of a dressing gown, and my thick plaits, and directed his narrow and piercing eyes straight into my own. The hall fell silent. On a side bench I noticed the headmaster of the school, Gulyayev, the director of the factory, Mavrin, and the king of food, Travkin. They were whispering something to each other. I felt strangely calm. I kept staring straight into the judge's eyes. That lasted for about half a minute.

"How old are you?"

"Fifteen."

They started reading out the charge. It took them a long time. Some candles were flickering on the red table, and shadows were crawling all over the red brick walls. There was no ice on the walls in that room. They went on reading something. My legs were shaking, as if heavy weights had been tied to them.

Why don't they let me sit down? My mother must be dead by now. Juozas is bound to be charged as well. In autumn, when we were busy unloading ships, he started pushing tinned food into his mouth, in the presence of all his bosses. He is tormented by hunger even more than I am; he finds hunger much harder to bear than I do. Yesterday he wanted to get up and crawl to the stove on his heels, because his toes were frozen, but he fell down and passed out. In the dark his beautiful face looked very white, and his thin body was light and helpless. My mother has died. Juozas will also die: he has already started passing blood, and this kind of diarrhea leads only to a pile of corpses.

Suddenly my mother's face appeared in front of my eyes, the face I remembered from my childhood. It was a beautiful and tender face, her eyes were huge, and the curls of her hair fell on her forehead. She was smiling at me. Mother, my mother, you must be gone by now, you must be getting cold, and I can't even close your eyelids. Juozas will be crying helplessly as he feels your cold body, small and thin like a child's, lying next to him. Why did you torture yourself for our sake? Did you want to prolong our suffering in captivity? Did you want us to put up with their scorn in prison, where they will send us tomorrow? You are no longer with us, and I don't care what happens to me now.

They were saying something to me. A thought flashed through my mind: how good it would be if they just took out a revolver and shot me on the spot. My body was powerless, and I was thinking only about reaching a speedy end. The quicker the better.

"I'm asking you, and you must answer me." I finally understood that the words were directed at me. "Do you agree with the charges?"

"Yes, I do."

There followed a pause.

"Do you understand Russian?"

"Yes, I do."

"Do you plead guilty?"

"Yes, I do."

The judge became confused. The hall grew restless. "Stupid girl." "What a child." "Defend yourself."

"Defendant, answer sensibly. Do you acknowledge your guilt in stealing planks from the storehouse?"

"Yes, I do."

My words were followed by a silence.

"Did you cut them up?"

"Yes, 1 did."

"Who made you?"

Žukienė closed her eyes and turned very pale.

"Nobody did."

"Did you go on your own?"

"Yes, that's right."

"Why did you steal?"

"To find something to burn."

"Do you know what state property is?"

"Yes, I do."

"Did you know that people are punished for this crime?"

"Yes, I did."

"Do you understand what you are saying?"

"Yes, I do."

"Where do you work?"

"I drag logs."

"They say you go to school."

"Yes, I do."

"Which grade are you in?"

"The seventh."

"Aren't you ashamed to be sitting on this bench here?"

A pause ensued. They repeated the question. The room was tense with a resounding silence. I heard somebody crying at the far end of the shed. Someone seemed to be feeling sorry for me. It was the voice of Lialė Maknytė, an eleven-year-old girl. She was shaking all over. For a minute, the court, the judge and the people disappeared, and another picture flashed through my mind. It was the twenty-eighth of May, 1941. I was fourteen, and I was hurrying to get to the theater. I was running across Vytautas Park. I was about to go down the steps there, when suddenly I stopped, as if under a spell. The sun was golden, a golden city spread out beneath my feet, and the smell of blossoms was enchanting. For the first time in my life my heart beat to the rhythm of spring, and my body responded to the spring of my life. I drew in air, closed my eyes, and felt enormously happy. My lips started to murmur, "Life, how wonderful you are. Youth, how good it is that you came, you are so wonderful! How charming life is!" Tears of joy welled up in my eyes. I ran down at full speed, summoned by the theater, music, joy and life.

Now I was standing again with my eyes wide open. But they were empty of any tears, either of joy or sadness; they were dry, and I could not weep any more. The beautiful picture of Vytautas Park had disappeared.

I felt how everybody was directing their curious gazes at me and watching me closely. Was I ashamed? Ashamed? Because I gave some water to my dying mother? Were you, well-fed Mavrin, Sventicki, and Travkin, expecting to see repentance in my eyes? Was I ashamed? You murderers, you should be ashamed and not I. The question was repeated.

"No, I am not ashamed."

"Sit down, please."

I flopped down on my seat. I heard turmoil around me.

Balamutas whispered into my ear, "Are you crazy, girl? What have you said?"

Žukienė was now being cross-examined. I heard some of her answers.

"No, it was the first time. She had never done it before."

It was certainly not the first time, Sventicki. If you collected all the boards I had stolen you would be able to cover all the roofs in Trofimovsk. The fool could not understand that we lived in the tundra, that there were no forests and no vegetation, and that a human being, even if he was a caveman, still needed fire. What could we do? Could we go down to get logs washed up by the river, a distance of ten kilometers? How could we ever bring them home? Could we use the corpses lying under our bunks? Better still, could we use those sick with dysentery and always dirtying themselves? Perhaps we could use Jasinskienė, who was always crying out in pain because her legs were twisted with scurvy.

The bench retired to discuss the matter. The discussion took a long time. I was overwhelmed with sleep, fatigue, and weakness. There was one thing that I desired more than anything else: to press my head close to somebody and fall asleep.

I was woken up by somebody prodding me in the side: "Stand up! This is hell!"

Riekus, Kobra and another Lithuanian were sentenced to two years in prison. At least that was what I understood. Because I was a minor and because I had pleaded guilty, I was allowed to go free. I felt that my teacher, Novikova, must have interceded for me. I was pardoned. What luck! Lialė was kissing me and crying for joy. What a beautiful soul you had, Lialė. Pretty soon life was going to teach you not to react so swiftly to pronouncements of good and evil, especially when the matter concerned other people and not yourself.

I crawled back and tore an entrance to the barrack with my hands. When I got in, I ran up to the bunks. I waited for a long time before daring to lift the rags. I climbed up and raised the rags covering her face. She was breathing! She really was breathing! I bent down and kissed her terrible, formless head and hands.

With my desire for life restored, I pressed myself closer to her, and blood started throbbing in my veins.

"Mother, you will recover, I know you will. Mother, they have not gotten me yet. Love is stronger than death. We shall live, do you hear? We may even return home. Mother, forgive us for not taking proper care of you, for allowing you to commit suicide." She was lying unconscious, but I believed strongly that she would recover. I believed that she would get back her strength, even though nobody else believed it, even though the team that collected the corpses had already come to our barrack and were ready to take her away. She was breathing, and I was sure she would continue to breathe.

I dragged some wood to the barrack and lit a fire. That evening they sentenced Albertas and Platinskas to three years in prison. Albertas' mother could not get up. Though hardly able to stand on his feet and constantly reeling as if he were drunk, Albertas could still walk. One day his mother had begged him to get some bread.

"Mother, where would I get it from?"

— "Steal it," came the reply.

At night, he and Platinskas quietly left the barrack, stole into the bakery and took two loaves of bread. When they saw so much bread, they became dizzy and couldn't even wait until they got out of the bakery. They started to gorge themselves. At that moment they were not thinking of the guards, or the trial, or prison. Each swallowed an entire loaf and might even have died of overeating. They wouldn't have noticed an earthquake. The guards caught them both finishing off a loaf. One loaf weighed about three kilograms. While the guards wrote out a charge and took them off to the cells, they were still gulping down their bread, wanting to have their hunger satisfied at least once. As Albertas put it, they did not feel satisfied, even though their stomachs had no more room for food. Two days after his arrest, his mother died, without tasting the hoped-for bread.

Dzikas and another Lithuanian were tried for forging bread coupons. Instead of getting bread, they got three years in prison.

Another day, Borisas Charašas was also tried for stealing planks. He was a very handsome sixteen-year-old Jewish boy. He followed my example by pleading guilty, but as the ploy was not new any more, he was sentenced to a year in prison.

IX

Our barrack had been turned into a hospital ward. Scurvy was bringing a great number of people down. Everybody was sick. Anybody who claimed that in the polar region noone got scurvy would just be laughed at. Everyone was ill, but with different stages of the disease. In the initial stages, the gums would bleed: they swelled up and the teeth turned blue. Afterwards, the teeth would start coming loose and fall out. It did not cause pain, and the roots of the teeth remained. Then cuts would appear on the legs. For months they did not hurt. It was even strange that those open wounds caused no infection, because our dirty trousers stuck to them. Maybe lice ate all the bacteria off the wounds. Joints and muscles, especially the knees and calves, began to hurt very badly. The only solution was to lie down less and move about more. In the morning it was hard to stretch out our legs; they seemed to be made of lead. We would crawl down from a bunk and start moving around on all fours. The pain was unbearable. It felt as if hundreds of knives had been stuck into our legs. When we went to work, we crawled out of our barracks on our hands and knees.

We started bringing back wood for the office, the bakery, and the bathhouse, which was about to start operating. Our team consisted of five people: Krikštanienė, Štarienė, Prapuolenienė, Nausėdienė and myself. I was always begging them to leave earlier in the morning because I didn't want to be late for school. I always was. One after the other, we crawled out of our barrack; we slowly put the harnesses over our shoulders and crawled, dragging the empty wooden sledges. Then we went gently down the hill. Our bent figures waddled, our legs were wide apart, and we did our utmost to prevent them from touching each other. Tortured by the pain, we covered the first kilometer with great difficulty; the knees simply refused to bend. Then I began to understand my grandmother, who had complained that because of the pain in her legs she found it very difficult to walk. She would waddle and walk very slowly; you could see that every step demanded a huge effort from her. In Trofimovsk we walked the same way, maybe even worse.

In front of us we saw the ice-covered mouth of the Lena. The river was several kilometers across. Where it was not covered with snow, the ice was as smooth as a mirror. We could hear a muffled thundering sound, as if produced by a cannon. Gigantic cracks would appear, covering the width of the river. We stopped for a short rest, even though we knew that later on we would find it even more difficult to move our stiff, leaden legs. Then we sat down on our sledges. We were a tiny dot against the background of the majestic, thundering mouth of the Lena. In the distance, the shore and Trofimovsk could be seen. We wanted so much to stretch our aching legs, which simply refused to take us any further. But if we stretched them, they might go completely numb. Who would drag us back to the barrack? We went on, dragging ourselves further. We were overtaken by Staniškis' team. Staniškis himself was very unsteady on his feet and walked with a lolloping gait. He seemed to be dreaming. He was followed by Šakalys, wearing the green coat of a Lithuanian army officer. Though I was always wearing mittens, my hands would usually go numb, and I would start hitting them against each other until I felt some pain, but none of it helped. My bladder was affected by the cold, but when the need arose I would have to let it run straight down my legs, for if I unbuttoned my trousers I would not be able to do them up again.

We covered a mere nine kilometers, though it felt as if we had crawled a hundred and fifty. With great difficulty, our wooden shovels pierced the hard snow; only seldom would we find a stick, a stump, or a small log washed up by the river. Štarienė would lay the sticks across each other and make a hollow pile big enough to hold a human being inside it. The sides were covered with stumps. It looked about two cubic meters in size, though in reality it would not have been even one cubic meter. We bound it together with ropes and harnessed ourselves in. The wooden runners, made from wide planks, slid with great difficulty. Staniškis was much better off than we were because he had horse sledges with iron runners, which he had gotten from Vanagas as a favor. Both men were from Panevėžys.

It looked as if the days were returning. The lightest moment was like a milky twilight. Even that was pleasant to behold, because for months we had been submerged in complete darkness. Step by step, with great difficulty and very slowly, some fifteen sledges, drawn by harnessed Lithuanian and Finnish slaves, went forward, looking like a funeral procession stretching over several kilometers.

Bent to the ground, nearly on all fours, we pressed ahead with all our strength. The sledges would not slide, and every step forced us to summon up our strength to the utmost. But for the loop I was harnessed into and kept hanging on to, I would have fallen. My hands and feet were frozen stiff. The small headscarf covering my face had been turned into a horn by my frozen breath and would not let any air through. My eyelashes seemed to be chained down, and would not let me see anything. We looked ridiculous and hopeless, viewed against the backdrop of the majestic ice mountains of the Arctic Ocean. We looked like Repin's painting of serfs dragging a ship.

Compared to those mountains of ice, with harnessed people resembling lice, Repin's picture would seem to be an anthem glorifying human labor. We were sure we would never reach Trofimovsk although it was very close to where we were at the time. Everything around us was trickery, or mockery of nature. It was always like that in the Arctic Circle: the hours dragged on as if they were years, or even an eternity. I felt that I had been pulling that cart since I was born, but it had hardly budged.

Again I remembered Repin's picture. Which of us would not have agreed to exchange places with those serfs? After the polar winter of Trofimovsk, dragging barges along the Volga would seem like a holiday on the Riviera. Somebody suggested that if we wanted to pass the time more quickly, we should think or dream about something.

The only thing was to think of Repin's serfs dragging that ship. Their exertions were like taking a stroll in comparison with our cavalcade. In Kaunas, I had often watched the old nags unable to pull their carts. I had tried to guess what they would be thinking. In Trofimovsk, I realised that they could not have been thinking anything. The head was absolutely empty. People moved mechanically; if they stopped, they might not be able to walk again. I felt I was slowly turning into an animal, dying on the ice, harnessed to a cart which I was unable to pull. The head was empty and free of any thoughts.

When we got to our destination, we would be able to gulp down our rations and our slices of bread, which were drawing us back to Trofimovsk like a magnet. We filled any holes in the outside of the hollow pile so the guard would not suspect anything. The mountain we had to climb was a real Golgotha. It was a Calvary. Straining on our harnesses, we stumbled and slipped. The ropes strained against our chests, and sometimes we had the feeling that blood was about to burst out of our mouths. For the first time in my life, I experienced an aching in the chest, as if somebody were pressing down on my heart. The young heart of an immature organism protested against the unbearable load. I felt faint and was on the point of losing consciousness. In comparison with that Golgotha, the hill of Trofimovsk, concealing its heaps of corpses, did not make any impression on me, nor did it arouse any fear in me. It was on that mountain that the first disgusting swearwords left my mouth. Each time, helplessly dragging our carts up the mountain, we would become furious beasts, ready to tear to pieces anybody who had enough to eat and did not have to work. But we had to grit our teeth and get to the top of the mountain.

I watched Vanagas as he counted up what was in the sledges. For any uncounted centimeter we were ready to beat him up. He did not seem to realise that every stick had been brought back at the cost of our blood and our lives.

When Mother was ill, it was my duty to buy the bread. But I could not spare the time to stand in the bread queue because there were so many people waiting outside the shop, and the headmaster might tell me off again if he caught me coming to school late. I returned to the barrack, grabbed my books and my ink, and with a completely empty stomach, slowly marched off to school. It was the second lesson already. I entered the classroom without taking off my frozen scarf or rubbing the icicles off my face.

"Why are you always late?" Gulyayev asked.

"I've just been collecting firewood. I've just come from work."

"I won't tolerate it any longer. You'll have to choose: either you study or you work. If this goes on, you will have to leave the school."

I kept silent.

"Dalia, have you really just come from work?" Ptitseva asked me.

I did not reply.

"Have you eaten yet?"

"No, Nastia, I did not get anything to eat. The bread queue was very long, and I didn't want to be late."

I experienced a strange sensation in my stomach. For the second day I had not eaten anything. I sat on the bench. During the break I did not have the strength to get up and walk to the stove. Hauling firewood seemed to have torn out my insides. I felt as if I were eighty years old. My feet were like two blocks of wood. I sat with my head in my hands and suddenly the present moment, together with the din of the classroom, disappeared. I thought I was sitting in my classroom in Lithuania; I could see the dear faces of R.Z. and B. School, Lithuania, home, childhood. Did I have a home? Did I have parents? Had there ever been people who took care of me, who worried about me going out into the street without wearing boots or going to school without my lunch? I could smell the tantalizing whiff of bread, which started to work on my nerves. Somebody touched my hand. Ptitseva was pushing something wrapped in a piece of paper along the bench. It must have been some bread. I knew her father was a fisherman, and they were not hungry.

"Take it, I don't need it."

The blood rushed to my head. What shame! I was being offered charity. And by my classmate! A demonic pride took hold of me.

"I don't need it, I have my own."

In her narrow eyes I could see deep compassion and an entreaty to take the bread. So, everybody thought I deserved their pity. I would have preferred to see hatred in their eyes, not compassion. Oh yes! I would have preferred to be punched, even not to eat anything for the next three days, but not to see that awful compassion in their eyes! Their sympathy struck deeper than the hunger!

I put my head down on the table, and tears started streaming out of my eyes. My throat felt squeezed by a shout on the way out. My notebook was wet, and tears were rolling down onto the bench. I could not even say why my tears were running down like that. I felt that in a minute I would not be able to stop myself from shouting; the screams would burst out of my breast, and I would start howling very loudly. There was silence in the classroom. All of us were adults, even though we were all just fifteen years old. Ptitseva was pressing herself against me. She had understood everything.

There were five of us in the class now. Semyonov had gone fishing a hundred and fifty kilometers away.

Then Kekonen was caught stealing, and Gulyayev expelled him from school. Gulyayev himself was notorious for the things he took home: the bread, the butter and cheese. His eyes turned white, and when he caught Kekonen by the scruff of the neck, he threw him against the door.

"Thieves are not welcome here!"

The boy turned to him and shouted, "Headmaster, you ... you are a thief!"

He rushed out through the door.

Tautvilas was demoted to sixth grade because he did not know Russian. Then there were three of us left in the class.

"I am closing the seventh grade. It does not pay to hire teachers just for the three of you. You may consider yourselves free."

My eyes clouded over as if I had received a blow to the back of my head.

X

Professor Vilkaitis and Staniškis died of dysentery. Vilkaitis had worked as a caretaker in Konstantinovka. Several days before his death, Zigmas Steponavičius, Vilkaitis' ex-student from the Academy in Dotnuva, had gone around all the barracks asking for a handful of rice for his old professor. Who could afford to give away rice when everybody else was also sick? Somebody had very aptly said that one could give something away only if one had it. Zigmas had asked Travkin to give him two hundred grams of rice, but Travkin was not one to give anybody anything.

Dysentery was a sign of the last stage of scurvy. Usually a sick person did not lose his appetite, and more often than not continued begging for food, claiming that he was tortured by hunger and that he was about to die of starvation. In fact, it was a hunger brought on by habit, because people sick with dysentery did not feel real hunger. The doctor prohibited people with dysentery from eating just anything. Their rations contained whiter bread than ours, but most of them would die anyway, one after the other.

Recovery was possible only one way: to consume as much fat and nourishing food as possible. The person was given his butter, five hundred grams of sugar, and American paté. He wolfed down the butter and the sugar, the paté and the daily ration of bread. The people around him would follow every mouthful with hungry eyes. They were sure that soon he would collapse, but sometimes, unexpectedly, a miracle occurred, and the dysentery was overcome. He started eating again and got better. In our barrack that happened to my brother and to Grockis.

Abromaitis and Tamulevičius' team took the corpses away. They constantly wove their way between the barracks and the hill with a heap of bodies on their sledge. Most corpses were naked, some were wrapped in sheets. Nobody could be bothered with burying them on the hill. They lay there frozen and piled up in a heap, like firewood. Because of the shortage of food, white foxes started to nibble them. Every night Misevičienė, the wife of a school headmaster, would go to the cemetery to try to put the scattered corpses in order.

In the seventh barrack, where some Jews lived, Gamzienė died. She was a beautiful Jewess of around forty years of age. In better times her family had been factory owners. In the Altai region we had shared a room with them. She was a very pretty and friendly woman, who loved her son, Nolia, more than anything else in the world. The boy was a tall, thin youth of eighteen, extremely capable and clever. Every evening all of us used to snuggle up close to the stove. In former times, when we were not so starved, we had all fostered the belief that we would soon return home. Gamzienė's son would close his eyes and sing to us in a deep voice.

Tamulevičius and his team entered barrack number seven to take her body away. The son was lying next to her. He was sick, and his toes were frostbitten from lying down too much and were already affected by gangrene. Lice were crawling across her face and bosom, and proceeded in the direction of the son and the neighbor on the right. Tamulevičius spotted a piece of bread, wrapped in rags, hidden in the dead woman's bosom. In the twinkling of an eye, he snatched the bread, quickly brushed off the lice, and shoved it into his mouth. Gamzienė's rags remained frozen to the ice-covered brick wall.

A day of torturous work had come to an end. I was sitting near the stove. Stolen planks were feeding the fire. We simply had to steal, though the trials were not forgotten. From that time on, two of us would go: one would take the planks and the other would stand guard. Only Nausėdienė could never bring herself to steal. Her very essence resisted, and she would not be able to take even a scrap that belonged to the state. She remained the way she had always been. At first we just wondered about her and considered her the black sheep of the group, but later her honesty started to get on our nerves. The rest of us were prepared to tear the roof off Sventicki's house.

Nausėdienė did not disapprove of our deeds; she simply said, "Believe me, I cannot do it."

As she was so unique, we decided to leave her in peace.

On Christmas Day, before we managed to reach the firewood on the other side of the river, a storm arose, but we could not bear the thought of returning home empty-handed. The way back turned out to be a real nightmare: the road was blocked, and we were surrounded by mountains of fresh, deep, soft snow. The wind hurled us down. Still attached to our harnesses, we fell over and rolled. The wind lashed our sides and carried away the sledge filled with firewood. It whipped out the sticks, which flew ahead of us, wailing and whistling. We lost our way. The dark polar night descended. We could not even recognize each other; we all looked like statues of ice and snow. There was snow in our gloves, in our trousers, and down our necks. Unprotected by her old, torn felt boots, Totoraitytė's toes froze. Her rope kept swinging about; she was barely alive and could not drag the load any further. We wanted to leave everything and each return on our own to the barracks: some of us might then survive this Christmas night. That seemed better than all of us perishing together. But Krikštanienė, a brave and excellent woman, who never lost her power of reason, ordered us to be patient. Soon we found ourselves in Konstantinovka and, with our faces turned windward, we crawled in the direction of Trofimovsk. Several times, the storm overturned us and our sledges, but the mountain that was our Calvary had been overcome.

Vanagas measured the wood with his eyes and ordered us to take it to the school. Trudging the last two hundred meters to the school was an extreme torment. Finally we stopped and, totally sapped of strength, the five of us silently disentangled ourselves from our harnesses.

Vanagas had crept back into his cabin a while ago. Nobody would notice if we emptied our load in that particular spot or somewhere else. Later, nobody would be able to prove anything. Our sledge began to move, and we started advancing towards the barracks. Nausėdienė's heart might miss a beat, but so be it; even she would likely enjoy warming herself by a hot stove on Christmas. On our way we met Mavrin, wrapped up in his fur coat. He must have thought that we were taking wood to the hospital. In five minutes the empty sledge was turned over and all the wood carried into the barrack. Shortly the fire was blazing. We had earned three rubles in wages as well as the firewood.

In that disgusting barrack, I stumbled on a pot again.... how revolting were the steam and stench of urine...

We were all frozen, our faces dotted with huge white spots, which we rubbed with snow. There were sores on our waists.

Krikštanis willingly expressed his readiness to chop the wood.

"Barniškienė, take your child away. I have to cut the wood."

Behind me was a stump on which we chopped logs. But there was something white lying on the stump. I approached it, bent down, and felt the corpse of a small child. It meant that Barniškiukas had died that very day.

"Where shall I put him?"

"Under the bunks."

The child's white body flashed before us for a second and disappeared.

Albertas crept into the barrack. He had come to say goodbye. He shook hands with everybody. I was sitting by the fire, and he sat down beside me, lighting a roll of tobacco. He gave me some tobacco to roll, and we sat there in silence.

"Dalia, I'm glad to be leaving this hell. It can't be worse in the prison camp at Stolb, it really can't. In any case, mother is already gone. I will persevere there for three years. Then I shall return to life. Then, Dalia, we shall live beautifully. I will persevere through everything. I never thought it was possible to desire to live so ardently."

Bringing his face very close to mine, he added with conviction, "We are young, we shall live. We have to survive."

Before going to fetch wood, I crept out of the barrack and stood on its roof. The roof was level with the snowdrifts around me. The barrack was buried in snow. The weather was uncertain. Snow was blowing across the ground, but so far there was no storm. The group of convicts, some thirty people, were walking downhill. There were many Lithuanians among them. I could see Dzikas, Riekus, several women, and Borisas. Petrikas, another Lithuanian, was carrying a gun and keeping guard over them. He had volunteered for that unpleasant job. I could also make out the slender figure of Albertas, dressed in a thin, blue autumn coat. It was madness!—he was definitely innocent. They would never be able to get far in this weather. One might as well expect them to stick their hands and feet in boiling water and not be scalded. He turned round and waved to me. Though the wind was quiet, snow was swirling more forcefully. The whole group soon disappeared in the whirl of a rising storm. Not only the distant Mount Stolb and the bank on the other side of the river, but even hillocks were invisible. Goodbye, once again, goodbye...but the wind suddenly howled and overwhelmed everything around me. Everything was in turmoil.

That night I dreamt about Albertas. He was crossing a meadow filled with beautiful flowers, picking them. Suddenly, straight in front of me, his face emerged, with its wonderful blue eyes. The eyes were sad, and his fair hair was tousled by the wind. "It's all over," he said, shuddered, and closed his eyes. I jumped up and screamed. A terrible wailing noise answered me. The sky was merging with the earth. Our barrack was shaking, the blizzard was dancing its mad dance through the holes in the ceiling, and snow was descending in whirlpools over shivering people, huddling close to each other under their rags. The polar elements were sweeping up, freezing, and killing everything in their path. The deafening wail became a shaking noise. The wild elements demanded victims.

They did not reach Stolb. God, cruel God, where are You? Where is Your mercy? God was helpless faced with that mad power. There cannot be a God. He is just a clay statue. Albertas ...

Slowly, the terrible howling subsided. Like an expiring animal, the storm began to die down.

Borisas and Riekus were the only ones to return. They had covered just five kilometers when the storm set in. They had not even crossed the Lena; nor could they distinguish the side of Stolb from that of Trofimovsk. Under those circumstances, the only option was to return home, but most of them erred from the path toward Trofimovsk. Everyone scattered in different directions, thinking that he alone knew which way to go. Finally, Borisas and Riekus somehow found themselves leaning against logs and crawled to the barracks.

Borisas' arm was frostbitten, and gangrene set in. It turned black. He lay in the seventh barrack, his black left arm thrust outward, hanging numb. The childish face of the sixteen-year-old boy was twisted in pain. He chewed his lips, holding back tears. He did not want to give in, and he sang out in full voice, but the arias were interrupted by shrieks of pain.

An emaciated Jewish girl with extraordinarily beautiful features pressed herself against him, her entire body trembling. In the darkness of the barrack, one could hear the ironical phrase "Laugh, pagliacci," followed by a silence. "My God," cried Borisas, "I haven't yet caressed anyone with this hand. Why have You taken it away from me?" Then he lost consciousness.

Riekus' feet were frostbitten, but he was hoping to escape gangrene. Nobody else returned. No team of huskies discovered any corpses. When they set off in different directions, they must have disappeared in the tundra near Trofimovsk, or in the labyrinthian estuaries of the Lena, or maybe in the cliffs at Sardakh, the icy tips of which glistened in the sun. One day, before the polar night set in, the corpses of Petrikas and Dzikas were found by accident. They were discovered by a Yakut and his huskies. He said he had buried them. That was what he said.

Goodbye, Albertas.

"We will live, Dalia. I feel that we will persevere, come what may..."

Goodbye, Albertas.

Translated by Izolda Geniušienė

D. Grinkevičiutė. *Lithuanians by the Laptev Sea* (Reminiscences, essays, letters). Vilnius: Lithuanian Writers' Union Publishers, 2002.

In the summer of 1953, Dalia Grinkevičiutė found herself in exile again, in Yakutsk. In 1954, having obtained permission to study in Omsk, she enrolled in the Medical Institute there. The following year, she returned to Lithuania and pursued her studies at the Institute of Medicine in Kaunas. From 1960 she worked as a doctor at the Laukuva hospital in the region of Rietavas (now region of Šilalė). The young doctor was continually persecuted. By order of Security forces in 1974, she was dismissed from work and evicted from the apartment that came with her position at the hospital.

Dalia Grinkevičiutė did not live to experience Lithuania's independence in 1990. She died December 25, 1987, and was buried in the Eiguliai cemetery in Kaunas.

COMPILERS' REMINISCENCES

Exiles in Kondoy: sitting (from the right) Adelė Kisielienė, Uršulė Miknevičienė, Birutė Merkevičiūtė-Jonkaitienė, Vytas Merkevičius (?), Viktoras Masaitis (exiled at age four); standing (from the right) Kazys Kurtinaitis, Gražina Jonkaitytė-Kralikienė, Miknevičienė's son Algis Miknevičius (exiled at nine), Marija Kurtinaitytė, and Liudas Jakubauskas. 1952.

Irena Kurtinaitytė, a middle school pupil in Marijampolė (then Kapsukas), 1956.

Kazys Kurtinaitis, Irena Kurtinaitytė, and Marija Kurtinaitytė in Kondoy, 1953.

Exiles in Kondoy: first row, from the left, Kazys Kurtinaitis, Algis Miknevičius, Ona Jonkaitienė; second row, from left, Gražina Jonkaitytė-Kralikienė, Irena Kurtinaitytė, Uršulė Miknevičienė; third row, from left, Marija Kurtinaitytė, Birutė Merkevičiūtė-Jonkaitienė, Romualdas Jonkaitis, Jonas Miknevičius. 1952.

Irena Kurtinaitytė

On March 25, 1949, eleven-year-old Irena Teresė Kurtinaitytė was exiled to Siberia together with her father, Kazys Kurtinaitis (1906–1988), and her aunt, father's sister Marija Kurtinaitytė (1905–2005). Her father was a farmer, who left behind thirty-eight hectares of land (ca. eighty acres). Her aunt, a teacher, was exiled under the falsified name Marijona Kurtinaitienė.

My father's side of the family harks from Pajevonis in the district of Vilkaviškis. His parents, my grandparents, Uršulė and Kazys Kurtinaitis, bought a thirteen-hectare farm in the village of Ožkabaliai in 1906. When my grandfather died during the flu epidemic of 1918, Uršulė Kurtinaitienė (1885–1976) was left with six children, of whom the oldest, Marija, was thirteen. My grandmother took charge of the farm with her twelve-year-old son, Kazys; she enrolled the girls in school so they wouldn't be limited to farm work when they grew older. Hardly making a living, even having to mortgage the farm at one time, she succeeded in providing the girls some education. Marija, Teresė, Eugenija, and Anelė became primary grade teachers, and Albina, an accountant. In 1937, when all her daughters were employed, my grandmother sold the farm, paid back the remaining loans, and let

Irena's grandmother Uršulė Kurtinaitienė with her children in Ožkabaliai, ca. 1932. In front, Anelė Bajorinienė, second row, from left, Teresė Vilkienė, Uršulė Kurtinaitienė, Marija Kurtinaitytė; third row, from left, Albina Šaulinskienė, Kazys Kurtinaitis, Eugenija Tamulienė.

Irena's mother, Veronika Kurtinaitienė, 1931.

her son marry and move to his bride's village, Pavilkaujai.

Unfortunately, World War II and the successive Soviet occupations of Lithuania destroyed the family's hopes for a good life. In 1944, Kazys' wife and my mother, Veronika Kurtinaitienė (b. 1913), died. Eugenija's husband, Juozas Tamulis, emigrated to the West, and their newborn son died in an unheated hospital in Vilnius. In 1949, Teresė's husband, Vincas Vilkas, was arrested and deported to a concentration camp. He was initially imprisoned in Karaganda, where he worked in coal mines; later he was forced to labor in the digging of the Volga-Don canal. Anelė's husband, Kazys Bajorinas, who had recently earned a law degree, was constantly persecuted by the Soviets. Albina Šaulinskienė's family lived on the brink of poverty in Marijampolė. My father, Kazys, my aunt Marija, and I, Irena Teresė, were deported to Siberia in 1949.

My schooling began in the village of Antupiai, nestled by the highway between the towns of Marijampolė and Vilkaviškis. My first teacher was Vincas Zeikus, who taught at the Antupiai elementary school for many years. However, I did not attend school during winter months, for at age six, I could not make my way through the snowdrifts to the school. The second and third grades were accommodated at the Maziliauskas farmstead in our neighborhood; the teacher was Miss Lizdaitė. Fourth grade was, again, further from home, at the Skystimas farmstead. From that year, the fourth, I remember an ornery gander chasing children in the yard, and a no less ornery ram on the grass. I remember the teacher, Valentinas Bindokas, but the school work itself has faded from memory.

During my fifth year at school in Lithuania, I attended the first class of the Gižai middle school, four kilometers from home. I vividly recall the fall of that year: warm, sunny, and dry. We children of neighboring villages used to return home in groups. Passing by abandoned farmsteads, we' d steal into the orchards looking for ripe apples and pears. Occasionally, the teachers would warn us not to walk through the town square. Upon returning home, I would find out that the desecrated bodies of slain freedom fighters (partisans) were laid out on the pavement in the town square.

In winter, neighbors would sometimes take us children to or from school on a sled, but not regularly. Although I missed numerous lessons, I kept up with the school work. My Auntie Marija, a teacher, tutored me at home and taught me perhaps as much as I would have learned in school. She used to conduct a dictation almost every day because, in her opinion, daily practice in writing was imperative. However, I did not complete the first year of middle school; we were deported to Siberia in March of that year.

A string of cattle cars, which began its journey at the railroad station in Vilkaviškis, took us to the Irkutsk region and finally let us off at the Kutulik station. From Kutulik we were driven by truck about forty kilometers north, toward the Angara River. We were settled in a little Buryat village called Kondoy.

The collective farm established in Kondoy was so poor that the local inhabitants had almost nothing to eat. Even the well was a kilometer and a half beyond the village. After the war, only elderly folk, women, and children remained on the farm, so there was no one to do the farm work. Consequently, the exiles who were brought here were forced to do all kinds of work in the fields and with the livestock on the farm, as it were sentenced to work on this farm. They worked every day, from pre-dawn to sunset without days off or vacations. And yet the collective farm did not have any funds to pay for the work. The exiles survived on the food they had brought with them from Lithuania.

Who knows how the exiles' predicament would have played out if, in a year's time, the farm in Kondoy had not been combined with a Ukrainian collective farm in the neighboring village of Tyrgetuy.

Those Ukrainians were also exiles, but they had been there for about twenty years and managed to make something of the farm.

Our living conditions in Kondoy were wretched. For four years we lived with two other families in a small, one-room house. There were bunks in three corners of the house, with very narrow passageways between them. In one corner were Uršulė and Jonas Miknevičius and their son Algis, about nine-year-old. In another were the three of us, and in the third, the widowed Adelė Kisielienė. Our lives were spent on those bunks: we ate, rested, and slept on them at night. We children did our homework and played on the bunks. In the fourth corner of the house was a large Russian stove, where we baked bread and cooked all our food. We cooked soup in cast iron pots, procured I know not where.

In the middle of the room was a little table, serving as a counter for the preparation of our meals. In wintertime, we even set up a little metal furnace (*burzhuyka*) beside that table. Local people heated such furnaces day and night. Exiles, who worked hard all day, couldn't tend furnaces all night because they had to get some sleep. Therefore, in winter, our little house used to be very cold at night. We slept on straw-filled mattresses in our clothing, with felt boots on our feet and scarves wrapped on our heads or fur caps pulled over the eyes. Water in a bucket used to freeze overnight. The windows were ice-laden. To open the door in the morning, we had to ax through the ice in cracks formed by irregular jambs. The temperature at night during winter was usually – 40 to – 50° C.

Children who reached the age of fourteen in exile were forced to work along with the grown-ups. But I was only eleven, so I attended the Kondoy elementary school, a one-room school house, with one teacher for grades one to four. I was placed in third grade and later in fourth. Although I had completed that level of curriculum in Lithuania, the schoolwork was difficult for me. First of all, I had to learn Russian. I remember my painful experience one day when I could not understand what the teacher was saying. She kept repeating the word *pepel* and appeared to be asking us to form a sentence with the word, but I didn't know what the word meant. Finally, the teacher approached the huge Russian stove, scooped up a handful of ashes, and said, "This is *pepel*." All the schoolchildren, first- to fourth-graders, burst out laughing....

As I was only attending school and not yet working, I became the main cook for my family at age twelve. I remember preparing the same kind of dumpling soup day in and day out because we had a supply of flour brought from Lithuania. In southwestern Lithuania, this was a tasty milk soup, but in Siberia we had no milk and used water instead. The process of making the soup was as follows: I slowly poured cold water into the flour; then, taking bits of the mixture between my fingers, I kneaded smooth, tender little dumplings. I dropped the dumplings into salted boiling water, let them cook for about five minutes, and the soup was done. I must have grown very weary of preparing those dumplings, as well as eating them, for once, having set the pot on the stove and gone outside, I totally forgot about the soup I was preparing. When I returned to the house, instead of soup, I found... a frothy liquid mess flowing over the edges of the pot. What was I to do? It didn't occur to me to throw out this slop and make soup from scratch, for I had never thrown any food away. I knew not to waste food; otherwise, we would go hungry. When my father and auntie returned from work, cold, tired, and hungry, I served them the frothy liquid slop. At first they ate silently, as I did. But my aunt could not restrain herself. Suddenly, in a calm voice, she said, "Irutė, your Dad works so hard... and you serve him such glop.... He didn't re-marry for your sake, so as not to subject you to a stepmother." I didn't say a word, but I felt awfully ashamed.... After returning to Lithuania, I never again made dumpling soup, not even the tasty kind with milk.

When I graduated from the Kondoy elementary school at age thirteen, I had a choice between working on the collective farm with grown-ups and attending middle school in Tyrgetuy. The first alternative seemed horrible to me because I had already experienced work in the fields during summer and fall. But how could I attend school in Tyrgetuy, five kilometers away from our village? In winter

I wouldn't be able to reach the school every day, with early sundown, cold, snow, and wolves lurking by the wayside. Where could I live in Tyrgetuy if exiles were crammed like herrings in their little houses? Where would I get food? The situation was complex. My loved ones didn't even consider further schooling in Tyrgetuy. No. It was impossible. Meanwhile, local Russian and Buryat children were getting ready for school…. To this day, I can't understand the source of my desire for education, but I was adamant in my demand: "I just want to attend school!" I climbed up to the little board attic in our house and did not come down for two days. I would not eat. I cried and cried… until my aunt finally called to me: "Come down! You'll go to school!" It was my victory; on the part of my family, letting a child attend school under the circumstances in our village was, indeed, a heroic venture…. I wonder if I thanked my loved ones sufficiently during their lifetime: thanked them for being literate and educated.

The first winter in Tyrgetuy, I stayed in a little room with Ona and Vincas Šulinskas. I slept on some kind of bench set next to their bunks. The second and third winter, I lived with a Ukrainian family, together with two Russian girls from our neighborhood, the sisters Tatyana and Yelena Salikova. In the home of the Ukrainian family, the Fedorinovs, life was lived on the floor, which they used to scrape very neatly with a knife. The floor was always clean and light.

Our hosts', the Fedorinovs', house consisted of only one room. Our hosts and their six-year-old daughter were settled in one corner. (The girl did not attend school yet.) We three girls, boarders, settled in another corner. In the third corner was a huge Russian stove, as usual in the houses of that area of Siberia; and in the fourth was a kind of animal shed and sheep-cot during winter. Here they kept a heifer, a few hens, and at night, even the grayish brown cow. In the middle of the room there was a table and, of course, a furnace. The housekeeper, Mrs. Fedorinova, did not work on the collective farm during winter months, so she could tend the fire in the furnace all night. The house was warm day and night…and wonderfully pleasant for us school girls.

After lessons on Saturdays, a group of us school children used to return to Kondoy. I was the only Lithuanian girl in the group. On Saturday evenings I used to wash up and do my laundry in pails of water from melted snow. Next day, Sunday, I would again join the group going to Tyrgetuy. Given some food to take with us, we'd load it into a bag or sack that we carried as a backpack. When the weather was very bad, one or another family would take our sacks to Tyrgetuy on a sled harnessed to a horse from the farm; of course, we would follow the sled on foot. I, a child exile, was then treated on a par with the local children.

Amid all that I might relate of my childhood in Siberia, all that I might remember and analyze, the most painful experience in the course of exile was the hard, and by no means childish, physical labor. From age thirteen, all children and teenagers, including those who attended school, had to work on the collective farm fields throughout summer and fall. Such were school children's "vacations" at the time: doing heavy field work along with grown-ups every day, from dark to dark, without any leisure days. During harvest, we used to pile up huge hay stacks with heavy wooden pitchforks we could hardly lift, all day, in the sun's heat. To produce animal fodder for winter, we pulled and dragged large, tangled sunflowers; working in pairs, we had to figure out how to load them onto a truck with those heavy pitchforks.

We used to work in grain-drying rooms not only during the day but also in night shifts—from dawn to dawn. After cleaning and filling bags with moist grain, we lifted them onto one another's backs and carried them upstairs to the drying stoves on the second floor. The immature spine and legs bent under such heavy loads. We constantly suffered from back pain. Exiles asked the collective farm supervisors at least to exempt children from work in grain-drying rooms; however, the collective farm lacked an adequate labor force.

In 1954, I graduated from the seven-grade school in Tyrgetuy. In October, after summer and fall work on the farm, I entered High school in Apkhulta. I stayed with Birutė and Romualdas Jonkaitis, who were raising their first-born, Gediminas, a toddler at the time. But I attended school in Apkhulta for only two weeks. When I received news that all children and teens who were born in 1938 or earlier were free, I left for Lithuania. My family seated me, together with four younger boys, on a train in Cheremkhovo, and we rode to Kaunas.

I am thankful to my Aunt Albina and Petras Šaulinskas, who sheltered me in Lithuania. Their family of five, living in a tiny house on the outskirts of Marijampolė, made room for me. With their children Nijolė and Mindaugas, I attended the Second High school in Kapsukas (now Marijampolė; the Rimantas Stankevičius School) for four years. Thanks to the Šaulinskas family, I graduated from High school in 1958.

I would note that my classmates from ninth grade at that school included Judita Sajauskaitė and Jonas Čivilis, who had also returned from exile in Siberia.

In 1957, my father, Kazys Kurtinaitis, and Auntie Marija Kurtinaitytė also returned to Lithuania.

Irena Kurtinaitytė Aras, Vilnius, 2011

Irena Kurtinaitytė Aras is an historian and a retired senior lieutenant of the Lithuanian Army. She participated in the independence movement of 1990-1991. For her merits in the formation and strengthening of the Republic of Lithuania's Army, she was awarded "The Lithuanian Army's Founder-Volunteer" medal; for her courage and service to the Republic of Lithuania, she received the "January 13 Memorial" medal and the LR Interior Defense Ministry's decoration "For Ousting the Russian Army."

She compiled (with Stasys Ignatavičius), authored chapters for, and edited The Los Angeles Juozas Daumantas Chapter of the National Guard: A History, 1964–2004 ("Los Angeles Juozo Dauman-to šaulių kuopos istorija. 1964–2004") *(2006). She also contributes articles to the Lithuanian press.*

Her daughter, Vaiva, and grandchildren, Tomas and Kristina, live in the United States.

Tomas and Kristina on the Hill of Crosses in Lithuania, 2009.

Vaiva Pechulis, Kristina, and Zina Markevicius, Los Angeles. 2005.

Irena, 2000.

Irena by the "Naujasis lankas" book exibit, LR Parliament, after presenting the Lithuanian edition of „Sibiro vaikai" („Children of Siberia"), June, 2011.

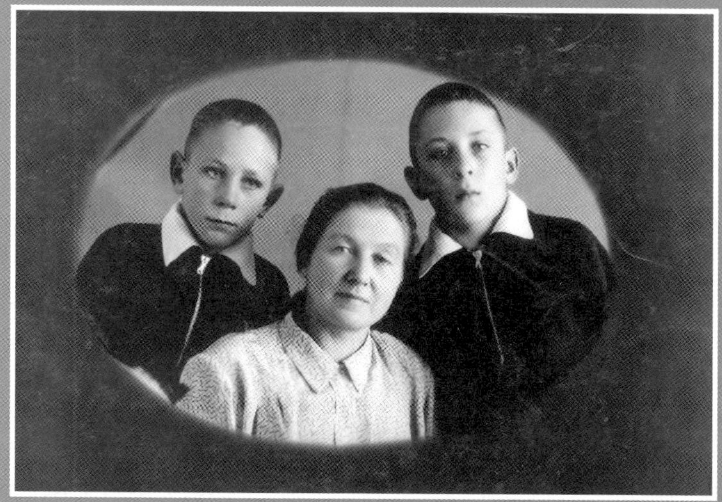

Eugenija Zavadskienė with her sons Vidmantas (on the left) and Arvydas in Bokhan, 1954.

Visiting with Lithuanians in Kharagun, 1955.
Sitting on the right is Stefanija Juodeikytė-Zavadskienė; in the third row, third from the left, is Eugenija Zavadskienė; in the top row, third from the right, is Jonas Zavadskis. In the photo on the left is Vidmantas Zavadskis.

Vidmantas Zavadskis

Four-year-old Vidmantas Zavadskis, his brothers Jorūnis (b. 1934) and Arvydas (b. 1942), and mother, Eugenija Zavadskienė, a teacher, were exiled from Viekšniai, district of Mažeikiai, to Siberia on March 25, 1949. His grandmother, Magdalena Juodeikienė, a farmer, and cousin Viktoras Zavadskis (b. 1939) were deported at the same time.

Vidmantas' father, Jonas Zavadskis, a teacher, had been deported to a concentration camp in Vorkuta in 1945.

I was born at a time of unrest, July 10, 1944, in the village of Slikiai, district of Kėdainiai, where my parents were schoolteachers. The Russians were attacking the Germans, bombarding Kėdainiai that day, and explosions were heard in Slikiai. Mother remembered how her loved ones tried to calm her down, saying it was the sound of thunder. I was the fourth child in our family. The eldest was Jorūnis; the second was Žygimantas, who died in infancy, and the third, Arvydas, two years older than I.

My father, formerly a teacher and a member of the National Guard, was arrested in 1945 and imprisoned in a concentration camp in Vorkuta. After serving an eight-year sentence, in 1953, he was detained there for two more years.

My early childhood memories are very diffuse, with only scattered retrievable episodes. We then lived in Viekšniai, where mother taught art and Lithuanian language. Arvydas and I were left at home alone when mother went to work, so I spent all my time with my brother, who educated me in boys' "street smarts." Snatching a red rag, we used to go tease a turkey penned up in the barn or cot. We rolled "cigarettes" from the leaves in a broom and smoked them, hiding behind a bed. I remember how Arvydas once tempted me to lick a frozen door knob and how badly my tongue hurt.

With the onset of deportations to Siberia, we used to go into hiding at night. I remember staying overnight in a house or farm where beans were being shelled in the evening. However, we did not succeed in evading the occupants' fury. In the spring of 1949, my mother, two brothers, and I, considered a "bourgeois nationalist's" family, were exiled to Siberia. Deported along with us were my maternal grandmother, *babunėlė* Magdalena Juodeikienė, who had lived on her farm in Zaventė (now Užventė), neighboring Viekšniai, and our nine-year-old cousin Viktoras Zavadskis. Viktoras' father, our uncle Stasys Zavadskis, like his brothers Jonas and Povilas, was already incarcerated in a concentration camp—from which he never returned. Viktoras' mother, Aunt Stefa, was hiding out at the time, and the "drivers" did not find her. Later, about 1952, she went to Siberia to seek her son and her mother, and she also became an exile. With Viktoras we are twice cousins because our fathers are brothers and our mothers, sisters.

I remember very little from those terrible days of deportation. I retained an image of the lights, way over my head, on the truck that took us to the railroad station. The long ride in the boxcar is totally blurred in memory, as if in a fog. But I do remember "knowing" that we were travelling to see father.

Our train ride ended in the Svirsk station, just beyond Cheremkhovo in the region of Irkutsk. From there we were taken to Kamenka, on the other shore of the Angara River, which was the locus of a "slave market." The "traders" from the collective farms were not interested in our family because, among the six of us, only mother was fit for work. Some kind of official had to intercede to persuade them to take us along with other exiles. In Kamenka, as I heard later, I nearly tumbled from an icy bank into the Angara River, but someone caught me just in time.

We found ourselves in a village called Kharagun in the vicinity of Bokhan (region of Irkutsk). Bokhan was a part of the Buryat-Mongolian Ust-Ordinsk national district, populated mainly by Buryats.

There were some Russians there as well. Exactly how many Lithuanians there were in Kharagun, I couldn't say, but they were all peasant farmers from the district of Mažeikiai. Among them were many of mother's former pupils, who persisted in calling her "teacher."

Life in Kharagun was very hard. We moved from one dwelling to another. Winters were very cold. The walls of our rooms used to be covered with frost, and we slept in our clothes. However, local Buryats were not much better off than we were.

The most difficult lot in exile fell to our mother. We children rarely saw her. Throughout the day, she worked in the collective farm fields, at the farms, or in the forest. Yet all that work did not suffice to feed us. In the evenings she used to sew for local people with the Singer machine she had brought from Lithuania. She used to barter some of our clothing for food.

As I remember, the bread we usually had tasted bitter and prickled the mouth while chewing. Mother, being a worker, sometimes got better bread. Upon waking in the morning, I used to find a piece of that delicious bread under my pillow. Another great treat consisted of boiled potatoes with hemp salt, that is, ground hemp seeds mixed with salt. It seemed to me an extraordinarily delicious dish.

Numerous memories of those years are associated with the Singer sewing machine. As our particular way of life resulted in infestations of various critters in our hair, mother used to comb our heads above the glossy, varnished cover of the Singer machine. When those critters fell out, we would charge at them with hunters' alacrity and crush them with our nails.

I learned to read quite early, with mother's help of course. As far as I remember, I learned to read Lithuanian before I read Russian. Those lessons also took place by the Singer sewing machine. Mother sewed while I read. It was something like the scene depicted in a sculpture I saw years later, Petras Rimša's "The School of Hardship" (Lith. "*Vargo mokykla*"), but instead of a spinning wheel, there was a sewing machine.

When we were departing from Lithuania, mother took quite a few books with her. (The soldiers who drove us noticed them and commented that it would have been better to take more food, clothing, and bedding instead.) My favorite among those books was one about Br'er Rabbit, a collection of stories from African countries, abounding with illustrations. I remember that book vividly, as if I were holding it in front of me now.

In 1951, I entered first grade, and I wanted to attend school very much. My first teacher was a Buryat woman. It's a pity I don't remember her name, her patronymic, or surname. I was in the same classroom with Arvydas, but he was in third grade whereas I was in first.

Fourteen-year-old Jorūnis and nine-year-old Viktoras began to work early on, while still attending school. They were also mother's main helpers with household tasks. Life was hard for them, as for grown-ups. I think exile was easier for those who were not involved in heavy physical labor.

We children, especially the little ones, quickly got used to exile and forgot about life in Lithuania. Nonetheless, when we used to come running home and grandma asked us where we had been, I remember answering that we had gone to Lithuania. The grown-ups' most urgent concerns revolved on the provision of food for their families. Children were not burdened with this problem. Though hungry, they explored the fields and went berry-picking in the woods in summer; in winter, they invented other pastimes. Local children made something that was a cross between a snow board and a scooter, and exiles replicated their handiwork. On a scrap of board rounded off in front, they spread cow dung; when this froze, they poured on water, which also froze and formed an icy crust on the entire board. Beforehand, they inserted a vertical rod with a crossbar into the board. Thus we used to skate, holding on to the handle and pushing against the ground with one foot.

We lived in Kharagun until 1952, when, by the commander's order, we moved to the regional center, Bokhan, nearer administrative surveillance. Mother, as a former teacher who knew Russian, used to defend harassed fellow Lithuanians and write complaints on their behalf. She had become an intercessor for them, in opposition to collective farm supervisors, for whom she had made considerable trouble. But we weren't the only ones ousted from the collective farm. The sister and brother Malakauskas were another undesirable family because hefty Bronius would never give in to the local Buryats and had often beaten them up.

Life was no less difficult for mother in Bokhan. For some time she worked for a group of geologists who were looking for oil-fields. Summer and winter, she dug foundation pits for drilling towers. When the geologists left, finding no oil, mother looked for another job. She sought work as a janitor in a pedagogical school, but she was not hired on account of her professional experience as a teacher. Later she found work in a kindergarden and other jobs.

Time passed. We children attended school and worked. My oldest brother, Jorūnis, graduated from High school and entered the School of Education and Culture in Irkutsk. Upon completing his studies, he worked as artistic director, and eventually director, of the Culture Center in Bokhan.

Father came to Bokhan in January of 1955, after serving his sentence and spending two more years of detainment in Vorkuta. He became an exile like us. I remember the cold day of his arrival and snow creaking beneath our feet as we walked to meet the bus from Irkutsk. Thus I became acquainted with father when I was ten years old. Oddly, I do not remember the moment of meeting father.

In 1958 many exiles were permitted to return to Lithuania, but our family obtained such permission only in 1965. Father travelled to Lithuania in 1959; he tried to find housing and work, but unsuccessfully because exiles were generally unwelcome there. He had to go back to Siberia, but of course not to Bokhan. He stayed in Suyetikha (now Biryusinsk), an industrial town sixteen kilometers from Taishet, in the western part of the Irkutsk region, where there was more opportunity for employment. Our whole family joined him there. We settled in a room with a little kitchen in a wooden barrack. There were many exiles in Suyetikha. For instance, there were six Lithuanian children in my class at one time.

In 1962 I graduated from High school and left for Tomsk to further my studies. I entered the Polytechnical Institute, where I studied until the end of 1967. After graduating, I worked in Omsk for a year. In the spring of 1969, having spent twenty years in Siberia, I returned to Lithuania, to Vilnius.

My parents might have returned to Lithuania in 1965, but they waited until I had completed my studies and went back in 1968. There was no warm homecoming for any of us in our country. Worse: we were considered strange birds in Lithuania, as we had been in Siberia…. It's a pity that neither of my parents lived to see the national rebirth of the late 1980's and Lithuania's independence in 1990.

The Zavadskis family after exile: Eugenija and Jonas; second row from the left, Arvydas, Vidmantas, and Jorūnis. Kelmė, ca. 1975 m.

Our family resembles many other Lithuanian families and shares the fate of many; it isn't exceptional in any way. My parents, of peasant stock, were first-generation intellectuals and patriots of independent Lithuania [1918–1939]. Their lives were ruined. The three Zavadskis brothers—Jonas, a teacher; Povilas, an actor, and Stasys, a military officer—were deported to concentration camps. Stasys perished there. Their parents, my grandparents Rozalija and Aleksandras Zavadskis, were exiled to the Krasnoyarsk region in 1948, and they died there in Siberia. My cousin Juozas Zavadskas was also incarcerated at a concentration camp. Another cousin, Benonas Zavadskas, a courier for the freedom fighters while still a high school student, was shot in the Šėta forest during a punitive military operation. Our family returned to Lithuania after many years of exile.

I will not speculate about our losses resulting from exile in Siberia during childhood and youth. But I know that we mustn't forget the past; our children and grandchildren must learn about it.

I have three grandchildren now: Rapolas, Arūnas, and Jurgis. As I write these lines, it occurs to me that the eldest, Rapolas, is the same age I was when we departed from Lithuania in the spring of 1949.... I cherish the hope that they, and all Lithuanian children, never suffer calamities of the sort we did when we were exiled to Siberia in childhood.

Vidmantas Zavadskis, Kaunas, 2011

Vidmantas Zavadskis is a computer engineer. After returning to Lithuania in 1969, he worked for institutions and companies in Vilnius and Kaunas, designing, implementing, and supervising various computer machinery, until 1993.

In the last twenty years, his life and work have been centered on book publishing. He is the Deputy Director of the printing press "Morkūnas and Co." and the Director of the publishing house "Nau-

jasis lankas." A considerable number of their publications are focused on the post-World War II resistance movement in Lithuania, deportations, and exile. Vidmantas is glad to contribute to the legacy of his fellow former exiles by facilitating the publication of their reminiscences and creating writung.

Vidmantas Zavadskis and his wife, Kristina Zavadskienė, raised two sons, Giedrius and Marius. Giedrius is a specialist in telecommunications; Marius is a sculptor and book illustrator.

AFTERWORD

Why and how the predicament of exile befell inhabitants of Lithuania are questions I attempt to explain in this closing chapter. I begin with a glance at present-day Lithuania and proceed to a brief survey of its thousand-year history, influenced by relations with neighboring countries. I also present aspects of the history of Russia, Lithuania's threatening neighbor on the east and source of dire misfortune for the Baltic countries. I conclude with some information about Siberia, which the tsars of Russia and later the communist government turned into a huge prison for people of various nationalities.

Lithuania in Brief

The Republic of Lithuania is a small country in Europe, on the eastern shore of the Baltic Sea. Within its territory is the geographical center of the European continent, according to the measurements of French scientists in 1989. Lithuania is an independent, democratic republic, a member of the European Union and NATO since 2004.

Lithuania's size: 65.3 thousand square kilometers.

Population: 3,043,429 (according to the census of 2011). About 84% of its population is comprised of Lithuanians.

Capital city: Vilnius, with a population of 535.6 thousand.

Currency: Litas.

Language: Lithuanian.

The Lithuanian language belongs to the Indo-European language group, which includes the Baltic, Slavic, Germanic, and Romance families, as well as the Indo-Iranian, thus numerous European and Asian languages: English, German, Russian, French, Italian, Sanskrit, Hindu, Urdu, and many others. Closest to the proto-Indo-European language are Sanskrit, Lithuanian, Ancient Greek, and Latin; among these, Lithuanian is the only living language. Lithuanian belongs to the Baltic family of languages, of which most are now extinct. It is related to Latvian, spoken in Latvia, and Prussian, which has dwindled to about 800 words.

Worldwide, about four million people speak Lithuanian today. They comprise ethnic minorities in Poland, Latvia, and Belarus, as well as Lithuanian communities in the United States of America, Canada, Australia, and the United Kingdom. In many countries there are Lithuanian Saturday schools, where children study their native language, history, folklore, and literature. Books are regularly published in Lithuanian, as well as newspapers and periodicals.

From antiquity to the present day, Lithuanian women have adorned themselves with amber. Miniature pieces of amber are scattered on the Baltic seashore—gifts of the sea—while entire strata of the precious substance lie hidden in the deep blue soil beneath. Amber is petrified pine resin, which abounded about forty million years ago. In times B.C.E., an amber trade route stretched from the Baltic Sea to the shores of the Mediterranean. Amber has been found in the tombs of Egyptian pharaohs and the sarcophagi of Greek kings. It was crafted as ornamentation by the inhabitants of Ancient Greece and Rome.

Throughout the centuries, Lithuanians have built their homes from wood. Talented wood-workers and carpenters, they constructed wooden churches and bell towers in their towns; by their homesteads and roadsides, they erected ornate wooden crosses and wayside chapels. These proliferated to the extent that they have become a constituent part and embellishment of the Lithuanian landscape. During the years of Soviet occupation, the construction of such crosses came to signify resistance against the oppressors and was in fact forbidden.

In the vicinity of Šiauliai, in western Lithuania, is the Hill of Crosses. Crosses were first erected here, on the Jurgaičiai mound, after the uprisings of 1831 and 1863, to memorialize the insurgents who perished in the onslaught of Russian troops. Later the hill was consecrated. During the years of Soviet rule, the government used to bulldoze the crosses, but they would continually reappear on the hill. Currently there are close to a hundred thousand crosses on the hill. Religious services and festivals are regularly held there. People pray and construct new crosses. After Pope John Paul II's visit to the Hill of Crosses in 1993, a Franciscan monastery was built nearby.

Lithuanians are lyrical and musical people. Their ancient folk songs are poetic, wistful, and sorrowful. In a region of eastern Lithuania, the tradition of performing multi-part songs, *sutartinės*, still thrives. *Sutartinės* are polyphonic folk songs, sung with instrumental accompaniment.

A wide variety of music events are regularly staged throughout Lithuania. There are numerous concerts by folkloric ensembles, along with folk art and craft fairs. Large scale song and dance festivals have been organized every four years since 1924. These are indeed theatrical performances. Present-day festivals involve up to thirty thousand participants, with hundreds of choral groups singing in unison and about nine thousand dancers joining in the figures of traditional dances. Three thousand singers and dancers might perform a musical program. Song and dance festivals are also held in Latvia and Estonia, Lithuania's Baltic neighbors. They have been recognized by UNESCO as treasures of the world's verbal and non-material cultural heritage. Similar festivals, but on a smaller scale, are organized by the Lithuanian communities in the United States, Canada, and Australia.

Lithuanian athletes have attained renown, especially the award-winning basketball teams and players. Indeed, Lithuania is referred to as the land of basketball. The sport is a source of national pride and on occasion has taken on political overtones. When the U.S. and U.S.S.R. men's basketball teams competed for gold at the 1988 Olympics in Seoul (South Korea), the winning Soviet team included four players from then occupied Lithuania: A. Sabonis, Š. Marčiulionis, R. Kurtinaitis, and V. Chomičius. Since independence, the men's basketball team of the Republic of Lithuania has won three European championships and three bronze medals at the Olympic Games: 1992 in Barcelona, 1996 in Atlanta, and 2000 in Sydney. A. Sabonis, Š. Marčiulionis, Ž. Ilgauskas, Š. Jasikevičius, and others have played for NBA teams. Lithuanian basketball players have been commemorated by the American-Lithuanian film producer Marius Markevicius in his 2012 full-length documentary film *The Other Dream Team*.

Flag and State Emblem of the Republic of Lithuania

A Map of Lithuania

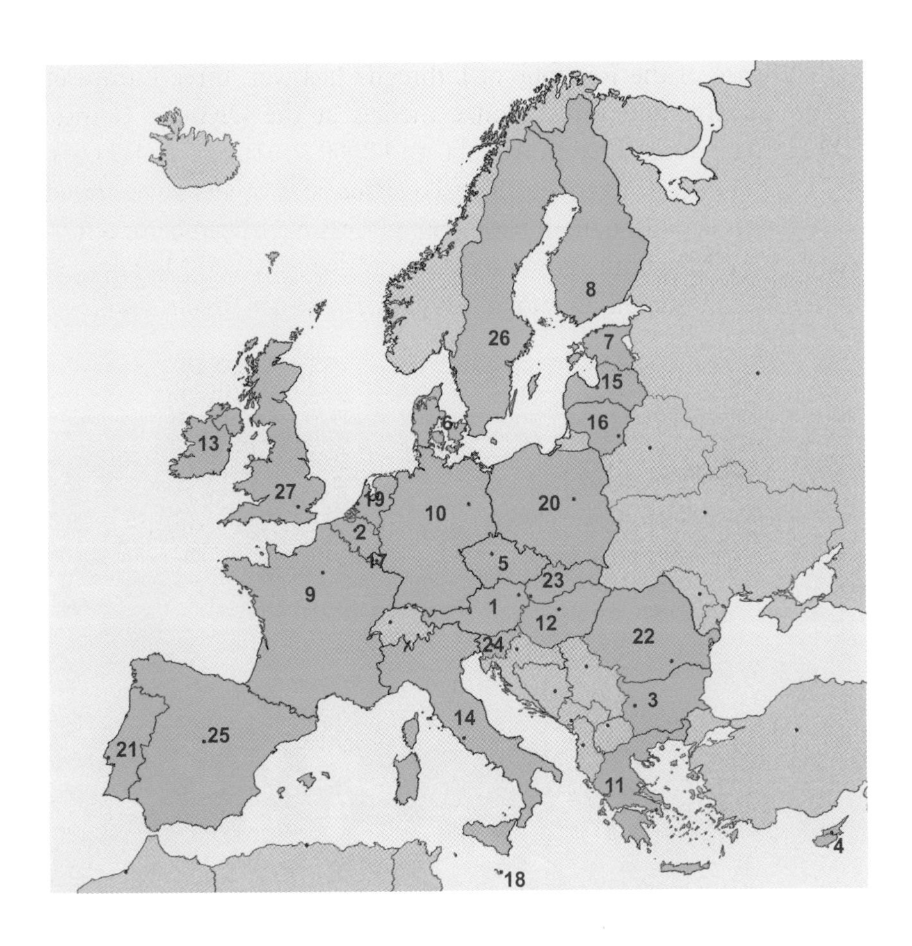

Member states of the European Union

1 Austria (1995)
2 Belgium (1952)
3 Bulgaria (2007)
4 Cyprus (2004)
5 Czech Republic (2004)
6 Denmark (1973)
7 Estonia (2004)
8 Finland (1995)
9 France (1952)
10 Germany (1952)
11 Greece (1981)
12 Hungary (2004)
13 Ireland (1973)
14 Italy (1952)
15 Latvia (2004)
16 Lithuania (2004)
17 Luxembourg (1952)
18 Malta (2004)
19 Netherlands (1952)
20 Poland (2004)
21 Portugal (1986)
22 Romania (2007)
23 Slovakia (2004)
24 Slovenia (2004)
25 Spain (1986)
26 Sweden (1995)
27 United Kingdom (1973)

A bird's eye view of Kaunas Old Town and confluence of Nemunas and Neris Rivers

The Hill of Crosses

A bird's eye view of Trakai Castle and Trakai Town

The narrow street in Vilnius Old Town

Vilnius Cathedral, late 18th century

Vilnius. St. Anne's Church, early 16th century

Lithuania to the 16th Century

Indo-European tribes in Europe, on the east side of the Baltic Sea as far as the Oka River, were first mentioned in the year 98 by the Roman historian Publius Cornelius Tacitus in his *Germania*. These people were referred to as "Aistians" (L. *aestorium gentes*). In the nineteenth century, the German scholar G. F. Neselman proposed the name Balts for these tribes, with regard to their geographical location by the Baltic Sea. Lithuania (*Lituae*) was first mentioned in 1009, in the Annals of Quedlinburg, a German city within the Holy Roman Empire. In 2009, Lithuania celebrated the millennial anniversary of this mention.

In the mid-thirteenth century, Duke Mindaugas united several Baltic duchies and was crowned the King of Lithuania on July 6, 1253. Thus 1253 is considered the founding year of the state of Lithuania, and July 6 is the State Day.

When King Mindaugas died, with no heir to the throne, Lithuania lost its status as kingdom. Dukes struggled among themselves for sovereignty. Moreover, they were constantly under attack by foreign enemies: from the north, by the Knights of the Livonian Order, which had consolidated its ranks within the territory of Baltic tribes, and from the southwest, by the German Teutonic Knights, which had vanquished the Prussian tribe and taken over its territory. In the southeast, Tatar-Mongols of the Golden Horde were devastating Slavic duchies and advancing on the borders of Lithuania. The struggle to preserve the state of Lithuania lasted 250 years. Fortifications built during this historical era—mounds, castles, fortresses—are still evident in Lithuania today.

In 1323 Lithuania's Grand Duke Gediminas (1316–1341) dispatched missives to West European cities, inviting traders, artisans, and landholders to Lithuania, proclaiming favorable conditions for settling in his country. Gediminas' letters include the first known mention of Vilnius. Although the city was already in existence, 1323 is considered the founding year of Vilnius and Duke Gediminas its founder. Vilnius has been the capital city of Lithuania since that time.

The dynasty of Gediminids, beginning with Duke Gediminas, ruled Lithuania until the sixteenth century. In 1385, Duke Gediminas' grandson, Lithuania's Duke Jogaila, married the Polish Princess Jadvyga and became King of Poland. So Lithuania's Gediminids branched off as Poland's Jagiellonian dynasty, which ruled Poland and a large part of Europe during the fifteenth and sixteenth centuries.

In Gediminas' time, Lithuania assumed the name Grand Duchy of Lithuania (*Lietuvos Didžioji Kunigaikštystė*, *LDK*). It spread eastward via diplomatic routes as well as attempts to gain influence in Slavic duchies. The marriages of Grand Dukes Gediminas' and Algirdas' (1345–1377) sons and daughters to rulers of Slavic duchies were milestones in this direction. Another noteworthy event, in 1391, was Grand Duke Vytautas' daughter Sofija's wedding to Moscow's Grand Prince Vasily I (1389–1425). The grand dukes of Lithuania, especially Algirdas, vied with the rising power of Moscow for influence in the Slavic duchies. These duchies often allied themselves with the state of Lithuania, seeking support for defense against the Tatar-Mongols' Golden Horde.

In 1363, Lithuania's Grand Duke Algirdas conquered the Tatar-Mongols in the Battle of the Blue Waters (on the shores of the Synyucha River, the left tributary of the Southern Bug, between the lower Dnieper and Southern Bug) and occupied extensive territory ruled by the Golden Horde. Later, toward the end of the 14 century, Grand Duke Vytautas annexed Tatar-Mongol dominated lands and reached the Black Sea. The Grand Duchy of Lithuania thus blocked the Golden Horde's route to Western Europe.

Descendants of the 383 families of Karaims, which Vytautas brought from Crimea still inhabit Trakai, a town and castle near

Vilnius. The Karaims were trustworthy soldiers of Grand Duke Vytautas and guardians of the island on Trakai Lake. They authored numerous legends celebrating Lithuania's Grand Duke.

Vytautas settled Tatar soldiers in the environs of Vilnius in order to defend avenues of approach to the city. Tatars' descendants inhabit Lithuania to this day. A Lithuanian Tatar's daughter, Loreta Asanavičiūtė, perished under a Soviet tank while participating in the defense of the television tower in Vilnius on January 13, 1991.

In 1387 Lithuania, the last pagan stronghold in Europe, was Christianized and converted to Catholicism. Christianization served as a link with West European culture and provided diplomatic advantage in defense against enemies, thus strengthening the state. However, during the second half of the fourteenth century, the Teutonic Knights and the Livonian Order continued to invade and devastate the country, especially western Lithuania (Žemaitija). They organized about a hundred campaigns into Lithuania during that time.

It was not until 1410, when Lithuania's Grand Duke Vytautas and Poland's King Jogaila consolidated their armed forces, that the Teutonic Knights were defeated. The cousins Vytautas and Jogaila led their armies to an overwhelming victory in the Battle of Grünwald (Žalgiris), within the territory of present-day Poland. Many knights, even leaders of the Order, with the Grand Master Ulrich von Jungingen at the fore, perished in this battle. The two hundred-year siege of Lithuania's territory by the Teutonic Knights then came to an end.

During the rule of Grand Duke Vytautas (1392–1430), the Grand Duchy of Lithuania became the most powerful country in Europe.

Lithuania from the 16th to the 19th Century

The sixteenth century was a cultural heyday in Lithuania, a time of urban growth and development in trade and industry. Brick construction became more prevalent in the cities. Grand Renaissance mansions were built, influenced by West European architecture. St. Anne's Church in Vilnius, a masterpiece of Gothic architecture from the sixteenth century, is still standing today. The capital city also abounds in splendid Baroque churches from the seventeenth century. Monasteries were established and schools founded along-side them. Book publishing was initiated in the capital city. In 1579 Vilnius University was founded.

The Union of Lublin in 1569 formed the Commonwealth of Lithuania and Poland, a Republic of Two Nations (*Rzeczpospolita*), which lasted until 1795. This was a complex period for the state of Lithuania, marred by wars with Sweden and Russia. In 1655 Lithuania was occupied by Swedish and Russian armies, which devastated the country and plundered its peasant folk. In the same year, the Russian army pillaged and set fire to Vilnius. Throughout the Northern War between Sweden and Russia (1700–1721), Lithuania, on account of its geo-political situation, was the locus of battles between opposing forces and so locus of destruction. This war brought famine as well as the plague epidemic of 1708–1711. The country's economy was ruined and farming villages abandoned. Lithuania lost about a third of its population.

The Commonwealth of Lithuania and Poland was undermined and, after three successive partitions, ceded to the dominion of Austria, Prussia, and Russia. Most of Lithuania's territory was annexed by Russia and remained occupied until 1915.

Yet another foreign army marched through Lithuania in 1812: Napoleon's French army of 153,000 crossed the Nemunas River at Kaunas enroute to Moscow; six months later, its hungry, exhausted survivors made their way home via Lithuania.

Lithuanians and Poles strove to liberate themselves from Russian occupation. Two large-scale insurrections were organized, in 1831 and 1863. However, the insurgents perished, outnumbered and overwhelmed by opposing forces. Entire peasant villages were exiled to distant Russian provinces in Siberia. In 1832 Vilnius University was closed. From 1864 to 1904, Lithuanian schools were closed, and the Lithuanian press using Latin letters was banned. Lithuanian books were then printed in Prussia, and they were secretly transported over the border between Prussia and Russia to Lithuania. That was a unique book smuggling operation, with no comparisons worldwide. The people who transported books to Lithuania were called "book-couriers" (*knygnešiai*). Many were also arrested, imprisoned, and exiled to Siberia.

Lithuania in the 20th Century

World War I, which rendered Lithuania a battle arena once again, nevertheless brought emancipation to the country. In 1915, German forces occupied the territory of Lithuania. On February 16, 1918, Lithuania's independence was declared, and it was subsequently defended and strengthened in clashes with the Red Army, the White Guards [Tsarist army divisions remaining in Lithuania and Latvia after the war, opposed to both Bolsheviks and local Balts], and dwindling German forces. However, in 1920 Poland occupied Vilnius, as well as the region of Vilnius, and retained control of this territory until 1939. During this time, Kaunas was the interim capital of Lithuania. In 1923, an insurgent populace re-incorporated Klaipėda (Memel) and its region into Lithuania. Although devastated by war and deprived of its capital, Lithuania was successfully rebuilt, its economy and agriculture revived.

In 1933 two American-Lithuanian aviators, Steponas Darius and Stays Girėnas, merited acclaim by their trans-Atlantic flight. They flew from New York to Kaunas in their small, two-seat plane "Lituanica" without radio communication, in bad weather. Having crossed the Atlantic Ocean, they perished near Soldin in Germany (now Polish territory) under mysterious circumstances. Nonetheless, their flight was a milestone in aviation history, attaining a world record in flight precision and second place for distance covered at the time. In 1937 and 1939, Lithuanian basketball teams won European championships, creating great celebrations across Lithuania.

After only twenty-one prosperous, peaceful years in the independent Republic of Lithuania, World War II erupted over the European continent. In March 1939, Germany occupied the Klaipėda region. On August 23, 1939, by the secret proceedings of the Ribbentrop-Molotov Pact, Germany and the Soviet Union apportioned Eastern Europe as their own. Most of Lithuania's territory was taken by the Soviet Union, which formally occupied the country on June 15, 1940. Terrible devastation of Lithuania's land and persecution of its inhabitants ensued. People were imprisoned, deported to the GULAG, exiled to Siberia en masse, or executed; their land, homes, and wealth were Sovietized.

On June 22, 1941, Nazi Germany proclaimed war on the Soviet Union. Crossing the border between Germany and the USSR on the very first day of war, the German army marched through Lithuania*. The Nazi occupation was also very hard on Lithuania. Vilnius University was again closed in 1943. Educated people, who opposed the mobilization of Lithuanian youth to the Nazi military regime, were deported to the Stutthof concentration camp. Lithuanian Jews were particularly victimized. Inhabitants of Lithuania since the fourteenth century, Jews had experienced neither persecution nor pogroms in this country until the World War II era; they had peacefully developed trade and industry and observed their cultural traditions. Vilnius was called the Jerusalem of the North. But in the course of the Soviet and Nazi occupations, the Jewish community in Lithuania was totally destroyed: their synagogues were closed, their organizations and cultural activities terminated, and their wealth confiscated. Lithuania lost 94% of its Jewish population.

---

* *In 1941, the population of Lithuania was 2.9 million.*

During World War II, front lines passed through Lithuania twice. Cities were ruined, villages burned, youths drafted by one or another invading army, and local food reserves commandeered by their soldiers. In 1944, as the Soviet front advanced toward Lithuania, approximately 120,000 people emigrated from the country. Some feared tanks, bombs, and starving soldiers; others feared the terrors of Soviet communism. Most of the emigrants hoped to return home once the war ended. However, the Soviet army did not withdraw at the end of the war. Lithuania continued to be occupied by the Soviet Union until 1990. There was no way back for Lithuanians who became displaced persons in war-torn Europe; they had to search for ways and means of settling elsewhere. They dispersed throughout the Western Hemisphere: Europe, North and South America, Australia. Those who remained in Lithuania found themselves behind the "Iron Curtain," comparable to being in a huge, miserable prison. Deportations to Siberia and the GULAG's forced labor camps were resumed and crimes against innocent civilians were perpetrated. Many Lithuanian youths opposed the occupant forces by joining the ranks of freedom fighters ("partisans") in the forests and waging rebel warfare. The freedom fighters were of course outnumbered, and by 1953 their resistance was quelled by the Soviet army.

The Soviet occupation of Lithuania was not recognized by the United States, the Vatican, and numerous Western countries. Embassies of the Republic of Lithuania were maintained in Washington D.C. and by the Holy See in Rome throughout the years of occupation.

In 1965, the U.S. House of Representatives and in 1966, the U.S. Senate passed Resolution Number 416, which states that the government of the Soviet Union forcibly deprived the people of Estonia, Latvia, and Lithuania of the right to self-determination and that by deportations and re-locations of the populace, the Soviet Union aimed to change the demographic composition of the Baltic States. The Resolution urged the President of the United States to bring worldwide attention to and to support attempts to restore the right to self-determination to inhabitants of the Baltic States, at the U.N. and other international forums. The Captive Nations Committee was formed in Washington D.C., with subcommittees in various cities of the U.S. The third week of July was declared Captive Nations Week.

Mikhail Gorbachev's proclamation of reform (*perestroika*) in the Soviet Union aroused hope for emancipation in Lithuania. A Movement for Reform in Lithuania (*Sąjūdis*) was organized in 1988. On August 23, 1989, two million Lithuanians, Latvians, and Estonians joined hands in a 620-kilometer chain from the Vilnius Cathedral to Riga and the Herman Tower in Talinn, demonstrating their opposition to the Ribbentrop-Molotov Pact and its consequences. Large-scale assemblies were called together in Lithuania. On March 11, 1990, Lithuania's Supreme Council, or Restored Parliament, chaired by Professor Vytautas Landsbergis, passed the Act for the restoration of an independent State of Lithuania. Consequently, Gorbachev's government declared a seventy-four-day economic blockade, depriving the country of food, fuel, and industrial raw materials. Military force was also employed to suppress Lithuania's independence. The Soviet army advanced on communications centers in Vilnius: the Press quarters, the Radio and Television Committee, and Television tower. Fourteen defenders of the TV tower perished in the Soviet offensive of January 13, 1991. On July 31 of that year, seven of the customs officials and border patrol officers on duty at the Medininkai border post were killed. Finally, not only Lithuania but all fifteen republics of the Soviet Union succeeded in liberating themselves from bondage in the "Prison of Nations."

ON THE RISE OF MOSCOW

The Duchy of Moscow—the Russian Empire—the USSR—the Russian Federation

The city of Moscow, founded by Duke Yuri Dolgorukiy in the twelfth century, grew to become the Duchy of Moscow in the thirteenth century. In 1238 the Duchy was subjected to vassalage in the Golden Horde's Tatar-Mongol state. Upon emancipation in the fifteenth century, it gained strength and began to form alliances with neighboring Slavic duchies. Duke Ivan III (1462–1505) was consequently bestowed the title Grand Prince of All Russia. Ivan IV (1533–1584), "the Terrible," instituted the title Tsar of All the Russias. Since the time of Tsar Ivan IV, Russia has sought possession of the Baltic coast and expansion into Europe as well as Asia.

To obtain "windows on the West," Russia had to reach the Baltic Sea and the Black Sea. Under the rule of Tsar Peter I (1694–1725), Russia came to resemble an immense war camp. Among numerous reforms based on West European models, compulsory military and civil service on the part of nobility was instituted; a new regular army was organized, composed of recruits obligated to twenty-five years of service. Tsar Peter founded the Russian Navy. He established military training schools as well as factories for the production of weapons, army supplies, and textiles.

At first Tsar Peter warred with Turkey but did not gain access to the Black Sea. Seeking an outlet by the Baltic Sea, he proclaimed war on Sweden and now met with success. In the course of the "Great Northern War" (1700–1721), Russia occupied Swedish territory between Lake Ladoga and the Gulf of Finland. By this Gulf and the Neva River delta, Russia built the Kronstadt military fortifications and ship-building facilities, as well as the city of St. Petersburg, which replaced Moscow as the capital city. It occupied the Swedish-owned eastern shore of the Baltic Sea, vanquished the Swedish Navy, and invaded the territory of Sweden. Having won the Great

Northern War and arrived at the Baltic Sea, Tsar Peter I was named Emperor, and Russia became an Empire. Before his death in 1725, Peter also occupied the cities of Derbent and Baku by the Caspian Sea and forced Persia to cede the southern and southwestern shores of the Caspian Sea to Russia.

Emperor Peter I's agenda was furthered by Catherine II (1762–1796), who was given the epithet "the Great" for her service to Russia. By means of aggressive foreign policy, she continued to expand Russia's territory, annexing more European and Asian lands. She completed Peter I's advance toward the Black Sea: after the war with Turkey of 1768–1774, she annexed the northern shore of the Black Sea; in 1783, she occupied the Crimean Peninsula. Catherine II also expanded the Russian Empire westward by joining a large part of the State of Lithuania and Poland to Russia.

The conquest of Siberia was most easily attained, for opposition by the small local nations was negligible. In 1741 the Russians reached the shores of North America, coming upon Alaska. They travelled south as far as San Francisco and built Fort Ross a few hundred kilometers to the north, by the Pacific Ocean. Russia governed Alaska from 1790 to 1867, when it was sold to the United States of America.

In 1864 Russia gained dominion of the Caucasus region; between 1864 and 1876, it succeeded in annexing Turkestan in west central Asia.

At the beginning of the twentieth century, Russia was exhausted by World War I. Tsar Nicholas II resigned from the throne in 1917, and the provisional government was overthrown by the Bolsheviks that same year. Tsar Nicholas and his entire family were executed by the Bolsheviks. The ensuing civil war lasted until 1922, when the State of Russia assumed the name USSR, Union of Soviet Socialist Republics (for *SSSR, Sojuz Sovietskikh Socialisticheskikh Respublik*).

Toward the end of World War II, the Soviet army forced its way deep into West European territory and did not withdraw after the war. By forming compliant subsidiary state governments, the Soviets established themselves in Poland, East Germany, Czechoslovakia, Hungary, Rumania, and Bulgaria. In 1955 the Soviet Union and its satellite states formed the Warsaw Pact military alliance. Lithuania, Latvia, and Estonia remained under Soviet occupation. To this day, Russia maintains interim governance of a part of East Prussia (Russia's Kaliningrad region).

Until 1953, the Soviet Union was under Josef Stalin's extremely harsh regime. Its foreign policy escalated the dissemination of communism as a means for the Soviet Union to gain world-wide hegemony. Cold war politics were actively pursued with the NATO countries.

In 1991 the Soviet Union disintegrated, ceding all its rights to the Russian Federation.

SIBERIA, LOCALE OF EXILE AND IMPRISONMENT

Siberia extends throughout northern Asia, about 7000 kilometers from the Ural Mountains east to the Pacific Ocean, and about 3500 kilometers from the Arctic Ocean south to Mongolia. The southern part of Siberia consists of steppes; the northern, of taiga overgrown with forests. A large section of Siberia lies beyond the Arctic Circle, in a land of permafrost and severe polar climate, a tundra with meager vegetation.

In the thirteenth century, all of Siberia, except for its northern borders, was colonized by the Mongol Empire. When this empire fell, some of the nations in Siberia were incorporated by the Golden Horde. At the end of the fifteenth century, the Siberian *khaganate* [cluster of states] was formed. The increasingly powerful Duchy of Moscow had launched military campaigns in Siberia during the fifteenth century, and by the mid-sixteenth century, made inroads for its conquest of the region. In the sixteenth century, the Russians vanquished the Tatars on the eastern side of the Ural Mountains and in the seventeenth century, the Buriat-Mongols by Lake Baikal.

Eventually they reached the Sea of Okhotsk; in 1648, they came to the Bering Strait. During the time of Peter I's reforms, in 1708, the province of Siberia was established, with its government centered in Tobolsk. By the mid-nineteenth century, Russia had taken possession of all Siberia, including its Pacific coastline in the east.

Siberia has been the place of exile for Russia's people since the seventeenth century and from the eighteenth century, also a locale for imprisonment. In the nineteenth and early twentieth century, Russian revolutionaries and dissenters, as well as people of occupied countries, were exiled to Siberia. To be sure, there were Russians who moved to Siberia voluntarily: hunters, traders, and those who sought refuge from persecution in Siberia's vast territory.

In the nineteenth century, the first steamboats appeared on Siberia's rivers. In 1900 the Trans-Siberian Railroad was completed, stretching from the Ural Mountains in European Russia to eastern Siberia as far as Vladivostok.

After the Bolshevik Revolution in the early twentieth century, the Soviet Union began to implement the "Great Construction Projects of Communism" in Siberia. Industrialization of the region commenced in 1920. Mining, logging, and drilling operations were set in motion in order to appropriate Siberia's abundant natural resources: coal, iron ore, copper, nickel, gold, diamonds, platinum, lumber, and oil. The Trans-Siberian Railroad was expanded to branch lines. Huge hydro-electric power stations were built on the Ob, Yenisei, and Angara Rivers in Siberia. The Soviet Union's Bolsheviks, possessed of grandiose schemes, even planned to reverse the courses of rivers flowing toward the Arctic Ocean.

The realization of all those projects required an enormous labor force, and this was procured by the exploitation of prison labor. Once the GULAG's system of forced labor camps was established, people were imprisoned without court trials or convictions. Indeed, the development of Siberian industry depended on unpaid prison labor, of both "corrective labor camps" and colonies. Moreover, entire families with children and grandparents were exiled to Siberia. Between 1929 and 1932, not only was a famine purposely induced in the Ukraine, but Ukrainian citizens were exiled to Siberia. After World War II, the Soviets exiled entire nations to Siberia: the Chechens, Crimean Tatars, and Volga Germans.

Having occupied new territories, the Soviets deported innocent civilians to the GULAG's labor camps or sites of exile in Siberia. They deported Lithuanians, Latvians, Estonians, Poles and Finns. In Lithuania, the word *Siberia* has come to symbolize terror, starvation, cold, torture, and genocide of an enslaved nation. The realities of Siberia during the years 1929 to 1953 were caravans of cattle cars, crowded with women, children, and the elderly, and the GULAG's labor camps, filled with hungry, freezing, ragged inmates.

To this day, an imperialistic mindset persists in the world; the struggle for possession of even the smallest of territories continues. New and ever more destructive weapons are invented and produced. After the break-up of the Soviet Union, Russia recovered. With vast territories in its domain, particularly Siberia, Russia has abundant reserves of natural energy: oil, gas, and numerous useful minerals. By developing its defense industry, Russia wields influence not only on the European economy but also world affairs. In Lithuania, this influence is demonstrated in various ways, but primarily in the exploitation of the country's dependence on Russia's energy resources. As Russia's state-regulated company Gazprom is the sole provider of gas for Lithuania, Russia sells gas to Lithuania at a higher price than to other countries of the European Union. Furthermore, two nuclear power plants are under construction near Lithuania's borders: one in the Kaliningrad region of Russia, close to the Lithuanian city Tauragė, and the other, financed by Russia, in Belarus, fifty kilometers (thirty-one miles) from Vilnius, the capital of the Republic of Lithuania. Taking into account the vicissitudes of nature—earthquakes and the permeability of terrestrial energy—there is no guarantee that these nuclear power plants will be safe. (In 2004 there was a 6.0 earthquake in the Kaliningrad region.) As we know, the causes of unforeseen calamities are most often human error and technological failure as well as natural disaster (for example, Chernobyl, Fukushima). Therefore, the construction of nuclear power stations near Lithuania's cities raises questions concerning manifestations of Russia's "good will."

Irena Kurtinaitytė Aras

References

A History of the Los Angeles Juozas Daumantas Chapter of the National Guard, 1964–2004 (Los Angeles Juozo Daumanto šaulių kuopos istorija, 1964–2004). Comp. by Irena Arienė and Stasys Ignatavičius. Kaunas: Naujasis lankas, 2006.

Lithuanian Encyclopedia *(Lietuvių enciklopedija)* Vols. 1, 16, 17, 34. Boston: Lietuvių enciklopedijos leidykla, 1953, 1958, 1959, 1966.

Lithuania's population in 2011. Results of the 2011 Census. (*Lietuvos gyventojai 2011 metais. 2011 m. gyventojų surašymo rezultatai.*) Vilnius: Lietuvos statistikos departamentas, 2012.

Makauskas, Bronius. *A History of Lithuania* (*Lietuvos istorija*). Vols. 1 and 2. Kaunas: Šviesa, 2006.

Mildažytė, Edita. *Lithuania on a First Date* (*Pasimatymas su Lietuva*). Vilnius: Tyto Alba, 2012.

Soviet Lithuanian Encyclopedia (*Lietuviškoji tarybinė enciklopedija*), Vols. 9 and 10. Vilnius: Valstybinė enciklopedijų leidykla, 1982.

Šapoka, Adolfas. *A History of Lithuania* (*Lietuvos istorija*). Vilnius: Mokslas, 1989.

Tininis, Vytautas. *The Establishment of the Communist Regime in Lithuania and its Crimes. The Second Soviet Occupation* (*Komunistinio rėžimo įtvirtinimas Lietuvoje ir jo nusikaltimai. Antroji sovietinė okupacija*). Vilnius: Margi raštai, 2009.

*INDEX**

* *The Index is limited to names and place names from the memoirs, pages 14–294.*

ACKNOWLEDGEMENTS

The compilers of this book and the publishers are very grateful to the authors of the texts and their families for permission to publish their authentic memoirs of exile in Siberia.

We thank Živilė Gimbutas for her diligence and dedication to the task of rendering a fine English translation of the book; Vita Milaknis Markevicius for the translation of the Foreword; dr. Izolda Geniušienė for permission to reprint her translation of Dalia Grinkevičiūtė's memoir; and Danutė Januta for careful reading and correction of the translated text.

For consultations and moral support, we thank Teresė Birutė Burauskaitė, General Director, Genocide and Resistance Research Center of Lithuania; Edvardas Strončikas, Chair of the Association of Lithuania's Political Prisoners and Exiles; Jonas Markauskas, Chair of the Brotherhood of Laptev Sea Exiles; Marija Augustine, President, Australian Lithuanian Catholic Federation, Editor of the newspaper *Tėviškės aidai* ("The Echoes of Homeland") in Melbourne, Australia; Marija Sandanavičiūtė Newsom, Director, St. Casimir's Lithuanian Saturday School in Los Angeles, dr. Anelė Butkuvienė, Historian, and Vaiva Pechulis.

Special thanks are extended to the Lithuanian Studies Society at the University of Tasmania (Australia), its President, Vincas Taškūnas and the Society's Founder, Dr. Algimantas Taškūnas, whose assistance and multi-faceted support made the publication of this book possible.

The Lithuanian Studies Society is a non-profit organization dedicated to raising awareness of Lithuania and its heritage. The Society encourages graduate research, at the University of Tasmania and elsewhere, on all topics related to Lithuania. The Society also publishes *Lithuanian Papers*, an annual English-language journal. Postal address: P.O. Box 777, Sandy Bay, Tas. 7006. Australia. E-mail: A.Taskunas@utas.edu.au

For financial support, we are grateful to the following:

Australian Lithuanian Foundation Inc. (Australia)
Australian-Lithuanians and their Friends in Australia
Lithuanian Educational Assistance and Relief Fund Inc. (USA)
The Fund for Research of the Genocide of Lithuania's Population and the Resistance Movement, for Support and Commemoration of the Victims
Morkūnas and Co Printing Press
Jurgis Valaitis (Baltimore, USA), Dr. Kazys Bobelis, Aušra and Henrikas Vilkas, Elena Monse.

Supplemented translation of the Lithuanian edition. The original Lithuanian edition, "*Sibiro vaikai,*" compiled by Irena Kurtinaitytė and Vidmantas Zavadskis, was published in Kaunas by "Naujasis lankas," 2011.

Children of Siberia features authentic reminiscences of Lithuanian child exiles. Finding themselves in the dire circumstances of exile, these children suffered hunger and want, exhaustion from hard physical labor, and humiliation. Their memoirs recall episodes of deportation, conditions of daily life in exile, early schooling in Siberia, and their parents' tribulations.

CHILDREN OF SIBERIA

Memoirs of Lithuanian Exiles

Compiled by Irena Kurtinaitytė Aras and Vidmantas Zavadskis
Translated by Živilė Gimbutas
Illustrated by Marius Zavadskis
Photos from publications and personal archives
Photos on pages 300–304 by Vytautas Kandrotas

Publishing house "Naujasis lankas"
Draugystės g. 17 LT-51229 Kaunas, Lithuania
Printed in Lithuania by Morkūnas and Co Printing Press.